THE POWYS BROTHERS

ALSO BY KENNETH HOPKINS

Love and Elizabeth: poems
42 Poems
Poor Heretic: poems
Collected Poems, 1935–1965

Llewelyn Powys: A Selection from his Writings
John Cowper Powys: Selected Poems

The English Lyric
The Poets Laureate
Walter de la Mare
Portraits in Satire
English Poetry: A Short History

The Corruption of a Poet
A Trip to Texas

Edmund Blunden: A Selection from his Writings
Walter de la Mare: A Selection from his Writings
H. M. Tomlinson: A Selection from his Writings
etc.

The
POWYS BROTHERS

A BIOGRAPHICAL APPRECIATION

by KENNETH HOPKINS

Rutherford • Madison • Teaneck
Fairleigh Dickinson University Press

Library of Congress Catalogue Card Number: 68-10855

Associated University Presses, Inc.
Cranbury, New Jersey 08512

6754
Printed in the United States of America

IN MEMORY OF

LOUIS WILKINSON

ILLUSTRATIONS

Between pages 52 and 53

The Powys brothers, about 1901

Shirley Rectory

Montacute Vicarage

White Nose, Dorset

Phudd Bottom, Hillsdale, New York

John Cowper Powys

John Cowper Powys

Louis Wilkinson

Llewelyn Powys in Africa

Llewelyn Powys

Theodore Powys

PREFACE

THERE have been a number of separate studies of individual members of the Powys family, but no general survey of their lives and works between one pair of covers; and this is what I have sought to supply. My book is a chronological account of the lives of John Cowper, Theodore Francis, and Llewelyn Powys, with discussions of their books as these arise in the chronological pattern, and to this I have added such supplementary information about other members of the family as seemed necessary, with some discussion of their work. I have sub-titled my book 'a biographical appreciation' because it does not claim to be exhaustively biographical of the three brothers, nor primarily a formal critical assessment of their work; it is modestly offered as a guide, or introduction, from which those readers who will may go on to the writings of the Powys brothers, and to the body of criticism which is beginning to be formed about them.

I first became aware of these brothers through buying for a few pence a secondhand copy of Theodore's *The House with the Echo*, in 1933 or 1934. I met Llewelyn Powys in 1935, and John Cowper Powys the following year, and with these two I continued an intercourse until their death; T. F. Powys I met only a couple of times, very briefly, and with him I enjoyed no intimacy. Later, I became acquainted with very many people who knew or had known the Powyses, and over the past thirty years an awareness of these brothers and their writings has been always at the forefront of my mind. I owe a debt to them in my own development as a writer greater than to any other contemporary source, and in these pages that follow I have tried to pay it.

I owe many other debts, too. The biggest must be to Louis Wilkinson (and I count it among John Cowper Powys's greatest kindnesses to me, that he introduced me to his old friend). From the day I arrived in London to seek my fortune in 1938, until today (when it has still to be found) Louis Wilkinson's urbane countenance and counsel have sustained, enriched and enlightened me; and in particular, in the present connection, he was an unfailing source of information about the Powys family, with which he maintained a close intimacy for almost seventy years. I had hoped soon to put a copy of this book into his hands, but 'vain are the hopes of man', and now he is dead.

I also owe much to Alyse Gregory for her sympathetic interest over the past thirty years, and her ready answers to my questions; and to Phyllis Playter, over almost as long, for the same forbearance and aid. Sylvia Townsend Warner has been generous in her help, and would have allowed me to print the whole of her unpublished monograph on T. F. Powys; but I felt that this ought to be separately published, and I hope that some day it will be. Miss Warner's reminiscences of the beginnings of Theodore's literary career have been of great value to me, and have been the source for pages I could not have written without them.

In following the Powys tracks in America I have been aided by the late Boyne Grainger of New York, who lived close to the centre of the Greenwich Village community of the 'twenties, and whose apartment in Perry Street was just over the way from Patchin Place; by Ruth Hoberg, who showed me not only the Powys haunts in and around San Francisco, but those of Robert Louis Stevenson for good measure; and Robert Blackmore, with whom I explored the backwoods of New York State, and in whose company I enjoyed the hospitality of Mr Albert Krick at Hillsdale, with his stories of his old neighbour J. C. Powys, and that of Miss Norma Millay and Mr Charles Ellis at Austerlitz, where we saw the cottage in which Llewelyn Powys completed *Impassioned Clay*.

Over the years also I have talked about the Powys brothers with many people, and have profited from these discussions—have gleaned an anecdote from Walter de la Mare, a hint from L. A. G. Strong, a line of thought from Kenneth Young, an insight from H. M. Tomlinson. For information and help of one sort and another I have to thank Eric Harvey, John Foster White, J. J. Curle, Thomas Davies, G. Wilson Knight, Lew D. Feldman, Lloyd Emerson Siberell, Louis Untermeyer, F. W. Roberts, Miss Betty B. Burkhalter, Mrs Sylvia Read, Mrs Isobel Powys Marks, F. P. French, and the late John Redwood-Anderson.

Naturally, I have profited from writers who have been in the field before me, but from none in the degree that I have from my friend Malcolm Elwin, whose *Life of Llewelyn Powys* is an essential tool for the study of all three of the brothers; and from 'Louis Marlow' (Louis Wilkinson) whose *Swan's Milk* and *Welsh Ambassadors* are pioneer studies which cannot be superseded.

K. H.

Liss,
    October 1966.

ACKNOWLEDGMENTS

The author and publishers are grateful for permission to quote from copyright material to the following:

The John Cowper Powys Estate, Macdonald & Company (Publishers) Ltd, and Laurence Pollinger Ltd for extracts from the works of John Cowper Powys; Mrs Violet Powys and Chatto & Windus Ltd for extracts from *An Interpretation of Genesis, The Left Leg, Mark Only, Mr Weston's Good Wine,* and *Fables* by T. F. Powys; Miss Alyse Gregory for extracts from the works of Llewelyn Powys and Philippa Powys; Mrs A. R. Powys for extracts from *The English Parish Church* and *From the Ground Up* by A. R. Powys; Chapman & Hall Ltd for extracts from *The Joy of It* by Littleton Powys; the late Louis Wilkinson for extracts from works by Louis Wilkinson and 'Louis Marlow'; Miss Sylvia Townsend Warner and Chatto & Windus Ltd for the extract from *A Chatto and Windus Miscellany* (1928).

I

THE VILLAGE of Shirley, in Derbyshire, lies off the main Derby–Ashbourne road, some four miles from Ashbourne, in a stretch of undulating pastoral country whose several small and remote villages remain today relatively untouched by twentieth-century conditions. The church is small and without features of great interest, although ancient, for it was enlarged and restored in the mid nineteenth century. It and the cottages group themselves pleasantly along the crest of a low hill, and westward and apart stands the largest house, the vicarage. This, like many such in small villages, is almost a mansion: a big, four-square eighteenth-century house in extensive grounds. The living is in the gift of the Earls Ferrers, of whom Shirley is a family name. Today the village has no separate vicar, and the vicarage is in private occupation.

Early in 1872 the Rev. Charles Francis Powys, curate-in-charge of the village of Bradford Abbas, in Dorset, was appointed vicar of Shirley. He was himself a Dorset man, the son and grandson of Dorset parsons. His father was the Rev. Littleton Charles Powys, rector of Stalbridge, another Dorset living. These Powyses came of a line of well-to-do country parsons and gentlemen, having a family connection with the barony of Lilford, and more tenuously with the ancient princes of Powysland, although this was largely conjectural, for the established line begins in the fifteenth century with one William Powys, of Ludlow.

About the time that C. F. Powys took orders he also took a wife. This was Mary Cowper Johnson, daughter and grand-daughter of parsons in Norfolk, who gave to her eleven children the blood of the poets Cowper and Donne, a fact which most writers about the family have noted as significant. To me it seems hardly so: the genius of the Powys brothers is much too strongly individual to be traceable to any

I

diluted influence from these two poets, and such affinities as may be found I consider merely accidental. The poet Cowper had no children, and the blood relationship with him comes through his second cousin, the Rev. John Johnson, a man who was Cowper's exact opposite in temperament. The connection with Donne also comes by way of the Cowper family and is additionally weakened by its remoteness in time. How much a strain of creative genius may be diminished in only one generation may be seen again and again when sons do not reproduce the talents of their fathers—contrast, for example, the poems of John Donne with those of his son John.[1] Even when the son outshines the father (as with Thomas and Matthew Arnold) there is seldom a further advance in the third generation. Genius transmitted by blood is not a tide, rising and retiring and again returning; but rather a ripple whose greatest force is at the centre and which grows ever weaker as it expands. The Donne blood in these Powyses was a ripple almost exhausted: their genius surely represents a new and independent ripple.

At Shirley were born the first five of the vicar's children: John Cowper (8 October 1872); Littleton Charles (1874); Theodore Francis (20 December 1875); Gertrude Mary (1877); and Eleanor,[2] who was born in 1879 and died in 1893 of appendicitis, the only one of the eleven who did not live a full adult life.

The birth dates of the other children may conveniently be noted here, though a little out of context. Albert Reginald (1881), Marian (1882) and Llewelyn (13 August 1884) were born at Dorchester, Dorset. Their father took a curacy there in 1879, when his brother Littleton, an army officer, died in India. The Rev. C. F. Powys felt he ought now to live nearer to his aged mother, whose home was at Weymouth. In 1885 he was offered the living of Montacute near Yeovil, in Somerset, which was convenient for reaching the Great Western line running into Weymouth; and at Montacute he remained for thirty-two years, until his own retirement to Weymouth, and his death there in 1923. At Montacute were born Catharine Philippa (1886), William (1888) and Lucy (1890).

It will be seen therefore that the accident of Derbyshire birth made little impact on the elder children, for when they left the county John, the eldest, was only seven, and Theodore was but four. It would be fanciful to see in them an element of the traditional Derbyshire stolidity

[1] In *Donne's Satyr* (1662), a collection not without interest, but displaying not a hint of the greatness of the Dean of St Paul's.

[2] This was the 'little girl' who gave to John Cowper Powys the *Poems of John Keats* which he mentions in his *Autobiography*.

lacking in the Dorset-born Llewelyn, and yet it would appear to be present in some degree in Theodore's slow caution and in John 'all fingers and thumbs'.

Certainly the major shaping influences on the whole family, so far as environment was concerned, were the Dorset and Somerset of their childhood; and the paramount influence on character their formidable father, and the phenomenon of ten remarkable children reacting upon one another.

An account of this family must begin with the father, a man of force quite out of the common. His sons John, Littleton and Llewelyn have all written about him, and to their family testimony may be added the impressions of a sharp-eyed outsider, Louis Marlow.

He was a man of massive simplicity; a countryman, with a clear uncritical faith in the broad principles of the Church of England and a cheerful acquiescence in the merit of the established order—a Victorian gentleman, to whom very properly every villager touched his forelock. A man exact in discharging his duty, and perfectly aware of what that duty was: to preach an uncomplicated gospel on Sundays; to visit the sick; to marry, baptize and bury.

His private life was equally direct, equally uncomplicated. He delighted in the country scene, and loved walking. He knew every bird and moss and flower: but not their Latin names—or, if he knew them, he ignored them. He was more interested in the country name, and the local use in cooking, or as medicine. He knew the seasons by observation and not from books. Indeed, he was not a great reader: for him the Bible sufficed, and Bewick's *Birds*. It was his wife who read to the children stories and poems; the Rev. C. F. Powys preferred to tell stories which he made up. He was a man of strong and conservative prejudices; he had no sympathy with progress for progress's sake, and a great distrust of science and book learning. It would be easy to overlook his virtues in listing his limitations, and to forget that he and millions like him were the backbone of England in a great age.

Mary Powys looks out from the photographs as a woman seemingly dominated by the personality of her husband; she appears the dutiful Victorian wife. But this lady was a personality also, and the impact of her very different character is to be traced in the children: the father's influence did not have it all the way. To her may be credited the strain of artistry and poetry, and perhaps her proud, withdrawn and melancholy spirit may also be seen to have contributed to the comparative failure of her children to be pre-eminent in the delicate arts—Gertrude was a good and an interesting painter, but not a great one; A. R. Powys a solid and competent architect, but not the designer of any important building; the strongly individual poetry of John Cowper almost everywhere lacks the note of definitive authority without which poetry cannot be immortal: he had genius enough for anything, except this. Llewelyn and Theodore, for all their graces, could do nothing in verse: here, if anywhere, may lie Cowper's mark upon them: a diffidence, a hesitation, in writing verse which he overcame in part, but they did not.

The vicar's, then, was very much the typical Victorian household as popularly understood—strong, stern but loving father; dutiful, submissive, gentle wife; large family of children; and the usual crowd of domestics. It is well to remember that this was the background against which the three writers grew up, for no matter where he afterwards goes, or what he does, a man cannot ever shake off the conditioning influence of his first fifteen or twenty years.

With the move to Dorset, Derbyshire virtually disappears from the family history. The children born there were too young to be much affected by the midlands scene before they left it for ever. John has a few early memories of Shirley in his *Autobiography*, and Littleton a page or so in *The Joy of It*; but both are subjective rather than objective in these passages, and the vivid physical impressions that might have been expected from Llewelyn are of course lacking, and although he was there years later and met his early love, Marion Linton, who was the vicar's daughter, in his magical evocation of their love in *Love and Death* the scene is set at Montacute.

But Dorchester, and Dorset in general, are indeed another matter. Llewelyn was proud of the ancient town of his birth, and it figures centrally in John's *Maiden Castle*, and obliquely in Theodore's stories. As a group of writers, these three are popularly identified with Dorset, although between them they range far more widely afield.

This Dorchester of the early 1880s was, however, not the Powyses' but Hardy's Dorchester—*The Mayor of Casterbridge* was published in 1886, and that is the book which evokes the scene into which the Rev. C. F. Powys now stepped. The statue of William Barnes had yet to be erected outside St Peter's, and the venerable figure of the Dorset poet was still familiar in the streets. Indeed, Mr Powys occasionally assisted the poet with his duties as Rector of Winterbourne Came, and Giles Dugdale [1] records that the Powys children were sometimes taken to

[1] *William Barnes of Dorset* (1953).

tea: and Llewelyn tells us that his mother carried him to Came to receive the poet's blessing.

For a brief time after accepting the curacy of St Peter's, the Rev. C. F. Powys lived in lodgings in Weymouth, but he then moved into the newly built Rothesay House, in South Walk, Dorchester. This was a somewhat overpowering mansion to house a curate: a solid villa in extensive grounds behind a massive feudal wall too high to be peeped over. Here Llewelyn was born.

Of the family life in Dorchester early records are scanty; here also John and Littleton remember mainly personal things: Theodore as always is autobiographically silent, and Llewelyn was not old enough to retain impressions. John is the most introspective of autobiographers, and Littleton's intense feeling for nature does not include any large tincture of the spirit of place: he recalls more easily the fields near Dorchester in which he chased butterflies, and his references to the buildings and streets are pious and perfunctory. Those early years at Dorchester, like the years at Shirley, left few indelible impressions, and even John's description of the town—which, owing nothing to Hardy's, yet may rival it—is rooted in experience gained in later years. The place of the family's childhood which made the deep and lasting impression was Montacute, just across the border in Somerset, to which they removed on their father's appointment as vicar, in 1886.

Montacute lies rather more than four miles from Yeovil, a little north of west, and on the road to Ilminster, which is some ten miles farther on. A parish, we learn—'St Catherine'—in the hundred of Tintinhull, and at the time of Mr Powys's preferment to the living, with a population of about eleven hundred. A proportion of these people were supporters of the Baptist and Wesleyan chapels in the village.

Montacute is a stone-built village, almost a miniature town, with a spacious and attractive square—'the Borough'—a handsome church, an ancient abbey now reduced to a farm, and the magnificent Montacute House, one of the glories of Elizabethan architecture, now in the keeping of the National Trust. The village lies in the shadow of Montacute Hill, with other hills beyond, including the famous Ham Hill with its quarries of warm-coloured stone. There is an accurate and affectionate description of the village as it was sixty years ago, in John Cowper's *Wood and Stone*, and it figures also less literally in *Wolf Solent*, in Llewelyn's *Love and Death*, and in the two brothers' autobiographical writings. A less direct description of the village and its surrounding countryside may be found in Philippa Powys's novel, *The Blackthorn Winter*, which evokes the Somerset scene without ever naming it. John Cowper has a poem 'To Montacute' in *Odes and Other Poems*, but it was perhaps too full of nymphs and dryads for Llewelyn's practical taste, for the younger writer's Montacute poet was Thomas Shoel, about whose verses he writes a characteristic essay.

When the Powys family arrived at the vicarage Montacute looked much as it does today, for change comes slowly there. The Borough had no red telephone kiosk, and there was no unending stream of cars passing through towards the seaside resorts of the west country; life moved in a more leisurely manner. But the tall gates of the manor stood open then as now at the bend of the road, the tall church tower rose above the roofs, and the birds circled around Montacute Hill, crested with its tower among the clustering trees. The Phelips family still lived at the great house which had been their home for three hundred years. A visitor to the village today may imagine himself back in the eighties as he sits in the sunny lee of the church or looks across the pond to the embattled Abbey gatehouse, or lingers along the side of the Borough. It is a pilgrimage many Powys admirers will wish to make, for the Rev. C. F. Powys was vicar here for thirty-two years, and there is no place so inseparably associated with the Powys name.

The vicarage, like the houses they had formerly lived in, was large and solid, with a big garden. The church was a fine building with a graceful slim tower, but not so impressive as some other village churches in the west country, because Montacute had never been a centre of commerce and wealth. The vicar once reduced an elaborate eulogy of the building to just proportions with the remark: 'We think that it is a very pretty church.'

Louis Marlow [1] gives a first-hand view of life at the vicarage in *Welsh Ambassadors*, and again in *Swan's Milk*; he dwells particularly on the great table at which the family gathered for meals: he saw them as one huge many-headed Powys as they sat there, confronting the single guest and stranger; and this is not entirely fanciful, for the stamp of their father was plain upon them all, and every one of them had the formidable Powys look. They were tall, handsome and powerful—every Powys was a personality in his or her own right, and I may say

---

[1] 'Louis Marlow' was, of course, Louis Wilkinson. The pen name appears on all but three of his books, but he used his real name on various shorter writings about the Powys family, and in broadcasts and of course when lecturing.

this with some freedom, for although I was not intimate with them all, I have seen eight of these brothers and sisters; not one of them could enter a room unremarked, though a crowd were there already.

Littleton Powys well describes the vicarage life in the first volume of his autobiography, *The Joy of It*:

Our father's character and personality went far in the making of this happy home; he was so strong, so independent, so simple, and so consistent; we always knew exactly where we were with him; he gave us a feeling of security such as I have never known since; he was the most honest man I have ever met; and he always took a great interest in what we did.

But he was not blessed with a great store of poetic imagination, and sometimes lost touch with the more active brains of some of his children. He had developed in him a very strong sense of duty; and few, if any, country parsons ever fulfilled their task more conscientiously and thoroughly than he. Down in his study every morning at seven-thirty he would deal with his letters; family prayers at eight; breakfast immediately afterwards; then a brief space taken up in wandering round the garden; dinner at one-thirty; at two-thirty he invariably set out to visit the sick in the parish, or those who needed help in any way; back home again by five forty-five; tea at six o'clock; then often to some meeting in the village; supper at nine and bed at ten o'clock.

Littleton also gives a glimpse of their mother:

Our evenings at home went quickly and happily enough; frequently our mother would get us together in the dining-room or drawing-room and read to us; when I look back I realise how excellent was her choice of books, and what a lasting effect this delightful time had upon each one of us. Later in the evening she would read to her husband who tired with the day's work would lie upon the sofa employing his hands in netting—making nets for all sorts of purposes.

But of course often she was not free, and then the evening was passed in reading to ourselves, or playing at games usually home made, invented by one or other member of the family. John would be directing the acting of some play, usually a play of Shakespeare, in which most of the family had parts, and he the most important; or he would be arranging some entertainment, in which his recitation of poetry played a great part. There was one great occasion when we joined forces with the Phelips family and produced *The Merchant of Venice*.[1] We had a game called Nebuchadnezzar, something of the nature of charades, in which scenes were acted without words, representing famous characters from history, from the Bible, or from literature. This game provided plenty of play for the imagination, and the walls would ring with laughter.

A little before ten would come evening prayers; after which my father would go to bed. Then my mother, having gone round the house and seen that all was well with the children already in bed would return to the drawing-room to enjoy what was her own private pleasure of the day—an hour or more of quiet, reading by herself. As we grew older, every now and then one or other of her elder children would be asked to sit with her, and she would either read aloud herself, or get him to read to her some selection of poetry or prose which particularly appealed to him; and I know what a great privilege I felt this to be, if I happened to be the favoured one.

The children were many, and because of this they felt little need for outside friendships; and perhaps in that day and place, outside friends would not have been easy to find, for between the gentry and the villagers there was the gulf of class, so hard to cross. They were fortunate to have lively and affectionate neighbours at the Abbey Farm, and at the big house. In his essay on Montacute House and its people Llewelyn points out that in those last days of the nineteenth century the squire was still a remote and feudal figure to the village folk; Mr Phelips was 'a highly cultured gentleman with a kindly disposition', but in his fields there were still clearly legible notices, 'Beware of Man Traps', and John recalls driving with the squire in his carriage when some of the villagers raised their caps and shouted and waved a greeting, and the squire remarked, 'We are being chaffed by the populace!'

The magnificent house is empty now, the family dead or dispersed; and all such emptinesses and dispersals, however changing times and ways may make them inevitable, are a diminishing and a narrowing in the character of England. Who is to say that the people of Montacute are the happier for having no influential despot watching over them

---

[1] Llewelyn says *Macbeth*, but perhaps there were two productions.

from behind the tall iron gates, which anyone may pass through now as of right, if only he pays a half-crown.

At Montacute the last children of the family were born, and the whole eleven of them grew up. In 1886 when they settled there John was already fourteen years old, Littleton twelve and Theodore eleven. The first two had been entered at the Preparatory School at Sherborne while still living in Dorchester, and they were now in the senior school. Theodore even thus early in life was taking a course independent of his brothers'. He went to a different school in Dorchester from the one they had initially attended, and although he was at the Sherborne Prep for a short time he did not go into the big school, and instead he was sent up into Suffolk, where the Rev. W. G. Wilkinson kept a private school at Aldeburgh. He was a friend of the Norfolk Johnsons, Mrs Powys's family, and father of Louis Wilkinson, whose life-long friendship with the Powys family had its beginnings about this time, although at first very tenuously, for between the little boy Louis, who was eight, and the reticent Theodore of fourteen, there could be but slight contact; but Louis recalls Theodore's 'inscrutable gravity' when some unknown artist left a graphic and unsuitable drawing on the lavatory wall, and in later years Theodore once observed that he didn't think Dr Wilkinson could have made much money out of the school, because the food was so good. He also claimed to have punched Louis's head 'for being the Headmaster's son', a convincingly Theodorian reason; but these are few details enough, compared with the wealth of detail supplied by John Cowper of his own schooldays, and the passages in Littleton's and Llewelyn's books. The other brothers were all educated at Sherborne, but only John, Littleton and Llewelyn went to university.

More than that of any of his brothers, the early life of T. F. Powys was bound up with East Anglia, for when he left school his father let him remain there working for a local farmer, and after this preliminary training the Rev. C. F. Powys bought Theodore a farm at Sweffling, in Suffolk. The other children made periodical visits to their Johnson kinsfolk in Norfolk, and some of them visited Theodore at Sweffling in due course, but only he of all of them made a home in East Anglia, although John uses the east coast for the main setting of *Rodmoor*, and writes the first two chapters of *Glastonbury* against the Norfolk background; he also has a sonnet 'Written in Sweffling Churchyard'.

Sherborne School is one of the most ancient in the country —

Littleton Powys, with the partial pride of an old boy and master, traces it back to the year 705; and it looks the part, for many of the school buildings are centuries old, and they lie in the precinct of the ancient abbey church. The town itself is a pleasant place, old-fashioned, and none the worse for that, having associations with Sir Walter Raleigh, whose ruined castle may still be seen, and with Sir Thomas Wyatt, traditionally buried in the north transept of the abbey after dying while on a mission for the king in the west country. Also in the abbey lie two kings, Ethelbald and Ethelbert, who died respectively in 860 and 866. But what the young Powys boys found most important was the fact of the school's location a mere ten miles from home, and John records how they would hurry across the hills to the Montacute vicarage of a Saturday afternoon and eat a great tea before setting out for the long run back before bedtime. Littleton recalls a more dramatic journey when, early in 1891, John was ill at school and he sent his brother home to say he felt he must leave; and leave he did, the very next day, when his father arrived in a hired carriage to take him home, never to return.

John tells of his school days with heightened effect in the *Autobiography*, and it is likely enough that public school life in the eighties was a rough affair; but he also speaks with generous appreciation of the masters, and so do Littleton and Llewelyn. Littleton gives a list of books borrowed from the library by John in his last term—a six-volume *History of the Christian Church*, lectures on other religions, sermons and theological works, and Coleridge's *Aids to Reflection*, among others; and this appearance of Coleridge prompts the reflection that the young J.C.P. resembled S.T.C. in a score of ways—in his nervousness, his learning, his eloquence, his enthusiasm; some of John's letters, with their exclamations, their underlinings, their range of thought and their brilliance, are irresistibly reminiscent of Coleridge; and I recall Mr Louis Untermeyer telling me that he met John Cowper only once, and that he never stopped talking, which is precisely what Hazlitt says of Coleridge.

Littleton, who was the most 'normal' of the Powyses, took the ordinary lad's interest in sports and the life of the school; his reading list at the same period contains six books on angling and ten Waverley novels; and his remarks on Sherborne dwell upon none of the horrors John endured. But it may be that public school life was unsuited to the temperament of the three brothers who became writers, for we have seen that Theodore did not pursue it, John did not enjoy it and

Llewelyn, so freely autobiographical on almost every phase of his life, is curiously reticent about Sherborne. He was slow at his work—both at school and at university—and although apparently popular enough at Sherborne he developed a secret life of his own, 'dreaming over my school books, my mind as dim and unlighted as the monk-haunted classrooms where I sat.' [1] For Llewelyn in after-life it is almost as though the years of his education made no permanent impact. His autobiographical writings in *Skin for Skin* and *Love and Death* begin with the onset of his consumption, as though that event were the real beginning of his life; and his detached essays on his childhood dwell lovingly on Montacute, and say virtually nothing about Sherborne or Cambridge.[2] He dismisses both school and university in six pages of *Confessions*, in contrast to a hundred and twenty-five on these subjects in John's *Autobiography*, and fifty in Littleton's *The Joy of It*. In *Apples be Ripe*, Llewelyn's hero, Chris, is shown to be wayward and unhappy at school, and although Llewelyn's published letters from school are too few to be decisive, it is hard to read into them any large enthusiasm for Sherborne. It is true that in *Swan's Milk* Louis Marlow quotes Llewelyn's zestful reminiscence, 'What days those were, what days!' in reference to their time together at Cambridge; but the reference is rather to personal friendships there than to the university itself. The conclusion must be that formal schooling paid a smaller part in the making of these three writers, John, Theodore and Llewelyn, than might have been expected.

Both the Powys grandfathers, and the Rev. C. F. Powys, had been at Corpus Christi College, Cambridge, and they were followed there in due time by John, Littleton and Llewelyn. At Cambridge, far more than at Sherborne, differences in age and temperament began to take effect. Littleton went up for his first year when John was already completing his last, and whereas John had no interest in games and no aptitude for them, Littleton at once took his place among the athletes, and before he left he was captain of both cricket and football at Corpus, and he later played rugby for Somerset. He records that his path and John's seldom crossed, and that on one occasion when they did his brother said to him, 'You never think, Littleton, why don't you think? You must think.' Littleton adds that John never said what he was to

[1] *Confessions of Two Brothers.*
[2] Some Cambridge reminiscences are in the essay 'Of Egoism' (*Earth Memories*), but they are not very full.

think about. John himself tells the other side of the matter in a different story, when he recalls making Littleton walk for some miles a few paces behind him. 'I explained that I *wanted to think* and that his breathing got on my nerves. "Let us think!" I would cry out in those days to anyone by my side.' [1]

Llewelyn's career at Cambridge was more nearly a mixture of thinking and doing; but the doing included too little at his books, and he failed his History Tripos, taking only a Pass Degree. When he got to Cambridge, John had already left, but Louis Wilkinson was there. He was three years Llewelyn's senior, and he exerted an influence on the less sophisticated Llewelyn which must have been entirely beneficent, although the Oxford authorities might not have agreed if consulted. Louis was a born rebel and nonconformist, over whom even John Cowper was apt to shake his head, and Theodore was quite positive that 'the Archangel' would be a dangerous ally for Llewelyn; John, walking near the college once with Llewelyn, proposed calling on Louis, and then, in an access of caution, 'Oh, no: we'd *better not!*' Llewelyn at that time had not met Louis, but he naturally lost no time in making this exciting and dangerous acquaintance, and a lasting friendship followed.

All the same, Cambridge had no greater permanent significance in Llewelyn's life than in John's, and John is quite specific: 'Take it all in all, the university *as* a university had not the least influence upon my taste, my intelligence, my philosophy or my character!' It was the brothers who did not go to university who knew best what they wanted to do in life, Littleton as always excepted. William never deviated from his chosen course, which was to be a farmer; like Theodore before him, he served an apprenticeship, though at a farm in Somerset, not East Anglia; he persisted in this work long after Theodore had abandoned it, and became a stock farmer in Kenya, where he spent the greater part of his adult life: a fact which was later materially to affect Llewelyn's prospects. Albert Reginald ('A.R.') was early apprenticed to an architect, and followed that profession with distinction for more than forty years, until his too early death. Even Theodore, although he finally gave up farming, was never in any real doubt what was his life's destiny: he only wanted to live in obscurity and to be left alone.

[1] *Autobiography.*

2

WHEN John Cowper Powys went down from Cambridge in 1894 he had, he tells us, no idea how he was going to make a living. He had given up the idea of entering the Church, which had been his parents' hope for him; and indeed he had travelled far from the simple and unquestioning faith his father held, although his sympathy with Christianity, and especially in later years with the Roman Catholic faith, was always stronger than that of Llewelyn, who was militantly a free-thinker, though never offensively so—indeed, Llewelyn's response to the poetry in the life of Jesus is an endearing element in writings which speak so scathingly of the antics of 'the cream dipp'd clergy'.

It was chance as much as anything that determined John's course of life for the next forty years. He was inquiring about schoolmastering possibilities when the scholastic employment agency mentioned an opening for a lecturer to girls' schools at Hove, and he tells us of his first delighted reaction: *schools of girls!* The idea of dozens, even scores of girls, all gathered in one place to listen to him was something new. He caught the next train to Brighton, he tells us. There were several schools at Hove all of which had been served by the same lecturer, who had just died. John Cowper had little difficulty in securing the vacant place, and at ten shillings a lesson, and two lessons a week at each school, he was made financially secure; especially as he also had the allowance of £60 a year given by the Rev. C. F. Powys to all his sons as they grew older, which in the eighteen-nineties was in itself almost enough to live on.

The vivid chapters in John's *Autobiography* which deal with this period in his life are much too good to paraphrase; the rooms over the Southwick grocer's shop in which he ate bread and milk and had prints of philosophers pinned over the mantelpiece; the ancient farmhouse near Lewes in which he read Swinburne in ringing tones to the housekeeper

who was 'happy to hear the dear Lord's name mentioned so frequent'; and the Burpham cottage with its 'Keep Out' notice which
brought up short the Duke of Norfolk, who owned all the land in
sight, including that which supported the notice; these and a hundred
pages in the *Autobiography* establish John Cowper's character at that
time far better than a later writer could do it. But he tells us very little
about his first venture into authorship, which happened about now,
or about his marriage.

Odes and other Poems, the author tells us, was published by the firm
of William Rider through the influence of Ralph Shirley, and he goes
on to call the poems 'conventional and imitative': well, so they are,
like those in very many first books of poems, but he is right also when
he says—looking at the book after a lapse of forty years—that 'a
certain faint feeling of spring emanates from it'. The forty years are
now more than seventy, but the faint feeling of spring still lingers:

> Music of rain on primrose-scented meads,
> Imperial daffodils that mock the wind,
> And laugh rude-shaken from their slumbers blind
> Beside the barren roots of moaning reeds,
> Anemones foam-fair and fairy-frail,
> Like gentle maidens won from dreamless sleep,
> That blush to cast aside their Beauty's veil
> And see the sunbeams thro' their curtains creep;
> And violets whose dim odours, like the voice
> Of Loves forgotten, steal our senses through,
> And carollings of larks that still rejoice,
> As did the morning stars when Earth was new.

Of the reception of this book by the Powys family we hear nothing.
John's father may have felt some pride in his eldest son's appearance
as an author, and his poetry-loving mother must certainly have
lingered over the pretty little green-and-gold volume in those late
hours of solitude when the household had retired, and she would have
seen behind and beyond the 'poor muse's thin scrannel-pipe' and may
perhaps clairvoyantly have detected the 'terrifyingly formidable
genius' to which she had given birth; but of all this we remain ignorant.
Even Llewelyn, so fiercely the champion of John's later poems, says
nothing of these; but the reception of the book cannot have been
discouraging, for in 1899 the same publishers were willing to put out a
second and larger collection under the simple title, *Poems*.

Odes had two effects at least, and one of them of great significance. W. B. Yeats, to whom one poem was addressed, wrote a long and appreciative letter (now lost) in which he gave the new poet careful advice; but more important was the invitation from Thomas Hardy to visit him at Dorchester, and this led to a friendship which lasted until the Wessex novelist died. I remember the pride with which John Cowper Powys told me that among the few books kept at Hardy's bedside in later years there was a copy of *Visions and Revisions*; and he recalls also that earlier moment of pride when he announced at the Montacute table that 'the greatest writer *now living on this earth*' was about to visit them:

> . . . and when in its slow, smooth, majestic manner the train belonging to the Great Western—monarch surely of all railways—finally drew up, and he, with the first Mrs. Hardy at his side, stepped out, what did I not feel! Do you think I have forgotten even what he wore that great day? Oh, most carefully was he dressed, consonant, in his Dorset-bred mind, with a formal visit to a Somerset vicar. He wore a light tweed suit, with knicker-bockers to match, and he had thin black stockings on, almost like those in which I had seen his friend, William Barnes, walking so stately down South Walk. Llewelyn, after his fashion, and in a manner that even I—John, the arch-imitator—cannot copy, has told how, when we took him down to the Robber's Castle under the high garden-wall, and called upon him to write his name in the band's archives, he wrote, in that clear classic hand I had seen in the manuscript of *Tess*, 'Thomas Hardy, *a Wayfarer*'.[1]

A third poem in *Odes*, addressed to Swinburne, appears to have provoked no reaction from 'The Pines', and the only member of the Powys circle to have any contact with the sage of Putney was Louis Wilkinson, who once helped Swinburne on with his coat in a pub, and was rewarded with 'Thank you'.

There is a considerable improvement in the second volume of John Cowper's poems, and in particular they are more original and individual. This may be in part because there is to be expected a natural improvement in the work of a young man upon his earliest efforts, and very likely many of the poems in *Odes* were written some years before publication, whereas those in *Poems* were presumably all new. But

[1] *Autobiography.*

some part of the improvement may be attributable to the influence of Alfred de Kantzow, whom John Cowper met at this time.

De Kantzow was an obscure and impoverished nobleman 'of some European country' (in fact, Poland) who lived at Portslade, and whom John's grocer landlord introduced him to; the old man was over seventy, a great character whom his disciple lovingly and vividly delineates in the *Autobiography* under the name 'Mr. de——'. Mr de —— was a poet of no small power. John Cowper says he never told the old man about his own *Odes*, but he took great trouble to get de Kantzow's poems into print, persuading first T. Fisher Unwin, and afterwards the Manchester firm of Sherratt and Hughes, to issue collections. The first, *Ultima Verba*, appeared in 1902 in Unwin's pretty 'Cameo Series', and the second, which is the same text considerably extended, was published under the title *Noctis Susurri: Sighs of the Night*, in 1906. These mainly philosophical musings on 'life, and death, and immortality' have, as John says in his autobiography, a real power, sombre and simple, and it would be interesting to see them reissued. Some influence on Powys's own *Poems*, and even on the verses he published twenty years later, may be noticed here.

MELANCHOLIA

The ground is ghostly with the dews that fall;
    Far in the sky there reigns unearthly light;
Fugitive spirit-clouds the sense appal;
    Give me back youth, O melancholy Night!

Ambition climbs in life's effulgent hours,
    Climbs oft in vain and visionary height;
No more I enter fancy's fairy bowers;
    Give me back Hope, O melancholy Night!

Hers was the grace of Helen, Ninon's bloom;
    She was a saint, she was my heart's delight.
Passion eclipsed casts all the soul in gloom;
    Give me back Love, O melancholy Night!

ELIJAH THE TISHBITE

It is enough. The cup of life I've drained
    Unto its lees. 'Tis hemlock at the last.
My sandals worn, my garments travel stained,
    Stretch the grey milestones in a vista passed.

It is enough. Now take away my life.
  My soul is noble by an accident.
With powers that quell me I am e'er at strife;
  Like sea-weed tossed, I drift—so Nature meant.

Enough—I am not better than my sires;
  Myself a mental cave-man wandering—
As I advance the Lord of Hosts retires;
  Eludes the arms that would about Him cling.

John Cowper says that *Poems* was issued 'with the combined help' of his father and cousin Ralph—that is, Ralph Shirley; which suggests that the volume may have been subsidized, and implies further that the first was also. This is a small matter; very many young poets have paid to see their verses in print, and not a few old ones. The two little books were kindly received by a not very exacting panel of reviewers —'there is a feeling of poetry in his writing which is absent from far cleverer verse-writers', the *Saturday Review* is quoted as saying, and the *Western Morning News* found that 'they surpass in poetic sentiment the usual run of published poems'. Be that as it may, the two books left no mark on nineteenth-century literature, and do not find even a footnote in the histories; and when their author says that at thirty he had neither written a book nor begotten a son, he is essentially in the right of it. He had done nothing—he says—but get de Kantzow's poems published: but this is something no reader of those poems will regret.

At this time John Cowper was making a living by his girls' school lecturing, and, the poems apart (and most sensitive young men compose verses), he had no thought of becoming a writer. He was enriching himself in those years by deep-rooted and long-lasting friendships with several remarkable men, and it is fair to say that the pages of his *Autobiography* which discuss the years around the turn of the century reveal the making of the novelist and philosopher.

The first of these was Dr Bernard Price O'Neill—'oldest and best friend of the family', as Louis Wilkinson calls him in the dedication of *Welsh Ambassadors*, in a phrase which he might himself have shared with Dr O'Neill. O'Neill was of mixed Irish and Welsh blood, and he passed his whole adult life obscurely as a general practitioner, the greater part of the time in Chiswick. But if he made no great personal mark in the world—and never sought to—none the less his lively and original mind, and his wide reading and clear thinking, left an indelible mark on the Powys family, and through them on their writings; in particular, it was he who first introduced them to the works of Rabelais, which influenced all of the writing brothers profoundly.

John says that he met O'Neill at the time of his marriage, but he doesn't say in what circumstances: 'without my marriage I should never have known this man of unique genius'. John's marriage was to Margaret Alice Lyon, sister of Thomas Henry Lyon, the architect under whom A. R. Powys learned his profession—and, many years later, in whose office John Cowper's son studied for a time. It would thus appear that O'Neill originally was a friend of the Lyons. John was married in 1896—the last little poem in his *Odes* is addressed to M. A. —(Margaret Alice). By 1899, when *Poems* appeared, he was close enough in friendship to Bernie O'Neill to dedicate the book to him— 'this country flask of vintage thin', he calls it—and over the years he dedicated to O'Neill two others, *Suspended Judgments* (1916) and *Rabelais* (1948). Louis Wilkinson reports—and no one who knew Dr O'Neill will doubt the truth of this—Mrs O'Neill's saying, 'I know who *could* have written as well as any. My husband.' But Dr O'Neill wrote nothing; he put the full artistry of his mind and spirit into living.

The next great influence on the Powys brothers was Louis Wilkinson. Louis Umfreville Wilkinson was born in 1881, and educated at Radley and at Pembroke College, Oxford, where he got into a scandal that led to his being sent down. It was a very unimportant scandal really, but blown up in size partly by the uncompromisingly bigoted attitude of the authorities, and partly because the magazine *Truth* took the matter up in a series of articles on 'A 'Varsity Star Chamber' and the like, so that Wilkinson and his friends got a great deal of publicity, most of it sympathetic. Their crime was 'blasphemy'—there was talk of black masses and of matters not mentionable, most of them also non-existent—and no appeal could be entertained. This in due course made it difficult for Wilkinson to gain admission at Cambridge; and it was only after several unsuccessful efforts that he learned privately that St John's College had not 'heard officially' of his Oxford scrape and would therefore consider his application. Accordingly he went to St John's in 1902 and was at Cambridge when Llewelyn went up in 1903. Wilkinson had met Theodore first, years earlier, at the Aldeburgh school, and he had come to know John through Theodore; he had doubtless heard of Llewelyn, and when the latter called on him 'in defiance of etiquette' the two quickly became friends. The fears of

John and Theodore about Louis's possible bad influence on Llewelyn seem to have acted the other way. Llewelyn needed no encouragement to be a rebel, and in fact Wilkinson, unwilling to be sent down again, hastened to lock the door one afternoon because of the outrageous things Llewelyn was saying. Recalling this in *Earth Memories*, Llewelyn adds that 'from that first afternoon we were always together, walking and talking and jesting, intoxicated with life'.

Louis Wilkinson, like Bernie O'Neill, became an inseparable part of the Powys way of life: for the next sixty years he and the family were in constant touch, visiting together, exchanging news and advice, borrowing and lending money—at different times he held a mortgage on Theodore's house, and Theodore one on his—and in general acting as one of the family.

Another potent influence at this time on John Cowper was John William Williams—'the Catholic', as they called him. He was a subtle and sophisticated apologist for the Roman faith, and John at this time was much concerned with Catholicism, to which his brother-in-law Harry Lyon had recently been converted. John never went so far, but his son later became a Catholic priest. This 'circle', as John loved to call it, of Bernie O'Neill, Louis Wilkinson ('the Archangel'), Harry Lyon, de Kantzow, Williams, was made up of men temperamentally poles apart, and their diversity had a profound effect on John Cowper after the years in which he was head and leader of a large family into the life of which strangers rarely entered. The influence would seem to have been greater than that of his wife, who remains a dim, enigmatic figure. There is no reason to suppose that they were not happy in the early years of marriage, and in 1902 she bore her only child, a son, Littleton Alfred. With John's life in America, which began shortly afterwards, she had little to do, and it may be that they drifted apart; her last years were clouded by persistent ill health, and she died in 1947.

While John was pursuing his strange profession as lecturer to schools of girls Theodore was about to embark upon the second phase of his.

It is usual to speak of a man 'going out into the world' when he reaches an age to leave his parents' home and take up a separate life; but it would be a reckless exaggeration to use the phrase in discussing the career of Theodore Powys. Certainly he was the first of the

brothers to leave home, and he felt (or seems to have felt) none of the
hesitations that troubled John and later Llewelyn on leaving the
university. Theodore went confidently into farming, but it might be
said that this was a gesture of withdrawing from the world, rather than
going into it. He had always been the solitary of the family; when the
children were young Marian, A.R., and Llewelyn had a secret hide-out
in the garden which they made themselves, and in which they had
feasts and gatherings—the 'Mayberlulu Castle'. But Theodore had
his own solitary fastness, 'Bushes Home', which was never the scene
of bustle or laughter: 'there he would spend hours by himself, thinking
his own thoughts undisturbed'. The farm which his father bought him
in Suffolk was remote indeed from the Somerset vicarage, and not very
close to his Norfolk relations. This was a 'Bushes Home' from which
could be heard no echo of the merriment in 'Mayberlulu'.

Theodore was not unsuccessful as a farmer, and the hard, monotonous life suited his temperament—years afterwards he wrote of
himself, 'Powys believes in monotony. He is happy when he does the
same each day'. But it is even more monotonous to do no work at all,
and perhaps that is why he gave up farming. 'The Sweffling experiment',
that period of his life might be called; it failed, and it was never
repeated.

But it is at Sweffling that we get our first glimpses of the mature
Theodore, for it was there that Louis Wilkinson first became intimate
with him, and he and John Cowper and Dr O'Neill were among the
visitors to the farm; and Theodore uncharacteristically allowed himself to be lured away occasionally, to visit Cambridge, where his
unconventional response to life delighted and puzzled Wilkinson's
contemporaries. In *Swan's Milk* Wilkinson gives us a picture of him
which, with minor modifications (like the disappearance later of the
moustache), may stand for him throughout the rest of his life:

In the early years of the century, T. F. Powys, who then wore a
heavy moustache, looked astonishingly like Nietzsche. I remember him as a heavily built young man with grey melancholy
eyes. His manners were courteous to the point of what seemed
to me an ironic deference. Always he was a countryman, and his
rural not rustic appearance made a sharply contrasting effect at
Dexter's dinner table. Among these young Oxonians and
Cantabs, these bright birds of rejoicing plumage, there was a
brown and earthy soberness in Theodore's aspect. His talk was in

contrast too: slow, rather timid sometimes, but ripe and bearing authority. No one could have been more alien to our kind of cleverness with its conscious precocity, our dapper 'wit', our studied French colloquialisms, our 'undergraduate chatter', to quote the phrase which Dexter resented him using later about one of his celebrated contemporaries. But his ironical humour fed silently on us, I am sure.

Already, Wilkinson tells us, Theodore was beginning to write, and he quotes a few sentences which are stamped unmistakably with the mark which might be called 'Theodorian' and which so notably distinguishes all his published work. But he was a slow writer, and not youthfully ambitious for print; in this he resembled an eighteenth-century author, rather than one of his own time—he was like some Thomas Gray, writing for a small audience or none, and suspicious of the printer: Gray, who would publish his poems only to save them from the indignity of being pirated by others. It was Louis Wilkinson and John Cowper who financed Theodore's first essay in publication, and it can be no accident that these two were associated with G. Arnold Shaw a few years later when he published Theodore's first solid book, *The Soliloquy of a Hermit*. It was Louis also who criticized, suggested modifications and to some degree 'edited' the early T. F. Powys stories, years before they were published. He says in *Swan's Milk* that his efforts to interest publishers and critics in Theodore's work met with small success; this may be true, but his aid to Theodore in other ways must be gratefully remembered, and the eventual publication of his stories must owe a great deal to Louis Wilkinson's persistent encouragement of their author: writing, with Theodore, was 'work', and he must always have felt a stronger incentive to stop than to start.

Theodore's moment of hesitation came when giving up the Suffolk farm. What should he do? That he hesitated is clear, for Louis Wilkinson records that he even 'gave a few lectures' at Eastbourne, where John Cowper was lecturing at this time at yet another group of his girls' schools. Theodore would never have made a professional lecturer: his thoughts were too original and too gloomy and too unorthodox to have endeared him to the average lecture audience; and he would not have excelled at discussing the thoughts of others at second hand. It is at once pleasant and awful to contemplate his delivering an oration on Mrs Humphry Ward, as Llewelyn was once obliged to do.

'Powys likes monotony.' He decided it would be possible to live on the allowance his father made him—Theodore's needs were modest. He took a cottage at Studland, a small village overlooking Poole Bay from the eastern edge of the Isle of Purbeck, surrounded by the last acres of Hardy's Egdon Heath where they reach the sea, and bounded by the grassy hills of Purbeck. Although Studland is close to the great sprawling conurbation of Poole and Bournemouth, it is still comparatively remote, for the waters of Poole Harbour cut it off from the busy trunk roads; and in 1902, when Theodore went there, it was indeed the end of the road, a village with an ancient church, a handful of scattered cottages, and a pub. Just the place for a man to do nothing, and think, it might be supposed; but Theodore found it 'too fashionable' and he moved on before long, seeking through the Dorset countryside for a place which was not fashionable. He came to East Chaldon, or Chaldon Herring as it is more picturesquely called, a village in a fold of the hills some way inland from the tall cliffs of White Nose and Bats Head. Ironically Theodore's choice of Chaldon for a home in turn made this village 'fashionable', and many famous artists and writers visited it—and in some cases made it their home. John and Llewelyn Powys, Gertrude and Philippa Powys, David Garnett, Stephen Tomlin, Elizabeth Muntz, Robert Gibbings, Sylvia Townsend Warner, H. M. Tomlinson, Valentine Ackland, Edna St Vincent Millay, R. C. Trevelyan—these are but some with whom the village and its whitewashed pub, The Sailor's Return, have associations.

Theodore's cottage at Studland had been opposite the post office, and at Chaldon he lived in a terrace of three cottages of which the post office was one. It is hard not to feel that maybe he considered it desirable to be able to keep an eye on the going and coming of the mail, but if this was so he gradually acquired a greater confidence, for he removed to another house—Beth Car, 'the house by the pasture', which lay on the western edge of the village, beyond the church, where the principal thing to be seen was High Chaldon, the hill he was to make known to thousands under the name of Madder Hill. This house had been built by Thomas Hardy's brother, and the tradition is that the architect was Hardy himself. The small square red-brick villa has no architectural distinction, but Theodore liked it, even to the black iron grate ornamented with 'three varnished iron sunflowers'.

In 1905 Theodore married a Dorset girl, Violet Rosalie Dodds, with whom he lived in entire accord until his death nearly fifty years later. That this lady exactly understood her strange genius of a husband sufficiently appears when we learn that from time to time she would say to him, 'Get along, you old teapot!'

At Chaldon—if his own testimony in *Soliloquies* may be believed—he walked the hills, dug his garden, and mended his broken fences. He also finished his first published essay, *An Interpretation of Genesis*, which was printed privately in 1907 and 'published'—for this is hardly the word—in 1908. It seems never to have been formally offered for sale, although some copies were sent for that purpose to John's publisher, William Rider; and almost all were accidentally destroyed by fire. The copies that survive are now among the rarest, and consequently to collectors the most costly and most desirable of all Powys items; the would-be reader may take heart, however, for an edition of 490 copies was issued by Chatto & Windus in 1929, and the text is therefore not completely inaccessible, although hard to find.

The book is little more than a curiosity, considered as literature; the 1929 reprint is handsomely produced, but the little squarish paperback pamphlet of 1908 really suits the essay better, for it is amateurish in execution and not altogether without elements of the cranky in conception. It might be a tract put out by one of the curious one-man religions of the nineteenth century; or it might be found akin to the equally odd writings being produced about the same time by Aleister Crowley. It is the only book by T. F. Powys which might have been written by somebody else—the only book of his not unmistakably marked with his unique genius.

An Interpretation of Genesis is a dialogue between Zetetes (who may be identified with the author) and a personage styled The Lawgiver of Israel. The Lawgiver quotes texts from *Genesis*, and gives as it were a running commentary upon them by way of interpretation and exposition; and Zetetes at first asks questions designed to further this elucidation, but as the discussion proceeds he ventures to tell the Lawgiver his own views and opinions, and so far as argument goes he gives as good as he gets. He is a seeker after truth, but he is not prepared merely to receive didactic exhortation.

If the book fails—and I think it does—it is not because the matter is without interest (although its interest is limited) but because the style is irritating: for nothing palls more quickly than an affectation of biblical language which does not succeed, and here it is sometimes painfully inadequate. Here is a quotation which is a very fair example of the whole; it is a comment by Zetetes on the Lawgiver's remarks upon Noah planting a vineyard and getting drunk on the wine it produced.

> I understand thee well: if man taketh from the Mother more than is necessary for him he becometh naked and a beast, and if man desireth all the Mother for himself, whether it be life everlasting, or goods, or comfort, or wine, or oil, whether he desire wives, glory, or praise, whatever he desire in this wise, it is nakedness unto him and he goeth into the beast again. And if any nursling or unlearned man see him that hath become a beast, the desire of the unlearned shall be the same as of the beast, and the unlearned shall be the servant of man, even as Canaan was: 'A servant of servants shall he be unto his brethren.' When man becometh naked by reason of his drunkenness, he hindereth the Truth in man, and especially he harmeth the youngest children, for children because of their tender years look unto their elders, even as the elders look unto their Father, and if the elders go contrary to the Truth they bear many of the younger children along with them, and because of the folly of the father the child is cursed. But the elder sons, although they hear of the nakedness of their father, will not be drawn unto him, for they know their true Father, and the Truth draweth them. Therefore were Japheth and Shem blessed, for they desired the Truth.

This was a harder nut to crack than John's juvenile poems, and it would be interesting indeed to know the Rev. C. F. Powys's comments; but I have not been able to learn what they were. On one occasion when John boasted to his father about the sins and temptations he was encountering the old man only answered by asking his son to help by reading the lessons 'during this season of long gospels'. He might perhaps have dealt with Theodore's unorthodoxy by a request to lead the responses.

3

LEWELYN took his degree in the last weeks of 1906, and was faced, like John before him, with the need to make a living and with no strong ideas how to do it. He had long since decided that 'the way of Jesus was not the way of Lulu', and although he probably kept the real force of his hedonistic convictions from his father, he did not respond to the suggestion that he enter the Church. His own immediate idea was to take up lecturing, in which John and Louis were already active. He even gave some 'practice' lectures, but although he returned to lecturing later for a time, in these first months after leaving Cambridge he gradually gave up the idea and drifted, as John had done, into schoolmastering, employing for the purpose the same famous and delightfully named agency of Gabbitas and Thring. But whereas John had heard through this agency of his exciting schools of girls, Llewelyn was less fortunate. All he could get was an under-master's job in a preparatory school, St Peter's Court, Broadstairs, and even this was only temporarily, during the absence of another master.

At first I was terrified at having to teach at all: all the little boys were cleverer than me. I used to have to steal along to the class room every night to get hold of a book 'with answers' so that I might work out the sums we would do the next day, in the seclusion of my bedroom. I also had to do this kind of preparation with the Latin Prose and French—French! that was always terrible to me; most of the boys had been abroad and knew how to speak it quite well. The 'Madam' who used to come over from Ramsgate twice a week to give conversation lessons, seeing my predicament got it into her head that it would be a kindness to let me attend her classes. A chair was placed for me at the end of the room and there I used to sit—like a great clownish dunce—while these clever children chattered away to each other and to the lady. The mere possibility of being called upon to pronounce the simplest word made me literally sweat.[1]

Llewelyn says that on the whole he enjoyed the three months at Broadstairs, but he noted and commented upon the 'objectionable and imbecile types' who became under-masters at preparatory schools. This was no flattering observation from the brother of Littleton Powys, who was already quite happily embarked upon a life as master, and afterwards headmaster, of a preparatory school. That may be why in his book Llewelyn is careful to say *private* preparatory school, no doubt to distinguish it from the public kind; and he had in mind probably the same ineffectual, defeated men whom we see in Hugh Walpole's novel *Mr. Perrin and Mr. Traill*, itself in part based upon early teaching experiences. It is interesting to note that Walpole was Llewelyn's contemporary at Cambridge, but they were never friends and Llewelyn's references to Walpole after meeting him years later in New York are not flattering.

Because he had enjoyed his experience of schoolmastering—'on the whole'—and more importantly because nothing else offered, Llewelyn looked for another similar job when the first came to an end. This when found was at Bromsgrove, in Worcestershire, and his second term of teaching taught him something also—that to be a schoolmaster was not for him. He decided to 'write for the papers'—a suggestion, he adds, 'vague enough to frighten anybody'. His intention was to ask Theodore for the use of a 'back room' and to live there on fifteen shillings a week while waiting for *Home Chat* and *T.P.'s Weekly* to open their columns to him. How far this experiment might have gone cannot be known, for before it was put into practice Llewelyn received the offer of a private tutorship to a lad of fourteen, at Calne, in Wiltshire. He accepted this and remained fifteen months, never at ease and never content; he gives a brief and somewhat guarded account of the experience in *Confessions* from his arrival when 'the discreet, ironic civility of the coachman who was waiting for me on the platform made me at once aware of my new social position—of the social position of a Private Tutor' to the last entry in his diary, 'Free at last!' The few happy hours he records are those he spent alone, when he was able— rather rarely—to escape and go walking by himself. 'I came across a farmer from our part of the country and longed to tell him to tell my

[1] *Confessions of Two Brothers.*

brother that *he had seen me in Hell.*' The non-success of this period lay
not only in Llewelyn's inaptitude for teaching, but also in the fact that
he could feel neither affection nor respect for his pupil, who had
'already acquired the insolent demeanour of the vulgar rich'. Speaking
of the guests at a house party he says 'they all had more money than
manners'.

During these months Llewelyn applied for lecturing to the American
University Extension authorities, lying sleepless after posting the letter
because he was conscious of having spelt the word needless with an
'a' for the second 'e'. John Cowper and Louis Wilkinson were already
working in America, and Llewelyn was inclined once again to follow
his brother's lead.

John Cowper Powys had extraordinary talents for lecturing; he
had great natural ability as an actor, and his tall figure and striking,
hawk-like head made his hold on an audience complete from the
moment he stepped on to the platform. Louis Wilkinson was also very
tall, with thick auburn hair and a deep, rich voice, and he too was no
ordinary orator. They both had experience with the Oxford Extension
programme before going to America, and they both settled down to
making this their main source of income for many years. As 'Louis
Marlow' Wilkinson had published his first novel while still at the
university; this was *The Puppets' Dallying*, accepted and published by
the firm of Greening and Co. in 1905, after being rejected many times,
so that Louis's friends had a little satirical chant, frequently sung, with
the dolorous burden, 'the Book's come back!' Greening published a
number of popular novelists of the day, including Cosmo Hamilton,
Guy Thorne, Edgar Saltus, Reginald Turner (with whom Louis later
became friendly, a man of charm and wit who made the wry joke,
'It's my *second* editions that are rare!'), and their list included Baroness
Orczy's *The Scarlet Pimpernel*. *The Puppets' Dallying* is in part a
school story and in part the story of adolescence, written with a certain
maturity of thought, but not of style. The writer occasionally uses
something of the mildly epigrammatic manner of the social chapters in
some of the Henry Seton Merriman novels, but without that writer's
professional competence. But no reader of *The Puppets' Dallying*,
aware of its author's later brilliant novels, could fail to see in the early
book, time and again, the germ which was to come so confidently to
fruition in *Love by Accident* and *Mr. Amberthwaite*.

John Cowper had taken up the English lecturing for University

Extension a year or so after his marriage, giving courses of lectures on
a set subject—'Shakespeare's Historical Plays',[1] or 'Carlyle, Ruskin
and Tennyson', to name a couple—and he speaks of journeying all
over England, sometimes giving lectures on successive nights in towns
two hundred miles apart; and when he became known he was invited
to do the same work in Germany, where he was a great success. Then,
in 1904, he was invited to America by The American Society for the
Extension of University Teaching, with headquarters in Philadelphia.
A year later Louis Wilkinson followed. Louis says of his first lecture
that it must have been pretty bad, but the audience of ladies evidently
looked upon him as an imported luxury, like English marmalade [2] or
Worcester sauce. Speaking of another lecture in which he fumbled and
hesitated, he says he learned afterwards that it was good if he could to
some degree antagonize his audience—'it gave him a grip, and, besides,
he liked the feeling'. Years later in advising Walter de la Mare on
lecturing, John told him to fix his attention on a man at the back of the
hall *whom he decided to hate*, and address all his remarks to him; but
L. A. G. Strong's advice to me when I began to speak in public was to

[1] Among the rarest of his publications are the printed syllabuses of these
lectures, and it may be of interest to quote a specimen lecture-synopsis to indicate
his approach. This is from 'Six Lectures on Shakespeare's Historical Plays'
(*c.* 1901):

Lecture VI.

The Roman Plays: *Coriolanus: Antony and Cleopatra.*

The attempt of the hero to stand alone,

> 'As if a man were author of himself,
> And knew no other kin',

and his overweening pride towards the people, the cause of the tragedy.

Shakespeare's political impartiality. His blame of both parties and kindness
to both. 'He reserves his scorn for the demagogues.' Volumnia compared with
Portia. Her stoicism more of the blood. Portia's of the brain.

Antony and Cleopatra. The most 'valiant', rich, and glowing in style of all
Shakespeare's plays. A play of the lust of love, with the wonders and luxury of
the East as a background. Compare it with *Romeo and Juliet*, a play of the passion
of love with the nightingales and gardens of Italy behind it.

Antony's very intellect enamoured of Cleopatra. He sets himself to live in an
embodied dream of pleasure. He plays with words as dice; but he is always the
Roman Antony.

Cleopatra, the most complex of Shakespeare's women. Compounded of a
thousand littlenesses, she becomes great by their united charm.

Antony wins our love, Cleopatra our wonder; but the cold-blooded Caesar
conquers the world.

[2] Certainly no marmalade-lover in America would eat the native concoction.

look for a pretty girl in the front row and direct my remarks at her!
Ultimately all such advice is profitless if given to one without the
temperamental trick—the *gall*, as John Cowper might say—to stand
up and talk. And this ability, which his friend and brother both had so
abundantly, Llewelyn lacked. He wrote to his mother after beginning
his first series in America in 1909 that his second lecture in New York
was more or less a fiasco, and 'one courteous American advised me to
take the first boat back to England, and others said likewise'. Louis
Wilkinson was present on that occasion and he says, 'Listening to it
was one of the most acutely embarrassing and distressing experiences
I have ever had, and delivering it was an evident agony to Llewelyn.'
He says that Llewelyn gasped, and paused interminably and read from
his manuscript without seemingly understanding what he read; and he
was completely floored by questions. Afterwards he was hardly able
to speak for misery and despair. But he persisted, and improved,
though never apparently to a point of being anything more than barely
adequate. He must at this time have gone through much expense of
spirit at the thought of successive failures when his brothers were
making their way serenely in their chosen professions. Willie the
farmer, Bertie the architect, both younger than himself, were firmly
set on their course; Theodore had come into a secure haven; Littleton
never doubting, marched breast-forward; and John was an obvious
success, exercising already his almost hypnotic spell from the platform, the author also of two published books, and of other writings.
He was engaged about this time on his *Life of Keats*, which was never
published, but its fate could not have been foreseen then. Louis too
was successful as lecturer and author. Llewelyn's moods of near
despair seemed to have sufficient justification, and he had not at this
time developed the resilient toughness of character which was to stand
him in good stead in later years, when his poor health often made
heavy demands on his philosophy.

Llewelyn's first American engagement was for three months, and
at the end of it he returned to England, still with his future undeter-
mined. There had been no offer of a renewal of his lecturing contract,
and all through the remainder of 1909 he was trying to choose between
various alternatives; in the meantime he spent some months at the
Sherborne Preparatory School where Littleton was already a master—
the school of which Littleton would afterwards be the head. Llewelyn
was happier schoolmastering at Sherborne, and with Littleton, but he
was under some pressure from his cousin Ralph Shirley, who wanted

him to go into publishing. 'Do not be irresolute,' Shirley wrote. 'Make up your mind to come to me—otherwise you will spoil your life.' But Llewelyn still had thoughts of 'writing for the papers', and he was also in expectation of a recall to America.

John Cowper was in England at this time, and it was now that he had the serious illness which almost forced him to abandon lecturing; the illness, which although it never crippled him as Llewelyn's illness crippled the younger man, was still a potent influence on John for the rest of his life—the nervous stomach disorder which played such havoc with his digestion and other internal processes, so that the graphic and sometimes horrifying details he gives of it in his autobiography leave the reader wondering how those marathon novels and 'mean-jump' lecture tours ever came to be completed.

For Llewelyn that was an itinerant summer; when the school broke up he went for a holiday with his brother Willie, and then he hurried to London to be with John, then back to Devonshire where his parents were staying at Sidmouth and where Llewelyn tried to arrange for John to abandon lecturing for a career as a writer—the *Life of Keats* was well on towards completion. With John much better, and the promise made that he would not return to America, Llewelyn set off to visit Louis in East Anglia, then back to London to see his brother Bertie and so to Burpham, in Sussex, where John was convalescing— and now again determined to resume his work in America. The restless Llewelyn was soon off again, this time to the old home at Shirley, where he fell in love with Marion Linton, daughter of the vicar who had succeeded Mr Powys. Finally, when the new school term began, he returned to Sherborne with Littleton, apparently reconciled to continue as a master.

It was at Sherborne, a few weeks later, that he learned that he was suffering from consumption.

It must be remembered that this disease was then one of the most prevalent and deadly of killers, and when Llewelyn wrote in his diary of the first signs of its appearance, 'That drop of blood is my death warrant', he was not being alarmist or dramatic. In those days few sufferers recovered, and most died tragically young; the mortality in England and Wales in 1908 was in excess of fifty-six thousand persons, and this figure represented more than 10 per cent of all deaths in that year. People with consumption expected to die, and usually did.

How Llewelyn came to be stricken with it is not clear, but certainly he had been living under great strain for some time—the uncongenial periods as schoolmaster and private tutor, followed by the near disaster of his American tour with its irksome duties in which he felt so little at ease, and thereafter John's sudden and dangerous illness: these had all placed a burden on Llewelyn which might well have exacerbated any initial weakness or tendency to the disease. He had also experienced emotional stress in the frustrations of a conventional morality which restricted his natural and healthier impulse to 'snatch, snatch at happiness with passionate intensity'. He had not yet shaken himself free of the taboos of his early upbringing, and it was in part the consciousness of his own youthful deprivations which later prompted some of his most eloquent pages, when, again and again, he 'appealed to youth' not to be deceived but to take every life-giving minute of love and sunshine and laughter, regardless of the disapproval of 'envious, defeated old men'.

Llewelyn's parents thought he would die, and were resigned. His mother wanted to keep him near her, and his father grumbled at 'exploitation' by the doctors. But John encouraged Llewelyn to fight for life, and he persuaded the Rev. C. F. Powys to send Llewelyn to Switzerland—to Davos-Platz, famous as the place where so many had come looking for health—the place where Stevenson had failed to find it, thirty years before, and where Flecker was to seek it in vain, a year or two later. In the event, Llewelyn was the luckiest of the three.

The accident of illness from consumption would affect the course of a man's life whenever it occurred, but the accident of its occurring to Llewelyn Powys at that particular time was of especial significance; a year or two later, and the whole course of his life would have been entirely different—or so it may seem to one looking back. For it appears likely that he was about to drift into schoolmastering, and a serious illness after a few years in that profession would very likely have served to keep him from taking up another, and might have left him ailing and frustrated, carrying on uncongenial work at Sherborne or elsewhere, unable to escape. This may sound a gloomy reflection to make of so sturdy and original a spirit as Llewelyn Powys, but I think his character was immeasurably strengthened by his illness, and by the illness coming when it did. His letters and diaries show that in the period immediately prior to falling ill he was much occupied with the formation of his personal philosophy; greatly concerned with thoughts of death, and with speculation upon the meaning of life; he had rejected Christianity, but had not yet found any beliefs to replace it; he was 'adrift on a wide, wide sea'. And now for seventeen months he was forced into inactivity in the sanatorium, with all the time he needed to read and think; and with several companions with whom to argue and debate and speculate—men of all nationalities, religions and viewpoints: women too—united by their common illness, but diverse in all else. How much he learned, and how much he profited by it, may be read between the lines of his writings about the sanatorium, whether in his contemporary letters or his later published essays. He went to Clavadel anxious, immature, unsophisticated; when he returned home he had advanced far towards the formidable, uncompromising and emancipated personality indelibly marked upon his later writings; but the young Sherborne master would never have written *Impassioned Clay* or *Love and Death*.

There are references to his illness scattered all through Llewelyn's writings, but the lengthiest is his account of its first onset, of the Clavadel 'cure', of the hot, lazy happy summer that followed, and of the sudden fresh attack which came in February 1912. *Skin for Skin*, dealing as it does with a bare three years of his life, cannot be called an autobiography in itself, although the whole content is autobiographical; it can be printed on a hundred pages. But within its scale it may be considered the most perfect autobiographical essay in English.

4

IN ALL families, even the largest and most united, there comes a time
when the familiar pattern breaks up—with the marriages of the
children, and their leaving home to embark upon individual careers.
That time had now come at Montacute. Already all the brothers except
Llewelyn had definitely moved away—Theodore was settled at East
Chaldon, Bertie was working in London, Willie was almost ready to
take up what would prove to be his life's work in East Africa, Littleton
was at Sherborne, and John was settled in Sussex with his wife and son,
and committed to the wandering lecturing life every winter in America.
Mr Powys's thirty-two years' ministry at Montacute was approaching
its close, although he would remain there until 1918. But the decisive
break came in 1914, when Mrs Powys died.

For Llewelyn, the eighteen months between his return after the
second stay in Switzerland and his mother's death were, despite the
great care he had to take with his health—care not always taken—
both busy and happy. The progress of his love affair with Marion
Linton is described with great sensitivity in *Love and Death*, and in the
summer of 1914 it had resulted in an engagement to marry. During the
same period he made his first successful essays in writing, and had his
first successes in publication; throughout his writing life he found a
place for his essays in rationalist and free-thinking journals, and this
began when he met with early encouragement from A. R. Orage, then
editing the *New Age*; at the same time his copious diaries provided
material for the *New Statesman*, whose literary editor was Llewelyn's
Cambridge contemporary, J. C. Squire. Malcolm Elwin records in his
biography of Llewelyn Powys that much of the material later gathered
into the volume *Ebony and Ivory* was written in and around the
summer of 1913, at Montacute—except for the purely African sketches,
which were of course the product of his four war-time years in Kenya.

The last settled European peace for half a century—perhaps for longer—was coming to its end, and it was in this closing Indian summer of a great and vanishing age that John, Llewelyn and Louis went to Italy. Louis had brought back from America an American wife, Frances Gregg, about whom John had written home excitedly and in some degree despairingly, for he also was in love with her; and Llewelyn when he met her fell under the same spell. The three friends and the girl went to Venice together: inevitably, there was extravagance, gaiety, perhaps excess—as Llewelyn's friends had foreseen: Bernie O'Neill (and he was a doctor) had warned Llewelyn against 'too much love-making' and the cautious Bertie had written of the Venice trip, 'All very well, but *don't do it*'. Frances dressed as a boy, and the four had a delightful time, ending up by being arrested under suspicion of nobody quite learned what, in that politically troublous time. Also in Venice they encountered the exotic Baron Corvo, a man hardly to John's taste—nor perhaps to Llewelyn's, although Louis no doubt contemplated that lively and sad figure with ironic detachment. It was John who put paid to the relationship: 'We're engaged,' he cried in response to the Baron's invitations. 'All the time! Up to the hilt!' As this holiday drew to a close, Llewelyn was taken ill again, this time in Milan; he moved on, slowly, to Genoa, and took ship home.

That Italian trip was made in summer, 1912, and through all the following autumn and winter Llewelyn was ill. In 1913 he remained at Montacute, quietly; and here again his illness may have had its influence for good, because he was unable to go far, or do much, and accordingly he was not tempted away from his writing, which made its first definite progress towards success during the summer. He was also able to carry on quietly and without excess his affair with Marion Linton.

Two events, one personal and one of wider implication, now dictated Llewelyn's course. The death of his mother affected him not only in its close relationship, the natural sad consequence of the severance of a long-rooted love; but also because it brought him yet again into the contemplation of the meaning of death; he writes of this death in some degree as though he were an outside, unimplicated observer.

Within a few weeks of the funeral war broke out in Europe, and Llewelyn made his decision to go to Africa. There was of course no question of his joining any branch of the armed forces, but by deputizing on the stock-farm for his brother Willie he was able to release Willie to enter the army—which he was anxious to do.

Willie—so he was always called—had completed his training in farm work and had taken a job at Gilgil, in what was then called British East Africa, 'a place twenty miles from the equator with an altitude of 8,000 feet'. This was in 1913, and it was about a year later— on 18 October 1914—that Llewelyn arrived to be his brother's deputy and temporary successor; give or take a few weeks, he remained there almost exactly five years.

A word may perhaps be said here about the Powyses and the war. John Cowper describes his own attempt to enlist, which failed on medical grounds; Littleton remained in the essential job of a schoolmaster. Llewelyn's health of course made soldiering impossible. Willie served in the army in Africa, and Bertie fought on the western front, and was a prisoner in Germany. Theodore's initial reaction was typically Theodorian and is described in a letter to Louis Wilkinson:

> . . . I was going to run off to Dorchester to join the ranks and serve MY country, only I happened to see a Corporal by the sea shore who arrested me for Bathing with my family. Such a Corporal! God! I would like to see him prod his little stick into your belly. Anyhow I have kept at home ever since and leave the country to serve itself.

This resolution, however, he did not adhere to, and afterwards made the journey to Dorchester—itself an example of tender patriotism, for the distance was all of twenty miles—and was not found acceptable by the army.

In the early months of the war John and Louis were both again lecturing in America, and it was at this time that they joined with G. Arnold Shaw, who had already 'managed' Louis, in forming the University Lecturers Association of New York, which John less grandly described as their 'circus'. There is an affectionate portrait of the eccentric Shaw in John's *Autobiography*—'if only we could mange our Manager'—but Louis speaks somewhat less tolerantly of Shaw's habit of leaving letters unanswered and losing lecture engagements worth thousands of dollars. It was Shaw who prompted John to his next essay in authorship, for in the winter of 1914 he produced a political pamphlet which had a wide circulation and provoked a good deal of discussion in America, and in England when it was issued there.

This was *The War and Culture*, subtitled 'A Reply to Professor Münsterberg', a hundred-page paperback, on the title-page of which the author is described, incidentally, as a lecturer at Hamburg, Dresden and Leipzig, which would seem to support his title to take issue with a German professor—especially as Münsterberg was practically an American after more than twenty years on the faculty at Harvard.

Münsterberg was a psychologist, but he wrote and spoke widely on many topics of public concern, as a few of his book titles demonstrate: *Psychology and Life*; *American Traits*; *Principles of Art Education*; *American Patriotism*; *Psychology and Industrial Efficiency*; and a dozen others. In 1910 he was appointed the organizer and first director of the Amerika-Institut of the German Government. The professor's viewpoint is clearly an anticipation of Nazi doctrine a generation later, as a short quotation may show:

> It cannot be denied, however noble the pacifist ideals are, their promoters have not succeeded as yet in proposing a single plan by which war would be abolished and yet at the same time possibilities given for the healthy growth of progressive peoples and for the historically necessary reduction of decadent nations.
>
> *New York Times*, 19 Sept. 1916

Münsterberg's *The War and America* was designed to show that Germany was entitled to America's sympathy and support; and of course there was and is in America a very strong element of German ancestry, which would naturally and reasonably incline to be pro-German. There was some arrogance in the professor's remarks, but their general tendency was to persuasion and reason, and in his reply John Cowper appealed also to reason; he gave fair summaries of Münsterberg's main arguments, and replied to them without heat and without bias—often indeed agreeing with the professor, or at least allowing that there were points to be made on either side. John's arguments are not so much anti-German or pro-British as a general assessment of the meaning of the war in terms of humanity as a whole.

The interest of this essay for the Powys student does not lie in what it says but in considering the style in the light of what came after. The first thing which will strike him is the restraint—here are no declamations, no excesses, no outpourings, no underlinings, no capital letters, no exclamation marks. The pamphlet proceeds with the decorum and gravity of a leader in the *Morning Post*. The style is hardly ever individual or recognizable—a detached paragraph printed anonymously would afford no clue to its author's name, and would arouse no curiosity to seek it. This is the interesting thing: that John Cowper could write so level and so balanced and so un-individual an essay; for he has told us of the extravagances of his *Life of Keats*, written a few years earlier; and nobody reading his published letters of the period will doubt that from the first he commanded a prose as personal and unmistakable as any in English. In *The War and Culture* he would appear to have imposed a restraint upon himself which he never felt the need to exercise again. All the same, there can be found in these pages the hint, in a phrase now and again, and in a longer passage less often, of the writer who was yet to be born in John Cowper:

> One cannot help thinking, sometimes, as this appalling war goes forward, with such incredible endurance and heroism on both sides, how good it would be for the race at large if non-combatant writers and professors could deal in the same heroic and elemental manner with the mysteries of life, wrestling, with tragic obstinacy, with the dark angel of truth. If indeed there is going to be any real light thrown upon the bewildering chaos of things by human thinking, it will be surely thrown by such thinking, drastic and adventurous and 'dangerous', rather than by such thinking as is self-satisfied and discreet. Nature gives up her secrets in the final result only to genius and to courage. Life gives up its secrets only to those who resemble life, in the large desperateness of their invasions, and the demoniac violence of their assaults. Culture, in the deeper issues, is no smooth, placid, academic thing. It is no carefully arranged system of rules and theories. It is the passionate and imaginative instinct for things that are distinguished, heroic and rare. It is the subtilizing and deepening of the human spirit in presence of the final mystery.

If John could not be a soldier—and perhaps he would have been no more effective in soldiering than was Coleridge, with whom he had so much temperamentally in common—he could come to his country's aid with words; and he was to do this again, a year or so later, not by his writing but by lecturing in England in support of the recruiting drives.

But first he did something of greater interest to us now. In 1915 Arnold Shaw published his first book of essays—*Visions and Revisions*, 'a book of literary devotions', and his first novel, *Wood and Stone*. The essays preceded the novel, but I shall speak of the novel first.

In his autobiography John tells us very little about his individual books; most of them he does not mention, even by name. But he does more than once—here and elsewhere in scattered references—speak of his desire to leave behind a handful of formidable romances, and despite the wealth of his critical and philosophical writing this was his prime driving force as a writer, this urge to tell long and comprehensive stories about groups of people acting and reacting upon one another; and his most sympathetic critical essays, and those in which may be detected the greatest insight, are perhaps those—a few essays on certain poets excepted—in which he writes of the novelists: of Hardy, and Rabelais, and Dostoievsky, and Melville, and Cervantes, and Balzac— the great *prodigal* chroniclers, the men who created not circles but societies, not communities but worlds.

Although the bulk of Theodore's work takes the form of fiction it was in John that the storyteller's instinct was strongest. He tells us how the Rev. C. F. Powys told interminable, rambling stories—a sort of endless serial—when the children were little, and how he himself began a similarly formless and unending tale about the fictional activities of his own early circle—about Alfred de Kantzow, and 'the Catholic'—'a mystic-humorous, Pantagruelian, Shandyan, Quixotic Romance' of which—its author tells us—he would take out the latest instalment in some pub where there was an 'incurious' barmaid, and read or show to 'the Catholic'. So far as appears, the grave John William Williams was the book's only reader.

Because of John's own reticence about his writings we learn nothing of the genesis of *Wood and Stone*, but it is a big book, not at all the kind of affair that could be dashed off in a few weeks, and Llewelyn refers to the completing of it in a letter from Africa dated 14 November —in fact the book was then already published in New York; Llewelyn's 'how excellent that you should have really finished it' suggests that the book had been some time in progress, and had perhaps been the subject of discussion between the brothers—which suggests further that this first novel might have had its roots in John's serious illness of 1909, when Llewelyn so urgently counselled him to give up lecturing and become a writer.

Wood and Stone is a most interesting book, which ought to be reprinted. The American edition can hardly have been large, and the small edition published in England by Heinemann in 1916 was only an importation of American sheets; this book and its successor *Rodmoor* may rarely be met with, but the Powys student can learn a great deal from it. As a novel it is unsatisfactory; it is loosely constructed, and often gives the impression that here is a sketch—a cartoon—from which at a more propitious time some great mural or tapestry might be constructed: which in effect is what happened—people, situations, settings, are frequently duplicated from *Wood and Stone* in *Wolf Solent, Glastonbury* and the later English novels. The tautly described complexities of an older-younger brother relationship sketched in *Wood and Stone*, and plainly based on himself and his brother Llewelyn, reappear ten years later in *Ducdame*, and then are expanded and broadened in the brothers Otter of *Wolf Solent*. The Andersons of *Wood and Stone* also contribute to the development of the Dekkers, father and son, in *Glastonbury*, and their relationship has its contrasting parallel in the cousins Crow of the same novel. Indeed, John Cowper returned again and again to these portrayals of close relatives, the one usually much younger than the other, and every time they may be traced back through the Andersons of *Wood and Stone* to John himself and Llewelyn—this in itself is interesting, for there is little suggestion in any of these pairs of characters of any of the others among John's brothers.

Also in *Wood and Stone* may be found the original of the worldly and dedicated industrialist, the capitalist enemy, the Philip Crow of *A Glastonbury Romance*, the Dog Cattistock of *Weymouth Sands*; here too are the solitaries, the eccentrics, the weak clergymen, the extremist politicians, who crowd the pages of the later novels. And, always present, protagonist and progenitor, the physical setting which influences and in part dictates events. In *Wood and Stone* it is Ham Hill, in *Rodmoor* it is the sea, as it is again in *Weymouth Sands*; in *Glastonbury* it is the Tor, in *Wolf Solent* the sinister pond, in *Maiden Castle* the prehistoric fortress. In *Wood and Stone* also we find, fully developed, John's marvellous power of evoking the local scene. His setting is Montacute, and he brings the village urgently alive. This loving and almost meticulous delineation of a remembered scene was always deliberately undertaken, as he himself tells us more than once. All these first novels—right up to *Weymouth Sands*—were written in America (even if a few chapters might have been written during visits to England) and the background scenery often enough sprang from a nostalgia which John nowhere denies; what he says in his preface to the 1961 edition of *Wolf Solent* might be applied substantially to them all: 'As I wrote *Wolf Solent* travelling through all the states of the United States except two, I became more and more intensely aware of the hills and valleys, the trees and various flowers, the lanes and hedges and ponds and ditches, of the country round Sherborne . . .' and that word 'intensely' is the key. In all his novels of England, and sometimes in the others, the descriptions of nature and landscape are at times ecstatic and always mystical, visionary and (again) 'intensely' personal.

There remains one final comment to be made on *Wood and Stone*, and that concerns the possibility of its influence upon T. F. Powys, in the character of the vile farmer, John Goring, whose unrelieved wickedness anticipates a whole gallery of Theodorian villains. There is also an occasional curious anticipation of Theodore in the dialogue:

As soon as Mr. Wone had gone, Mr. Taxater summoned his housekeeper.

'The next time that person comes,' he said, 'will you explain to him, very politely, that I have been called to London? If this seems improbable, or if he has caught a glimpse of me through the window, will you please explain to him that I am engaged upon a very absorbing literary work.'

Mrs. Wotnot nodded. 'I kept my eyes open yesterday,' the old woman remarked, in the manner of some veteran conspirator in the service of a Privy Councillor.

'As you happened to be looking for laurel-leaves, I suppose?' said Mr. Taxater, drawing the red curtains across the window, with his expressive episcopal hand. 'For laurel-leaves, Mrs. Wotnot, to flavour that excellent custard?'

The old woman nodded. 'And you saw?' pursued her master.

'I saw Mr. Luke Anderson and Miss Gladys Romer.'

'Were they as happy as usual—these young people,' asked the theologian mildly, 'or were they—otherwise?'

'They were very much what you are pleased to call otherwise,' answered the old lady.

'Quarrelling in fact?' suggested the diplomat, seating himself deliberately in his arm-chair.

'Miss Gladys was crying and Mr. Luke was laughing.'

The Papal Apologist waved his hand. 'Thank you, Mrs. Wotnot, thank you. These things will happen, won't they—even in Nevilton? Mr. Luke laughing and Miss Gladys crying? Your laurel-leaves were very well chosen, my friend. Let me have the rest of that custard tonight! I hope you have not brought back your rheumatism, Mrs. Wotnot, by going so far?'

The housekeeper shook her head and retired to prepare supper.

John Cowper Powys disliked reading his own books after publication, and when I once mentioned *Wood and Stone* to him I did not expect to hear very much in the way of criticism. What emerged was curious—an admission that in fact this was the only book of his he had ever read after publication—except for *Weymouth Sands*, which he was obliged to go through to make the changes required for transmuting it into *Jobber Skald*.[1] As for *Wood and Stone*, he employed 'the first printed copy' of that book to while away the time on a journey from New York to Atlantic City on the Pennsylvania Railway.

While John was 'commencing author' in New York, Llewelyn in Kenya was gathering a thousand impressions of the violent and beautiful country in which he found himself. His letters and diaries show how great was the immediate impact of Africa upon him, and his later more formal essays show how long it endured. But he was far too busy with the work of the stock-farm to do much more than gather and garner his impressions; the 'Llewelyn Powys who writes about Africa' was resident in New York, later. Throughout his stay in Africa he had to be always conscious of his health, and the tenacious disease that held him was at best only kept at bay. In Kenya, especially after Willie joined the East Africa Rifles, Llewelyn felt cut off. He had little in common with his employer, the Hon. Galbraith Cole, although he respected and in some degree admired him. Contrasting their respective characters, he says in a letter to John dated 20 February 1916 that Cole was a strong character and a man of intellect, and a man it was possible to talk to; but 'I am by nature a writer, and man-of-letters, and not a sheep farmer . . .' and his sketchy knowledge of his duties, and not always efficient discharge of them, made him always conscious of being a misfit. It was while he was in Africa that Marion Linton wrote to break off their engagement. She had decided to go into a nunnery. Although Llewelyn said at the time that he would never marry anyone else, his regret at losing her seems to have been rather perfunctory—unless he felt more deeply than he allowed to appear in his letters. His main enduring reaction was annoyance at

[1] As discussed further below (page 204).

having been defeated by the Church. 'No circumstance will ever persuade me to forgive the Church after this. Let me get well and my craft and wickedness will startle everyone I encounter.' Even this protest seems half humorous, but after all his lost love was in any case some thousands of miles away. 'I see in the background three Kikuyu girls who have come from far. I shall perhaps select one when I come back from dinner tonight.'

5

THE year 1916 is a notable one in Powys annals, something indeed of the order of a 'year of wonders'; John published three books and had a half-share in a fourth; Theodore now came before the public in a substantial way, after the tentative and restricted publication of 1908, and Llewelyn had the satisfaction for the first time of seeing his work between hard covers. In addition, two other publications are of interest to the Powys student—Louis Wilkinson's pamphlet, *Blasphemy and Religion*, and his novel, *The Buffoon*.

It seems probable that Shaw commenced publishing at John's prompting; he never had a wide list of books, and he never had more than a handful of authors. His first major production was *Wood and Stone*, and no doubt that book's success—it went quite quickly into a second edition, and even thus early critics compared John Cowper with Thomas Hardy and noted his affinity with Dostoievsky—was an encouragement to Shaw to continue publishing. His first list includes books by John Cowper and Theodore Powys, novels by Ian Campbell Hannah and L. B. Stoughton Holborn, and other books by the last two authors, who were members of the team of lecturers, specializing respectively in art and world affairs.

The Soliloquy of a Hermit Shaw announces as 'deliberately chosen' to be his first publication of 1916, and Louis Wilkinson's pamphlet appeared at the same time. No correspondence has been published to support speculation about Theodore's appearance in Shaw's list, but it seems likely enough that John would have told Shaw about his 'hermit' brother, and that he would have told Theodore about his new venture with Shaw; and that Theodore replied that he too had material ready for the printer, and what about it? Mr H. Coombes notes in his book on T. F. Powys that the *Soliloquy* was written in the spring of 1915, and although he gives the writing date for *Mr. Tasker* as winter

1916, there is some evidence that it may have been ready earlier, for Shaw announces for publication 'a novel by Theodore Francis Powys' in his list for September, and in a letter to Louis Wilkinson dated 26 January 1916, and in another dated 3 February, Theodore speaks as though the completed manuscript were already in Shaw's hands, ready for publication but subject to such revision as Shaw might advise and Louis undertake. At all events Theodore was now actively writing, and he would have embraced an opportunity to be regularly published in a manner calculated to 'produce gold'.

Louis's curious little pamphlet was intended to do just this, we may suppose. It is marked 'price 10 cents', but the conclusion must be that it was circulated as an advertisement. (A rather odd advertisement, in a way, because it exalts Theodore's book at the expense of John's, but the publisher and the authors might have hoped that it would contrive to extol both, for the sake of sales. This little pamphlet was no doubt one of the main planks in Llewelyn's platform from which he proclaimed Louis's treachery to John over the years: a 'treachery' John never recognized and one certainly that Louis never consciously practised.)

The pamphlet was issued in January 1916, and I will describe it in some detail, for it is now excessively rare—probably one of the two or three rarest of all Powys items. It is printed on a creamy, rather thick paper, in green ink, making with the outer covers of the same paper sixteen pages $4\frac{1}{2}$ in. high by $5\frac{1}{2}$ in. wide. The full title appears on the cover—'Blasphemy and Religion, a dialogue about John Cowper Powys' *Wood and Stone* and Theodore Powys' *The Soliloquy of a Hermit*'—and the text begins immediately on page 3. The dialogue is between the 'Marquis' and his son, Remy. The Marquis upbraids Remy for reading 'unpardonable novels' when he might be reading a work of art like the *Soliloquy*; and Remy protests that Theodore writes like a rustic, has a very limited vocabulary and shaky grammar— 'harassed meditation', he calls the *Soliloquy*, and the Marquis retorts that *Wood and Stone* is frivolous; John Cowper is 'forever breaking into spiritual sweats', he has nothing of his own, 'nothing to evoke, nothing to realize, nothing to enhance, nothing to guard—nothing that is sacred'; the Marquis adds that his digestion is troubled, the penalty for speaking of *Wood and Stone* so soon after dinner. The son is no match for the father in eloquence, and we get a rather perfunctory defence of John Cowper; but the Marquis says brave things about Theodore, and these are early expressions of Louis's own lifelong loyalty and devotion to his friend's extraordinary genius. It is this devotion to Theodore rather than any strong 'treachery' directed at John, which in my view dictates the bias in the argument.

The *Soliloquy* itself appeared at the same time—in January. It may be noted in passing that the slight modification in the title— 'soliloquies' for 'soliloquy' in the English edition—is of no large significance. The text is the same,[1] but the word 'soliloquies' is perhaps a little more exact, for the book is not in fact one single theme developing, but several themes proceeding together: meditations upon God, and man, and nature. As with all these Powyses—in their several ways—what is said is not at first so decisive in its impact as the manner of the saying. They were completely different from one another in style, these three brothers; but each of them commanded a style which holds the attention, and beguiles a reader on, even in passages the content of which he disagrees with, or is not persuaded by. Since they were indeed so different, these brothers, it is in fact hard to agree with them all, as one reads; and every reader must choose for himself among their beliefs and philosophies. But equally every reader will extend a suffrage of respect and admiration to them *as writers*—though perhaps in differing degrees. Where there is antipathy it is usually strongest in respect of John's style, with its sprawling untidiness: the defects here are at once obvious and irritating, but in so vast a body of work defects are liable to appear exaggerated, and it must be remembered that the merits are also on a heroic scale. It would be impossible to describe any work of John's as 'a small classic', but this might be the right way to speak of Theodore's *Soliloquy*. It is short, it is perfect in scale, it promises well for better things to come, it announces with authority the arrival of an original thinker and stylist; as the Marquis says, it is a work of art. But it is not *Wood and Stone*, and I must declare myself of the party of Remy.

Oddly enough, as the attentive reader of *Wood and Stone* may notice occasional similarities of expression or thought to Theodore, so readers of the *Soliloquy* may catch glimpses of Llewelyn looking over the author's shoulder—as, for example, here: 'I have discovered that all movement is a begetting and creating, and that when I only move my feet I bring to birth new wonders. We cannot overrate too much mere existence. Simply to be set dancing by the sun is something.'

Perhaps the most notable long passage, in the eye of a later student, is the account of 'Mr. Thomas', which is a very exact portrait of

---

[1] In the second English edition, 1926, chapter numbers and headings are added.

Theodore as he appeared to himself—and exact, too, in showing the
man seen by others; it is a 'character', essentially true to the life. The
book is nowhere solemn, and Theodore's delightful and unexpected
humour is constantly breaking in. It is an essential study for any
reader who wishes to come close to Theodore, and it contains the
germ of all his later philosophy, although that is presented at greater
length and with full maturity in his novels and stories. It is interesting
to read the *Soliloquy* at the same time as one reads Llewelyn's *Impassioned Clay*, the essay in which he expresses most concisely and
most eloquently his deepest belief; for in these two books may be seen
most clearly the contrast between these two brothers as thinkers and as
writers.

When he heard that John had found a new publisher Llewelyn in
Africa naturally thought to turn the situation to his own advantage.
He suggested that Shaw might publish a collection of his tales and
sketches, but nothing came of this. Instead, John raised the matter of
Llewelyn's work with another publisher, Claude Bragdon, whose
Manas Press was at Rochester, N.Y., where John had first met him at
a lecture. The passages from Llewelyn's diaries it was proposed to
publish made too small a book, and John hastened to contribute a
long essay in autobiography, so that the book appeared under the title
Confessions of Two Brothers. If the contrast between Llewelyn and
Theodore may be studied as I have suggested, that between Llewelyn
and John may be found here between the same two covers. As an
autobiographer, Llewelyn sets himself squarely against a background
of the visible world, and he discusses himself in the light of what he
has experienced: 'By day and by night no sight that we see, no sound
that we hear, but has its own poetical burden', as he tells us in *Impassioned Clay*. But John creates an image of himself out of himself,
and it would be essentially the same if he had written in exile, alone, in
a darkened room. John's 'confessions'—characteristically, they occupy
the larger share of the book—are not so very different in content and
manner from the full-scale *Autobiography* of twenty years later, but
Llewelyn's—equally characteristically he says they are 'vague autobiographical ramblings' rather than confessions—are notes and
sketches from which in later writings he was to produce fuller and
maturer essays. Unfortunately, this book also is now rare, and few
readers have access to it. It is a significant milestone, and one may hope
it will eventually be reprinted; its American circulation must have
been quite small, and in England it was not published at all. But how

surely and clearly and immediately do we recognize each brother from the very first sentences that he writes. So, John: 'It is the little thing, the unrehearsed gesture, the catch in the breath, the droop of the lip, the start of surprise, which really reveals. We may analyze ourselves in volumes and remain undiscovered; and then—by a yawn, a tilt of the head, a sob of exhaustion, a flash of hate—we are betrayed and unmasked for ever.' And Llewelyn: 'To be suddenly born, to suddenly acquire consciousness on the surface of this unsteady and amazing planet, that is a chance indeed to justify everything.' Add to these a random quotation from the *Soliloquy*, and it will be seen how at this time of setting out as writers each of the three brothers was already recognizably himself: 'I know how men move under the shadow of the moods of God, and I know how I move. Some try to hide in the Garden, and some try to hide in the beast's belly. I have tried to hide amongst the grassy hills; but the moods of God have hunted me out.'

From the first, and until late in life, Louis Wilkinson's main impulse as a writer was to the creation of character and situation: he was first and principally a novelist, a satirical commentator. He would seem never to have wished to translate his lectures into essays, as John did; he never collected his poems, although over the years he wrote a fair number, and it was not until he was fifty-three that he made the first of his essays in autobiography—which (again, characteristically) took the form of a novel. He was more detached than Llewelyn, and infinitely more detached than John, in the expression of his reflections about himself; but once pen had been set to paper he was as unreticent as either. We must suppose that *The Puppets' Dallying*, written at twenty-two, was largely autobiographical, no matter how modified; and the central character of *The Buffoon* again is Louis himself, in the name of Edward Raynes; that Raynes was the buffoon appears in the very first sentence: 'It seemed inevitable that all contacts with Edward Raynes should shake his cap and bells.' But Edward Raynes is no self-portrait of the order of Dexter Foothood, in *Swan's Milk*. The early novel is definitely a novel, and not a disguised autobiography, and it would be a mistake to look upon Raynes as merely 'drawn from' his author. The character unmistakably 'drawn from' a recognizable original is, of course, Jack Welsh; and no student of John Cowper Powys can afford to miss that graphic representation of John as he was in 1916. Llewelyn may protest as much as he will at the 'malice' of this portrait—and I think he protested too much, as to malice—yet it

remains a portrait and not a caricature. I did not know John in 1916—
I was indeed but two years old—but I knew Jack Welsh and met him
again and again in the John Cowper Powys of 1936 and after.

The plot of *The Buffoon* is slight—really not much more than
enough to furnish out a short story. Edward Raynes, approaching
middle age, becomes aware that his apparently settled and comfortable
life is a failure; in earlier years his sufficient income, his love affairs and
his attempts at writing had satisfied him, but now he realizes that he
will never be a writer of any standing and he faces loneliness and frustration. It occurs to him to marry, and he chooses a girl whom he has
met through Jack Welsh. It never occurs to Edward that she will
reject him, and throughout his wooing he is concerned rather to
determine if in fact he will have her; and if so, what changes for the
better he must make in her. The girl puts a period to all this by getting
engaged to someone else, and as the book closes Edward is left with
nothing: alienated from his closer friends and deprived by death of
Jack Welsh, the closest; and with his vague literary ambitions mocked
by the girl's gesture in rejecting him in favour of a poet. He cannot
foresee the future as his settled world crumbles around him, but we the
readers know that the outbreak of war—it is 1914—may resolve as
many difficulties as it creates. Edward's future probably lies among 'the
poplars of France, under a misty dawn'.

Very many of the characters in this book are based largely or to a
smaller degree on the 'Powys circle'—on people whose real names are
known to every reader of John's autobiography: Harry Lyon, Tom
Jones, Bernie O'Neill, 'the Catholic' and so on. They do not all appear
directly, but the constant reference to them creates in a reader familiar
with the *Autobiography* a feeling of familiarity, of being among known
faces and places: here is the little street girl Lily, and Mr De —— the
poet, and Theodore 'who is a hermit', and 'my brother Lulu' and the
wicked Archangel. What Louis has done is to re-create the 'Circle'—
twenty years before John did so in the *Autobiography*—and use it as
cast for his own fictional comedy.

Certainly the book is a comedy—the chapter in which Edward
proposes to Eunice is an example of light satire brilliantly handled and
triumphantly humorous—but like all true comedy it is shot through
with pathos, if not with tragedy. The chapter—xxxi—in which
Edward begins to see that to be accepted in marriage is but a beginning,
and not the end of the wooing, produces no laughter, and may leave
the reader looking uncomfortably at himself.

Frank Harris, in his 'Contemporary Portrait' of Louis Wilkinson, says that Louis, 'disgusted by the imperfections of his first novel', made no serious attempts to write from 1905 until 1914; and that *The Buffoon* was begun in the summer of 1914 at Siena. This is Harris's only comment on the book, and he reserves his high praise for the two novels that followed; but I think *The Buffoon* deserves more consideration than this. It makes enormous strides over *The Puppets' Dallying*, while retaining the original excellences. The epigrams are no longer slightly suspect, but crisp and inevitable; we are reminded now no longer of the faded wit of Henry Seton Merriman, but of the sophisticated cynicism of Somerset Maugham: 'reminded', I say, but I do not think there was a direct influence. The natural turn of Louis Wilkinson's mind was to this kind of wit, and it was an accident that Maugham was exercising it at the same time. No doubt it was this affinity that sustained a long friendship between the two men in later years.

The Buffoon has another excellence not common: it contains not 'dialogue' but conversation—genuine conversation: talk. To handle a group of four or five speakers sitting or strolling and just talking is a very difficult exercise and one many writers never succeed in; here first, and in his later novels more assuredly, Louis Wilkinson shows himself entirely at ease in it. He shows also another hard exercise fully mastered, the creation of a character in vignette; he has a chapter describing one of the nights with Tom Jones in Liverpool which John talks of in his *Autobiography*, and he creates the small, unrecurring characters admirably and just to scale—the girls, the landlady, 'Tom Fielding'—so that they come briefly but unmistakably alive. For a later generation of readers it is inevitable that the Powys connection will make *The Buffoon*, as they say in America, 'required reading'; but those who approach it for the sake of Jack Welsh will lay it down having received from it a great deal more than they came for.

In 1915 John had published *Visions and Revisions*, the first collection of his literary essays, and in 1916 he followed this with *Suspended Judgments*; the first, after many years out of print, was reissued in England in 1955 with a new preface, and is therefore known to a good many readers; the second has yet to be reissued, but may be said in the main to resemble its fellow, except that whereas all the essays in *Visions and Revisions* are concerned with individuals—all are 'literary devotions', in the author's phrase—in *Suspended Judgments* the subtitle is 'essays on books and sensations' and we get in 'The Art of

Discrimination' an early example of the author's handling of the relationship between letters and life. These essays were something new in criticism. They were far removed from the arid academic essays of the professors, but they bore no resemblance to the 'gossip in a library' of such popularizers of literature as Edmund Gosse or Augustine Birrell. Let me say here that I condemn neither: they each have their place and use; I am only saying that John Powys extended the frontiers of literary criticism by such essays as these: essays *in which the author is passionately involved*, sometimes almost embarrassingly so. It is hardly surprising that the professional critics cried 'charlatan', nor is it surprising that today John Cowper's writings on aspects of literature and art are not cited or discussed in 'books about books'. I recall only recently talking with a lady who was making an extended study of Dostoievsky; she was a scholar in several languages, including Russian, and she had read scores of books, in fact 'everything' on the subject, but she had not read the book by John Cowper Powys, nor did she intend to; she dismissed it as obviously of no account, unread. There are naturally exceptions, but in general the academics will recognize John Cowper Powys as a literary critic only when they are forced to by prevailing opinion; for there is no shop more tightly closed than this. For the general reader it is another matter: for him these short critical studies have one cardinal merit: they send him to Lamb, to Dante, to Hardy, to Goethe, to Milton, with an entirely new capacity to appreciate, to understand, *to enjoy*. And the power to enjoy great literature was never in greater need of stimulation than it is today.

6

I HAVE said earlier in this book that the village of Montacute remains hardly changed today, except in details, from what it was when it was the centre of the Powys family life. The same is broadly true of the village of East Chaldon, although it now lies almost under the shadow of an atomic power station. Chaldon must always rank with Montacute as a place of Powys association, for it was the home of T. F. Powys for some forty years, of Llewelyn Powys for about fourteen, and for a short time also of John. It was also a place to which all the 'Powys circle' came from time to time.

Like Shirley in Derbyshire, Chaldon is approached along narrow lanes that lead nowhere else in particular, and the busy main road—in this case, the one from Bournemouth to Weymouth—lies sufficiently far away to be no distraction. In Chaldon it is usually safe for a cat to cross the road. The village centre is a small triangular green flanked with cottages and farm buildings; the road comes in from the village of Winfrith and branches at the green, left for the church, right for the inn. The hills rise on either side, those on the left, or south, as the approach is made from Winfrith, lie fold upon fold between Chaldon and the sea. On the right is the ridge over which a narrow road climbs, past the tumuli known as the 'Five Marys' and down beyond to the Weymouth road. The left-hand branch of the road passes the church and a few more cottages, and then wanders on to the hamlet of West Chaldon before more or less petering out. Something of the antiquity of the place may be seen by a reference to the church at West Chaldon (or Chaldon-Boys) having been amalgamated with East Chaldon (or Chaldon-Herring) because it had fallen into ruin—West Chaldon never, in any case, had more than a handful of people. This amalgamation was effected in 1446.

But the Chaldons have no written antiquity, no battle was fought here, no lord chancellor was born here, no queen slept here. There is no separate lord of the manor, and the living of the church of St Nicholas oddly enough is in the gift of a Roman Catholic family, the Welds of Lulworth. All around Chaldon lies a remoter past, in the upland slopes and valleys, buried in the tumuli and marked by the stone circles and village sites, some of which A. R. Powys and others were to excavate.

Part of the village is built of stone and thatch, part of brick and slate. It is small, and even the smallness is scattered. The old church lies on one flank, the thatch-and-whitewash pub—The Sailor's Return —on the other. T. F. Powys lived in the little square detached house called Beth Car, beyond the church. Llewelyn lived at Chydyok, a pair of cottages high on the downs, a good half-hour's climb towards the cliffs and the sea; Llewelyn and Alyse had one cottage and Gertrude and Philippa lived in the other, but this was later in the story. The third Powys home in Chaldon was Down Barn, or Rat Barn, which lies in another valley between the village and the sea. Here John lived for a time on first returning from America, and it was used off and on by other members of the family.

Our first glimpses of East Chaldon are to be found in Theodore's *Soliloquy*, and of course he used it again and again in his stories and novels: Beth Car looked out across the road to the hill of High Chaldon, so often a centre of the scene in some tale of Madder and its people. Llewelyn too delighted to depict the slow-moving progress of the seasons across the Chaldon downs, but John never travels so far east in his stories, and it made too small a part in his early life to occupy a place in his *Autobiography*. Only in *Ducdame* do we come close, perhaps, to this southerly boundary of Egdon Heath; but the setting and landscape of that novel are not clearly identifiable with a known original in the sense that those of *Wood and Stone*, *Wolf Solent*, *Weymouth Sands* or *Maiden Castle* are.

The Chaldon landscape exactly suited Theodore. It was open, remote, unpeopled. The great shoulders of the downs were always green, the banks of clouds never ceased to march across the sky from west to east, throwing their dappled shadows down. Here were no shanty towns, no rash of bungalows edging the cliffs and the sea, but a silence stretching back to prehistory. 'Let us think!' John tells us used to be his own cry, and at Chaldon Theodore was able to do just that, without distraction or interruption. On these hills a man may walk for miles and never meet another.

The brothers, about 1901. *Left to right:* John Cowper, Littleton, Theodore, Albert, Llewelyn and William

Shirley Rectory, the birthplace of John Cowper and Theodore

Montacute Vicarage

Kestins, Weymouth

White Nose, Dorset

Phudd Bottom, John Cowper's house at Hillsdale, New York

Portrait by Allan Chappelow, M.A., F.R.S.A.

John Cowper Powys, about 1956

Bust by Hugh Oloff De Wet

John Cowper Powys

Louis Wilkinson

Llewelyn Powys in
Africa, 1915

Llewelyn Powys

Crown Copyright: Central Office of Information

Theodore Powys

In the years since the printing of *Genesis* Theodore had gone on with his writing, and a letter of December 1914 written to Louis mentions a group of stories which Frances Wilkinson had been trying to sell in America. In January 1916 we hear the first word of *Mr. Tasker*; Theodore writes to Louis that he has sent the first part of a 'domestic novel' to Arnold Shaw, and that John thinks Louis would be a good man to prepare the book for the press; Theodore adds cautiously that he is not prepared to pay for this service—not with eggs at $3\frac{1}{2}d.$ each—and furthermore, Louis is not to lose the manuscript. In the next letter he relents and promises to pay 'something—afterwards'. This novel was announced for publication by G. Arnold Shaw in the advertisements at the end of *Blasphemy and Religion*, and this means that Shaw must have made his decision to publish it within a few days of receipt; he even went so far as to give a date, September. But September came, and no publication of *Mr. Tasker's Gods*; and when the book did appear, it was in England, after the publication of three others and not until 1924.

The reason would seem to lie in further hints that may be found in Theodore's letters. Louis Wilkinson was good enough to send me the complete unpublished text of his letters from Theodore, from which we learn that Theodore's conception of 'preparing for the press' included extensive rewriting, if necessary. He asks Louis and his wife to deal with the manuscript as they think fit, by cutting, fusing, transposing, adding, modifying. It might seem therefore that what he had submitted was rather shapeless and inconclusive as it stood, and Frances and Louis may well have had difficulty in carrying out their task. Not until October does Theodore write thanking Frances for 'finishing' *Mr. Tasker*, and now Shaw must have withdrawn, for we find Louis offering the book to his own publisher, Knopf, and later there is talk of another American publisher, Huebsch. All these negotiations support the proposition that to Theodore writing was 'work'. He never wrote swiftly and easily, like his brother John. *Mr. Tasker*, although as published a powerful and impressive book, is never spontaneous, has neither flourish nor grace. T. F. Powys was to achieve these, but not yet.

While Theodore was learning, painfully, and by trial and error— the book he worked on next, *Amos Lear*, was never published and in later years he did not wish it to be—Llewelyn was learning too. He was not learning to write—as John later said, Llewelyn from the first wrote spontaneously, as spontaneously as he walked, talked, ate, drank, breathed. But Llewelyn was not a dealer in abstract meditation, he was no voyager in strange seas of thought, as Theodore was. Llewelyn related everything he wrote, everything he wished to say, to what he had himself seen and experienced; and when he took flights into speculative philosophy it was always from some solid earthly jumping-off point—like holding the veritable skull of Yorick in his hand as he mused on the ways of mortality. So in Africa, although he wrote a little, he was engaged more fully with experiencing and recording—in his diary, or in his mind—things he would have occasion to write about later. Right to the end—apart from what he wrote directly about Africa—there are allusions and references in his work which indicate how deeply the raw and cruel Kenya life had entered into his consciousness.

Africa brought home to Llewelyn as nothing earlier had, not even his illness and the illness he had seen at the sanatorium, the desperate terms of life on earth, for every living thing. In Africa he saw indeed how red nature is in tooth and claw, and he refers frequently to things seen and remembered from those crowded stock-farm days—references to the dead being disposed of by being dragged while still dying to be eaten by the hyenas; to constant shooting and killing of bullocks and monkeys and porcupines and leopards: 'W. shot a wild duck. I picked it up. It wagged its tail, stiffened its webbed legs and opened and shut its round brown eyes, but I did not care.' Again, 'Caught an eagle in a gin.' Again, carrying home a dead leopard, 'Willie carried it home on his back. I walked behind stuffing stones into the hole in its skull to keep its brain from falling out.' Well might Llewelyn in after years quote not once but often, 'Have not I in my time heard lions roar?'

He must often have felt cut off, as the war dragged on and he saw nothing of his brothers, save only Willie sometimes at home for a few days on leave. Llewelyn felt perhaps that much in life was passing him by: books were being published, girls were being loved—but not by him. He may not have realized then how great a store he was accumulating of marketable experience. He was also now 'a success', that is he was demonstrating that he could do an exacting and difficult job—uncongenial too—in a workmanlike manner. When his employer had to return to England in 1917 owing to ill health Llewelyn carried on alone as sole manager of the farm—miles from another white man—and this not in a merely administrative capacity, but with day-long manual work. It must be remembered that he began as an amateur, with no aptitude and no great interest, and it was only his brother's action in joining the army that ever made the work permanent for Llewelyn; and it must also be remembered that although his illness gave comparatively little trouble during these years it was ever present in the background, ready to spring. 'I am not a sheep-farmer', Llewelyn wrote, very rightly; and we may admire the determination and courage which carried him through. We may also sympathize with his longing to be away—away from sheep, and disease, and bodies which however graceful were always black. He was living for the day when he could be with John in New York.

And in New York, and in the United States generally, John meanwhile was making a double reputation. He was now well known all over the country as a lecturer; in *The Buffoon* Jack Welsh's income from lecturing is given as five thousand dollars a month—at that time over £1,000; this may possibly be greater than John commanded in real life, but it is an indication that he was now well established. His books may have been comparatively less profitable, but they too were bringing him rewards and reputation. He was a public figure of sufficient stature to be a witness in 1917 at the *Little Review* prosecution over the publication of James Joyce's *Ulysses*.[1] He was also, incidentally, an early and eloquent apologist for Joyce's greatest work, but his long analytical essay on *Ulysses* is not discussed by later commentators, nor is it to be found in the bibliographies: matters which are not a reflection on John Cowper Powys.

The making of a double reputation involved him in living a double life. His lecture tours took time and energy, but even a rapid writer could hardly produce nine books in four years without similarly demanding calls on energy and time. In addition, John spent the summer of every year in England, and during the later war years—having been rejected by the recruiting board—he travelled extensively about the country lecturing on war aims and assisting recruiting. It may be doubted if this sort of oratory would have counteracted the influence of the rude corporal on Theodore, but it is certainly a fact that he also made a move to join the army at this time. He reports the affair to Louis, and mentions that on arrival at Dorchester Barracks he asked to be allowed to sit down—'What a situation!' as Alfred de Kantzow might say. He then found himself moving naked from place

[1] A year earlier John Cowper had been influentially active on Theodore Dreiser's behalf in the controversy following the appearance of *The Genius*.

to place, being prodded and eyed and measured on the way by various orderlies, until at last a doctor told him to put his clothes on 'as if he were doing something indecent'. And the result was rejection on account of a weakness in his heart.

I have mentioned 'nine books in four years' as John's output at this time, and it will be well here to glance at those not already noticed: two collections of poems, a second novel and his little guide to good reading, *One Hundred Best Books*. The taking of short cuts to culture by means of advice on what to read, or hear, or admire in literature, music and painting represents of course nothing new, but it came to its fullest influence with Sir John Lubbock's famous list of the hundred best books, published in 1891. Lubbock died in 1913 and thus did not live to comment on John Cowper Powys's list, as perhaps he might have done; but John by implication comments on Lubbock's: he says in his brief preface, 'This selection of "One hundred best books" is made after a different method and with a different purpose from the selections already in existence. Those apparently are designed to stuff the minds of young persons with an accumulation of "standard learning" calculated to alarm and discourage the boldest. The following list is frankly subjective in its choice; being indeed the selection of one individual, wandering at large and in freedom through these "realms of gold".' The list is indeed subjective, on two levels; first, in omitting a large company of the great unreadable which one can only suppose and hope that even Sir John Lubbock never read— Wake's *Apostolical Fathers*, say—and next in including a preponderance of fiction. Only about a dozen authors appear in both the Lubbock and the Powys lists, and those the ones that must seem inevitable— Shakespeare, Cervantes, Homer and the rest.

What is surprising is the comparatively few poets in John's list. Elsewhere he calls Wordsworth his 'great master', but he does not include him here. No Coleridge, no Keats, no Shelley; no Pope, no Dryden; Tennyson, Browning, Swinburne, not admitted. There are very few plays, and those, Shakespeare apart, are nearly all foreign. Philosophy, despite John's own interest in this subject, is also a subordinate division of the list. Sir Thomas Browne appears for his style rather than for his matter, and Nietzsche is to be read 'with the due pinch of Attic salt'. The classic philosophers from Plato downwards do not appear at all.

These are not criticisms; in his introductory essay the compiler makes his intention reasonable and clear. He wants his prospective reader—one who theoretically has read nothing—to come to books not primarily for profit, for culture, for learning, for, so to say, 'what he can get out of it'; not in pursuance of the cult of 'becoming a superior person by reading the best authors'. Instead, let him find reading a pleasure, a recreation, a refreshment, a solace, a comfort, a joy.... 'The secret of the art of literary taste, may it not be found to be nothing else than the secret of the art of life itself—I mean the capacity for discovering the real fatality, the real predestined direction of one's intrinsic nature and the refusal, when this is found, to waste one's energies in alien paths and irrelevant junketings?'

Some measure of the value of this list may be seen in its success. The original edition was several times reprinted, and other editions have followed. In this year of 1967 the book is still in print in the United States, although it has never appeared in an English edition; this may in some degree point to a difference in national temperament, and a greater willingness in the Americans to be instructed and to learn. It might be said that such a publication, from Powys's point of view, was in the nature of a job of propaganda, supporting his role as lecturer. But he was quite incapable of any work having the effects of a pot-boiler—haste, inattention, superficiality—and his commentary on the various books and authors, brief though it is, is full of pointed and arresting observation—it has something of the condensed wisdom of Lamb's notes on the dramatic poets.

The war years saw John Cowper's most productive period as a poet; the two war volumes contain together almost two hundred poems, and the small 1922 volume adds a score—this one, *Samphire*, was a winnowed selection made under Llewelyn's editorial influence, from which it may be supposed some poems of inferior standing were left out.

Wolf's Bane (1916) is subtitled 'rhymes'—'bitter stammered rhymes', the author calls them in his introductory stanzas, but he suggests that they have a place in the 'infinite stream' as the individual expression of one mind, one soul. And they do indeed express an individual viewpoint on life's fundamental verities of love, religion and death, and on the shifts a man is put to to confront them. They have a cumulative effect on the reader; hardly more than two or three single poems stand out in the mind and are separately remembered when the book is laid aside, but the collection as a whole is not forgotten when it is returned to the shelf. Many influences may be noted along the way —Wordsworth, Whitman, Coleridge, Hardy, Poe—but in the main these are superficial; they occur in the application of a stanza form, or in a reminiscent turn of phrase. The mind reflected in these poems is John Cowper Powys's own. As a full selection from them has recently been made available,[1] I will not quote extensively here, but a few small specimens will serve to indicate their quality.

THE DEATH-BIRDS

Will the rain on the drenched mould
    Never have rest?
Never—never—wail the death-birds in their flying.
  Will the vulture of night never fold
    Its wings on its breast?
Never—never—wail the death-birds in their flying.
  Will the wind that teases the trees
    Never be stilled,
Or the pain at the heart of all these
    Never fulfilled?
Never—never—wail the death-birds in their flying.
  Will the earth never cease from its moan
    Or the sea from its crying?
Never—never—wail the death-birds in their flying.
  And the whisper of their dirge
  Blends with the ocean-surge,—
  'Christ's heart is turned to stone;
  And God's pity gallows-high
  Under the weary sky
  Like a corpse stark and bleak
  Can only whistle and creak.'

KNOWLEDGE

The wild swan over the marshes knows
    On what cold reed-bed
The witch-girl pressed the rook-boy's lips
    Until they bled.

The wild owl over the mad-house knows
    In what padded place
The loveliest form that ever breathed
    Lies on her face.

[1] *Selected Poems of John Cowper Powys*, Macdonald, 1964.

The wild hawk over Golgotha knows
　　Whose patient heart
Cursed day, night, earth and heaven, before its curse
　　Rent it apart.

The wild kite over the wold's edge knows
　　To what piteous end
All joy, all hope, all love, all wisdom, all desire
　　In swift procession tend—
Yet none the less it soars and flashes free
Across the glaciers of eternity!

The poems in *Wolf's Bane* are 'personal', but they deal mainly with a personal reaction to matters of general application. In *Mandragora* (1917) there are many more poems arising out of matters nearer home, out of private feelings and relationships; here indeed much is said in few and simple words:

Oh that at this last hour
　　The word might be given to me
To tell you the power—the power
　　That you have over me!

The nine short lines of 'They Say' express exactly and finally one of the common moods of love:

They say the sky is azure fair,
　　I do not know;
They say the spring is in the air,
　　It may be so.
They say the crimson-throated shrike
　　Will nest this year in Alder Dyke—
'Tis very like, 'tis very like.

The spring? Oh God, in heaven above,
Let the spring go—give me my Love!

Llewelyn was always strong in sympathy with John's poetry, but he thought *Mandragora* inferior as a collection to *Wolf's Bane*. He writes contrasting the two books, finding the second series 'too artificial'—'you have been drifting down a by-path and these poems reveal it'. His summing up may be quoted in full, although not all readers will share his view of the comparative merits of the two books.

Llewelyn feels that John has been distracted from his true course in poetry by the intrusion of a passing and unimportant love affair and he thinks that John should see such matters in a more accurate perspective:

> Write other poems and treat all girls as they should be treated, they have none of them ever cared for either of us. You mustn't allow them to divert your mind from the things that really matter—from the general situation—they are celandines by the way and celandines however beautiful should not be allowed even partially to reconcile us to the universe. You must not fritter away your time with shilly shally—gather your mind together, and like Samson once more strike out for the last time in a formidable desperate way. I like to think of your following the wind, but I don't like to think of your taking little shoes and frocks too seriously.

When Llewelyn got to America he kept a close eye on his brother's poetical activities. John tells us that the poems in *Samphire* were largely written for Llewelyn—that is, at Llewelyn's prompting—and that Llewelyn was the moving spirit in getting them published, after what was probably rigorous editing, also by Llewelyn. The book is but one-fifth as long as its predecessors, but the contents are all of the author's best; such poems as 'The Ultimate', 'The Old Pier-Post' and 'Metaphysic' are unique in English.

> An author's *second novel* when once again after however many years it is that divide 1916 from 1949 he opens it has a very remarkable effect on his mind; an effect that I can only describe by the word '*Romantic*'. But as the *first novel* of an author reflects his erotic tendencies and his longing to describe the people who press on him in his life with love and hate, so in his *second novel* he takes hold of these things more freely and projects them to a greater distance from himself, and thus he grows more free of them, and independent even of his reactions to and from them.

So wrote John Cowper Powys when inscribing a copy of *Rodmoor*, and whatever the general application of his remarks might be so far as they apply to other novelists, they seem appropriate to the contrasts between *Wood and Stone* and *Rodmoor*. In the first there are indeed evidences among the characters of real-life originals pressing on the author with love and hate—Luke Anderson, based closely on Llewelyn, and Francis Taxater, based on 'the Catholic', and even subordinate characters like Witch-Bessie, whose original was the old Montacute crone, Nancy Cooper. In *Wood and Stone* we detect also the 'pressing on' of the physical environment, the close approximation of Nevilton with Montacute.

John Cowper is right when he says (at least so far as his own example is concerned) that in his second novel he freed himself of these dictates, whether of people or of place. It is the novel in which we find the characters least subjective, least projections of himself or his close friends; even the study of an intimate family relationship which occurs almost always in his work here is not brother and brother, father and son, but 'projected to a greater distance' by concerning two sisters. The background, a sea-coast town of East Anglia, no doubt can be shown to lean on his early memories of the region, but it takes a subordinate place: only to an unimportant degree does the nature of the terrain condition and influence events. In so far as it does exert an influence, the influence comes from the sea: and seas do not vary greatly from shore to shore.[1] The sea off the Norfolk coast in which Philippa is drowned clutching and embracing the body of her lover is hardly different from the sea in which Dog Cattistock is nearly drowned in the storm off Portland Bill, in *Weymouth Sands*.

But if *Rodmoor* displays an advance in the respect mentioned, it also displays all the characteristics that distinguish *Wood and Stone*— the gallery of odd and eccentric characters, the overwhelming problems of the principals, the loves that run unsmoothly, the ambitions frustrated, the hopes unfulfilled. And here, more I think than in *Wood and Stone*, we find the beginnings of that power of evocation from the inanimate which distinguishes some of the finest passages in the author's later work:

> . . . Sorio did not hear him. All his attention was concentrated just then upon the attempt to burst another seaweed bubble. The bell from the unseen buoy rang out brokenly over the water; and between the side of their boat and the stake to which the man was clinging there came gurglings and lappings and whispers, as if below them, far down under the humming tide, some sad sea-creature, without hope or memory or rest, were tossing and moaning, turning a drowned inhuman face towards the darkened sky.

[1] 'Wherever it flows', Sylvanus Cobbold is quoted in *Weymouth Sands*, 'it's always the same sea.'

7

For Llewelyn, as for millions of others, the ending of the war brought the need for a new beginning. The years of his 'African exile' had imposed certain disciplines upon him, but they had also freed him from others. The problem of what to do for a living was temporarily shelved and temporarily forgotten; the farm work was a full-time preoccupation for Llewelyn, especially in the years when he was virtually single-handed. But now Willie returned from the wars to take up his job again, and Llewelyn was released; his first thought was to return to England. He had some savings, and when everything was paid he expected to be left with about £250, a respectable sum in 1919 and enough certainly to buy him time to write one or two books and get established 'writing for the magazines'. He landed in England on 2 August 1919 and remained until 14 August 1920, when he sailed with John for America.

After five years' unbroken absence in Africa Llewelyn's first programme was for a round of visits. His father was now living in retirement at Weymouth, in the care of Gertrude, and Llewelyn made their house his base, going from it on various trips to see his old friends. He had his old garden shelter dismantled and sent from Montacute, and he set it up 'on a round hill by a ruined house above the coastguard' on the outskirts of the town, and announced to John that he would live and write and sleep there, keeping in touch with his father and sister at Greenhill Terrace. He began to write a novel based on life in Africa, but it went slowly and very soon his letters to John contain renewed doubts: '. . . I now know that I cannot ever expect to write a novel. *I cannot do it.*' 'I have tried and tried to begin a novel but I can't.' 'I hate my novel really and that's why it is such a thin bloodless thing. I have not written a word of it with any real pleasure.' He says ruefully that the case was quite different over at East Chaldon: 'Theodore can write novels all right, there is no stopping him.' But Theodore also had his problems, for although the writing of novels did not stop, the publishing of them did not begin; and in fact Llewelyn was not altogether right in suggesting that Theodore wrote with ease, for the novel he was working on at this time, *Georgina, a Lady*, was to remain unpublished even after the others in the cupboard had been taken out and put into print.

Llewelyn had a few successes—with the *New Age*, with the *New Statesman* and in New York with *The Dial*, which paid him £13 for a story; but where money was concerned he had crippling reverses. He invested in German marks at Louis Wilkinson's suggestion, and lost his savings; and he records that when he had only £50 left Louis borrowed it! The question of taking a job of some kind was raised again in family discussions, and Llewelyn applied for one in which a young man was to be escorted on a trip round the world, but his application was not successful. Finally, in the early summer of 1920 he went again to Sherborne to help Littleton, after writing in despair to John, 'I don't want to be a schoolmaster again!' It was to be his last stint. John returned to England for a holiday that summer, and Malcolm Elwin tells us that it was on the wharf, as the ship docked and the brothers met at Southampton, that the decision was made that they would return together to America.

John Cowper had published no new book since *Mandragora* in 1917, but he now had in the press in America the first of his long essays in didactic philosophy—*The Complex Vision*. It is interesting to contrast the philosophical writings of the Powys brothers. Theodore was satisfied to record the conclusions he reached; Llewelyn hoped to persuade readers of the value of his observations; but John, the lecturer, may be said to have preached. All his writings have in their eloquence something of the actor declaiming, the rhetorician expounding, but this appears most clearly and most forcefully in the philosophical essays. His inclination always was to take far-reaching problems or themes and relate them to the individual—to himself initially, and through his own reaction to the reaction of others. He would offer counsel, give advice, tell his reader how to meet this situation or that. Right at the beginning he makes his aim clear: 'It has come to be fatally clear to me that between the great metaphysical systems of rationalised purpose and the actual shocks, experiences, superstitions, illusions, disillusions, reactions, hope and despairs, of ordinary men and women there is a great gulf fixed.' It was not so much to bring philosophy as it existed within reach of the man in need, as to create a new philosophy that would never be out of his reach that John Cowper wrote, over the years, his eight books in this field. How far they were successful is not easily judged, for the influence of writings of this sort is cumulative and cannot be assessed from the remarks of reviewers, or judged by the number of copies sold. Only one seems to have been widely noticed, and widely distributed, and that is *In Defence of Sensuality* (1930) which may owe some of its initial success to an arresting title. Certainly with the passage of time John Cowper came ever nearer to the viewpoint of the 'ordinary man and woman'—*The Complex Vision* is, in its complexity, nearly as remote as the metaphysical systems of rationalized purpose it is supposed to replace, but the essays in *The Art of Growing Old* (1944) or *In Spite Of* (1953) really come close to everyday perplexities and stresses, and offer working and workable solutions, not indeed practical for everyone, but tending to a broadly practical application. There is, however, more in *The Complex Vision* than its content of philosophy, for many readers will turn to it in order to learn how the author's development as a writer may here be studied; it was his first sustained venture into this field, and he began to exploit a quite different style from that used in his novels: a style closer to the lecture platform, with its 'I', 'you' and 'we' bringing the reader into the argument, and its colloquial use of such phrases as 'I do not mean', 'Let us consider', and 'It cannot be denied', phrases of oratory as much as of letters. When in the novels he speaks directly to the reader —as he often does—it is always as a writer, through print, never as a speaker in the same room. But here in the philosophical writings he seems sometimes to 'wait for an answer' before proceeding and he deals with imagined objections and interpolations as he goes along. This serves to save his style from the stiffness that might be imposed upon it by the abstract and even abstruse nature of his material. *The Complex Vision* is not an easy book to read, nor are its principles easy for an 'ordinary man or woman' to follow; but the difficulty is never occasioned by the manner in which it is written. Often enough, indeed, the reader who is nowise convinced will be insensibly beguiled to read on:

> There is no doubt that the sons of the universe found in Jesus a soul so uniquely harmonious with their own that there existed

between them a sympathy and an understanding without parallel in the history of humanity.

It is this sympathy which is the origin of those unequalled words used by the son of Mary in which he speaks as if he were himself in very truth an incarnation of the vision of the immortals. The whole situation is one which need have little mystery for those who understand the nature of love. In moment after moment of supreme ecstasy Jesus felt himself so given up to the will of the invisible companions that his own identity became lost. In speaking for himself he spoke for them, and in the great hours of his tragic wayfaring he felt himself so close to them that, by reason of his love, he knew himself able to speak of the secret of life even as the immortals themselves would speak.

It may be that the writing of *The Complex Vision* shows John to have been, consciously or unconsciously, at a crossroads in his development as a writer. It was over four years since he had published *Rodmoor*, and it was to be another five before he published *Ducdame*; thus a promising beginning as a novelist was to be followed by an interval of nine years. *The Complex Vision*, although the longest, was not the only excursion he made at this time into speculative philosophy. In 1923 he published his essay on *Psychoanalysis and Morality*, and in 1925 *The Religion of a Sceptic*, and over the years 1923–28 three 'Little Blue Books' with the Haldeman-Julius Company of Girard, Kansas— *The Art of Happiness*, *The Secret of Self Development*, and *The Art of Forgetting the Unpleasant*. These small paper-bound booklets of up to sixty pages must have circulated in tens of thousands during the next forty years, and as I write this are still in print. These little essays are indeed an attempt to formulate 'a philosophy for every man'. They are phrased like a discourse from a soap box at Speaker's Corner—nor are they the worse for that:

> The truth is, people have got a completely wrong idea of the nature of culture. They regard it as the luxury of the leisured; whereas it is as much of a necessity for everyone as is love. As a matter of fact, every human being is compelled by the pressure of the life-urge itself to acquire some degree of culture. Culture is simply the name we give to a premeditated and calculated response to the mystery of life when such a response is directed *toward life as a whole* rather than toward any practical end.

... The most uneducated peasant or factory-hand, if he has developed an original and sensitive response to life, is in reality more cultivated in the truest sense of that term than many a college-bred professor. And the more deeply cultivated a person is the fewer will be the books he will read. For he will gather the great select spirits of the ages about him and meddle very little with contemporary fashions. He will carry the Sonnets of Shakespeare in his pocket as he goes to his office ...

(*The Secret of Self Development*)

When it came to writing on philosophical themes both Theodore and Llewelyn took account of the unchanging problems that have always exercised thinkers in every age and nation, but only John was closely aware of matters happening in the contemporary world—his essay on *Psychoanalysis and Morality*, his debate with Bertrand Russell on modern marriage, his *Religion of a Septic*, written directly because 'the old controversy between Fundamentalists and Modernists has recently broken out again', and of course his crossing of swords with Münsterberg being examples. *The Complex Vision* has a chapter on 'The Idea of Communism', and a quarter of a century later we find him still keenly aware of political events and developments, in *Mortal Strife*. Llewelyn, on the other hand, occupies himself rarely with current issues—except when he writes disapprovingly of the Oxford Group—and he was so far out of touch with mere dates that he didn't realize his abridgment of Anthony à Wood was appearing in that worthy's tercentenary year until an accident brought the fact to his attention. Theodore's concession to modernity takes the form of allowing God to drive a Ford car. The three viewpoints are understandable; Theodore, by choice and environment, was out of touch with the ordinary life of the world; Llewelyn, living by his pen, would naturally write about what most interested him, and about what he best knew; [1] but John, constantly travelling, meeting new people every day, and above all being questioned after his lectures by a varied cross-section of the people, was continually being brought up against the burning questions of politics and affairs, and being obliged to have views upon them.

When the two brothers landed in New York they went first to live

---

[1] Llewelyn was interested in world affairs, and concerned by them (witness his writing to President Roosevelt) but they made little impact on his professional work.

with their sister May. Marian Powys had made a unique career for herself, by determination and spirit. Early in life she had refused to be a 'stay-at-home', in the Victorian manner, and had learned shorthand and typewriting when those two accomplishments were rare among girls. She had then taken up lace-making, and afterwards studied lace-making in the European centres before emigrating to America in 1912, where after a short time she opened a lace shop in New York. Over the years this establishment prospered and expanded, and Marian's skill and learning in her subject kept pace, so that she became recognized as a leading authority; she also in later years published an important book on lace-making.

Marian was busy with her shop, and John had returned to his lecture programme, and at first Llewelyn was somewhat solitary in New York. In *The Verdict of Bridlegoose* he tells of his first weeks there, when it appeared certain that he would never make a start with his writing, and he could not face lecturing or schoolmastering again; but the employment agencies had nothing to offer, until finally, '. . . I seriously considered accepting a job offered to me by a firm of Philadelphia undertakers. I knew that in Africa the task of consorting with the dead was allotted to the lowest pariahs; and as my value in America seemed exactly nought, it appeared to be an occupation to which I might with some justification aspire.' But instead he was given an introduction to Harry Dounce, who had just joined the New York *Evening Post*, and Dounce commissioned him to write articles on Africa. These soon became a popular feature of the paper, so that some months later when Llewelyn had occasion to take a room in an hotel the reception clerk, reading his signature in the register, said: 'Are you the Llewelyn Powys who writes on Africa?' All through the winter Llewelyn remained in New York, making steady though slow progress with his writing; in a letter to his sister Philippa in February 1921 he says he has made £100 in five months—which at least covered his living expenses—and adds: 'I am very happy here, the life suits me exactly. . . .' In the spring, however, he was ill with influenza, and when he recovered he set off to join John in the mid west and go on to California.

Inevitably, thinking and writing of this journey, one's thoughts turn to Stevenson, going the same way half a century earlier; but times had materially changed. The world of *Across the Plains* was no more, and the train took only a fraction of the time needed to transport Stevenson. Llewelyn dismisses the journey in a few pages, probably because his response to a landscape could be complete only if he were a part of it, and things seemed remote and unreal seen through the windows of a train. They travelled the southerly route, through Arizona, and this great desert waste did prompt Llewelyn to a page of speculation in which he saw 'William Blake walking here naked, holding high converse with Los. . . . We might, I thought, have been passing over the surface of Uranus . . .'

At San Francisco they avoided the main city and crossed the Golden Gate to the small town of Sausalito, then cut off and accessible from the city only by ferry: for the great suspension bridge had yet to be built. The town rises steeply from the waterfront, and looks inwards across the harbour with its back to the sea; the hotel Alta Mira has a terrace with a panoramic view over waters and islands to the distant hills, and everywhere there are tall trees. The marine panorama might remind an Englishman of the view across Plymouth Sound from the Hoe. Again Llewelyn wrote enthusiastically, 'This is a splendid place and suits me exactly', and he exclaimed at the notion that these were waters not of the Atlantic but of the Pacific, and he must have noted their 'melancholy, long, withdrawing roar' as the breakers came rolling in from the empty wastes between California and Japan.

John Cowper, after so many years of travelling up and down the United States, had friends in many cities, and here he introduced Llewelyn to the poets George Sterling and Charles Erskine Scott Wood, with whom they spent a good deal of time, and Sarah Bard Field, Wood's collaborator and editor. Here too Llewelyn first met Theodore Dreiser. San Francisco is an exciting city, with a long and strong literary tradition, and while enjoying this Llewelyn also made long walking expeditions into the pleasant surrounding country, and also fell in love. But he found it more difficult to sell his articles in New York and the literary centres of the east—'The mere fact of heading my letter with the word California seemed sufficient to ensure the rejection of the manuscript, the editors concluding out of hand that I was just another weak amateur of letters, such as dwell in their thousands amid the orange groves of Santa Barbara and Los Angeles.' Marian feared that his health would be affected by the more rigorous climate of the east, but now he met with a reverse even in the glorious sunshine of California, for the dreaded blood-spitting returned.

There was at this time a celebrated practitioner in San Francisco,

THE POWYS BROTHERS   69

Dr Abrams—a man suspected by the orthodox in his profession as a quack, but none the less highly successful in effecting cures. His treatment brought about an immediate improvement in Llewelyn, and a 'cure' which lasted for three years and left him strong and active for the most of the remainder of his time in America. Fortified by this accession of health, Llewelyn returned to New York.

8

THE Powys base in New York was always Greenwich Village, and if these countrymen born had to live in the city, perhaps no section of it could suit them better. The Village, as New Yorkers call it, has a life and character all its own. It lies on the south-west of Manhattan, with something in it of London's Soho, something of the Paris Left Bank, something of Chelsea, something of Montmartre, but the roaring bisecting 6th Avenue—'Avenue of the Americas'—to remind everyone that this is also New York. Thus far down, the other famous street, Broadway, is dull and narrow, lined by obscure and dirty warehouses and office buildings, with none of the lights and glamour of the 'great white way' it becomes a mile or so farther north. But the Village has its lights too, its little theatres, its cabarets, its restaurants, its clubs, its galleries; the shops and cafés are open late into the night, and the Village never sleeps. Certainly, this aspect of it would not have a great appeal for John and Llewelyn, but the infinite human variety of the place would be another matter—the Jews, the Germans, the Italians, the Greeks—Greenwich Village was a teeming ant-heap of humanity, and for Llewelyn in particular its study was a never-failing delight. The Village was also a convenient place for walking, with the pageant of its streets, and the docks and river not far away; here were the ferries, the one to Staten Island being in particular a favourite, for the island was then still semi-rural, and on its beaches New York seemed far away. Llewelyn, with his constant need for the countryside, found even the disciplined lawns of Washington Square a solace, and he took delight in the great trees, under which he would sit and write, with the running children about him, and the old men sitting at their open-air checkers games near by. Perhaps he remembered that a former resident of the Square, Henry James, had spoken of detecting here 'a kind of established repose which is not of frequent occurrence in other quarters of the long, shrill city'. In his own essay on Washington Square Llewelyn refers to the 'rich, mellow atmosphere' of these 'happy purlieus', and a few sentences will demonstrate his power, at the very beginning of his career, of evoking from unpromising material a vision of the enduring verities:

Of the various trees in this part of the town it is perhaps the English elms that are most stimulating to the imagination. There are two especially fine ones in the Square itself, one near Fourth Street and the other at one corner of the east end. Many a forlorn, heart-sick European who has allowed his eyes to wander upwards along their dark, rough-barked timber, must have felt their generous influence prompting him to forget if but for a moment, the cark and care of workaday life, as his mind, in lovely retrospect, harks back to far-off days in distant harvest fields, where under just such lofty branches horses and men take their rest among cool shadows. There is indeed one other tree capable of soothing unhappy and deflowered minds, a tree especially typical of certain aspects of New York. In Washington Square, in Patchin Place, in almost every insignificant back garden of the neighbourhood, the lovely ailantus or 'heaven-tree' grows up bravely, spreading out its delicate palm-like leaves—leaves such as one might fancy were strewn under the hoofs of that gentle animal which bore our Lord into Jerusalem—as a constant and consoling reminder that even out of dust and ashes, out of arid brick and desolate pavement, beauty can and will force its way up in all its loveliness towards the calm, eternal stars.[1]

This tree, the ailanthus, springing up so unexpectedly from area and alley, moved John Cowper also and he made it the subject of a sonnet published in *The Dial* in 1926.

In Greenwich Village also there was a constant though ever-changing population of writers and artists—actors, sculptors, musicians, poets, novelists, journalists, dramatists, painters; and to Llewelyn, after five years of African loneliness, the good talk must have been a wonderful blessing. Every writer sometimes needs to meet and talk with his peers: even the hermit Theodore received visits from fellow writers, and assuredly benefited from them even if he never expressed very convincing regret at seeing them depart again. Llewelyn made friendships with many American writers, with Theodore Dreiser,

[1] *Honey and Gall* (1924).

with Van Wyck Brooks, Edna St Vincent Millay, Marianne Moore and Arthur Davison Ficke, and with some of the writers from Britain then living in New York, notably Richard le Gallienne and Padraic Colum. Apart from those who became his friends he met also scores of others with whom he had a more transitory intercourse—Amy Lowell, Bertrand Russell, Edmund Wilson, Scott Fitzgerald. His comments on some other celebrities in *The Verdict of Bridlegoose* are not always flattering.

At first both brothers lived with their sister Marian on West 21st Street, and they also at one time had a room together at 148 Waverly Place—this was the great bare empty room which was barricaded by an immense anti-burglar lock which Llewelyn installed, although neither of the brothers had anything worth stealing, except Llewelyn's overcoat; the lock nearly succeeded in keeping the brothers out too. John's absences on lecture engagements left Llewelyn much alone, but this no doubt served to keep him at his writing, and he contributed to a good many journals in these first months, so that by the time he had been in America a couple of years he had enough material to make up several books, and these essays were used in several subsequent volumes, including *Ebony and Ivory, Thirteen Worthies, Cup-Bearers of Wine and Hellebore* and *Honey and Gall*.

When Llewelyn had been living in New York about a year he received a letter inviting him to tea in Patchin Place—'No suspicion, no inkling, did I have that the white page . . . was the first token of a relationship that was to have so much significance in my life.' But the letter was from Alyse Gregory, whom he would marry. Miss Gregory was at that time a freelance writer, and shortly after this meeting she became Managing Editor of *The Dial*, one of the most notable and influential of literary magazines.

Llewelyn speaks of his discovery of Patchin Place as producing, or at least coinciding with, a 'bettering' of his fortunes. Certainly his immediate response to Miss Gregory's personality brought him a happiness he had not experienced before, and this broadened into love. He tells of the influence of the cosy rooms and their owner upon him. Patchin Place itself is a haven in the roar of New York. It is a short blind alley-way with a double row of old houses, not more than a score, under the looming shadow of the towering apartment and ware-house blocks of the main thoroughfares. No car enters Patchin Place, and wrought-iron gates across the narrow entrance keep out all but foot traffic. The houses are terraced, and have stood, one may suppose, for not less than a hundred years, perhaps for a good deal longer; they are flat-fronted, three-storey buildings, with dark basement areas from which spring the leaning ailanthus trees. They are such houses as may be seen by the score in Kensington, Chelsea and other parts of London, and in such cities as Bristol and Brighton, but in New York—even in Greenwich Village—they are a rarer growth. Llewelyn writes of the interior of the rooms, with their coal fires brightly burning, as a haven and a retreat, and says he was reminded of the interior of a fisherman's cottage on Chesil Beach, so snug and warm within, while a great tempest raged without—there, a tempest of the sea, but in Patchin Place the never-ceasing tempest of traffic and the town.

The bettering of Llewelyn's fortunes lay not only in this new security but also now in the brighter prospects for his work; Alyse was able to introduce him to editors and publishers, and the first substantial result was the publication, by American Library Service early in 1923, of *Ebony and Ivory*. Theodore Dreiser was then at the height of his celebrity, and the preface he contributed, so generous in its terms as it was, must have impressed many prospective readers. 'I wish for this little book all that its intrinsic merit deserves,' he wrote. 'If that wish were granted the author would never need complain.' He remarked that no doubt the author would be recommended to write a novel, and he went on: 'Why a novel? . . . since the things he offers are immensely beyond the value of most novels and sketches. They present a temperament, an emotion, a taste, a judgment and an understanding altogether artistic and therefore distinguished.' These words must have been especially good reading for Llewelyn himself, conscious that his talent for writing novels was a thin one. In the English edition of the book, which was published later in the year by Grant Richards, Dreiser's preface was omitted for one by Edward Shanks, who like Dreiser is impressed by the 'beautiful and sonorous prose' of these 'unexpected masterpieces', but he takes up a point not stressed by Dreiser—the pain and cruelty of these essays and sketches: 'The sensitive reader is not to expect anything but pain', and I recall my own determination, maybe thirty years ago, never to read the book a second time. It is a determination I have not held to, but there are still pages and paragraphs which leave me uneasy and distressed; pages in which cruelty is not only recorded, but seemingly accepted without protest. And yet—the reflection comes—in the face of monstrous things occurring daily what are the protests, often enough, but sentimental sops to a conscience only superficially troubled? These essays make the reader uncomfortable perhaps because he does not wish to know of such things.

Later in 1923 the same two publishers, in New York and London, put out another book of Llewelyn's, *Thirteen Worthies*, to which he had originally added the subtitle 'whimsical, wise and wanton', and the three words illustrate the approach he made to the great figures of literature. Much as he valued their writings, he was always concerned first to come at the man. It was indeed for their wisdom that he came to them, but the quirks of character, the ironies of their lives, the eccentricities they displayed, these were his constant study and delight; and he wrote in his best and happiest manner of the odd-men-out, the flamboyant, the nonconformist, the rebels and the underrated figures—of such men as Thomas Deloney, Anthony à Wood, Tom Coryat, Burton, Rabelais, Bewick—'grave, gentle, honest, lusty and curious men', Van Wyck Brooks calls them in his preface. Over the years Llewelyn Powys wrote appreciations of very many books and writers of the sort gathered into *Thirteen Worthies*, and many of them remain uncollected. They have not the immediate value as literary criticism of the more elaborate essays of John Cowper Powys; they are not interpretations of great and complex thinkers, but rather familiar discourses designed to send readers again, or for the first time, to writers not always in literature's main stream: writers easily overlooked, or easily known only superficially, or only in part; how many readers of the essay on Nicholas Culpeper are hearing of him for the first time? And how few of them turn the pages unrewarded! Llewelyn's approach to the criticism of his worthies' writings is unacademic, and must have seemed valueless to some who practised an austerer discipline, with commentaries on prosodic influence and comparative symbolism and the use of imagery. There is nothing of that here, and yet it might well stimulate a reader to interest and sympathy in coming to the poetry of William Barnes:

In his poetry there can be found no trace of that black salt of disillusionment, bitter to the taste as the milk of dandelions or the roots of certain weeds, that seems to have become so inseparable from the work of the poets of these latter years. Never for one single moment does he suspect the world of concealing for human life yawning gaps and ghastly insecurities! Nothing but what may be called 'natural sorrows' ever darkens the brows of the simple folk whom he portrays from the time when, as

swaddled children, they are held over the 'hallowed stone' of the
baptismal font till the hour when their bones are laid to rest
amongst those of their fathers and of the old men before them...

No one, not even Hardy, can conjure up more surely the picture
of a sweltering hayfield at the time of the Feast of St Barnabas:
the hard-working labourers, 'Wi' their eärms in white sleves,
left an' right,' the glittering farm instruments, the swathes of
wilting, sweet-smelling grass, the slow-worms, the mice, the
little green cold-backed frogs:

'Or in the day, a-vleèn drough
The leafy trees, the whos'se gookoo
Do zing to mowers that do zet
Their zives on end, an' stan' to whet.'

John Cowper, in these years of Llewelyn's first permanent residence
in America, was less active in authorship than in the closing years of
the war. Between *The Complex Vision* of 1920 and *Ducdame*, which
came in 1925, he published only the small collection of poems called
Samphire (1922) and three little pamphlets, although it is true he wrote
some long papers and reviews, including the notable study of James
Joyce. He was now lecturing under a different management, Arnold
Shaw having retired, and his long absences from New York removed
him from the urgings of Llewelyn, always anxious to persuade him to
write more and lecture less. The three little pamphlets are small
indeed: *The Art of Happiness* [1] is the first of John's 'Little Blue
Books'; *Psychoanalysis and Morality* is a 48-page essay of which only
five hundred copies were printed, and of these two hundred were lost
by fire and a few were reissued later in New York by Random House;
and *The Religion of A Sceptic* is an essay of similar length published
in 1925 by Dodd, Mead, of New York. These represented indeed a
slender output from a writer usually prolific both in variety and length.
As for the *Art of Happiness*, that too is an essay of some fifty pages—
about 20,000 words.

The Little Blue Books merit a word of comment. They were published by E. Haldeman-Julius from the little town of Girard, Kansas.
The books were in paper wrappers of pale blue (sometimes in later
years buff, salmon-pink and other colours appeared) and were about
five inches by three and a half; they were printed not very clearly on a
newsprint-style paper which goes yellow-brown with age; and they

[1] This title appeared again in 1935 on a larger and quite separate book.

were sold at ten cents. The slogan some of them carry, 'A University in Print', is justified by the extraordinary range of titles and subjects, from the philosophy of Plato to 'do-it-yourself' medicine. The series contains nine titles by John Cowper Powys and two by Llewelyn, and must have drawn the attention of thousands of Americans to those two authors, as to scores of other authors in the series; for these little books circulated in places where more pretentious volumes were less easily come by; and of course they long preceded the flood of cheap paperbacks which was a product of the 1939–45 war, and only took a strong hold in the forties and thereafter. The Little Blue Books do not hold the place that once was theirs, but their place in the history of popular education in America is secure.[1]

[1] Their significance has not been overlooked, and an almost complete set has been assembled for study at Colgate University; doubtless others are preserved elsewhere.

9

IN THE autumn of 1922 T. F. Powys wrote 'out of the blue' to Messrs Chatto & Windus, enclosing what he described as a short novel, 'The Left Leg'.[1] He said he had other similar stories which could be published with 'The Left Leg' to make up a volume. The publishers replied that they would like to see further stories, and over the next few weeks they received, separately, *Black Bryony*, 'Abraham Men', 'Hester Dominy' and 'Tadnol'. On 7 February 1923 Chatto & Windus wrote to suggest publication of 'The Left Leg', 'Hester Dominy' and 'Abraham Men' in one volume; on 20 February Theodore returned the publishing agreement signed, and a long association in writing and publishing had formally begun. Chatto & Windus thereafter published all his full-length books in England; in America he was published initially by Knopf, and later by the Viking Press.

But why did Theodore write out of the blue to Chatto & Windus, when he might have tried John's London publishers, at that time Heinemann, especially as they were Louis Wilkinson's publishers

[1] I *think* T. F. Powys sent the book, but there is some confusion in the accounts. Mr David Garnett, in his autobiography, says that he read the three stories and sent them 'with a recommendation' to Charles Prentice, of Chatto's. Miss Sylvia Townsend Warner, in her unpublished study of Theodore Powys, tells of taking the stories to Mr Garnett, but seems to imply that he suggested sending them to Chatto, rather than that he actually sent them himself. The reason why I favour the suggestion that Theodore sent them is that the earliest by date of the references is a letter from Charles Prentice to Miss Warner, which she has been good enough to show me, in which Prentice—writing in 1927, only five years after the event—states precisely that Theodore sent 'The Left Leg' on 22 September 1922, and that the other two stories which made up the published volume of *The Left Leg* came one from Theodore and the other from a literary agent within a few weeks of the first. The point is a small one, but it illustrates the difficulty of coming at the truth in writing biography, even when discussing events upon which contemporary authorities may be consulted.

also? To find the answer, it is necessary to go back a year, to mid 1921, when the sculptor Stephen Tomlin took lodgings in East Chaldon with a view to working there. Tomlin quickly noted that in the village there lived a very remarkable man, a hermit who read Dostoievsky, and he communicated this intelligence to Sylvia Townsend Warner, together with a request that she send him one of her plays 'because Powys would like to read it'. Manuscripts were exchanged, and Miss Warner (who had already read the *Soliloquies*) found herself in possession of *Mr. Tasker's Gods*. The book 'enthralled, frightened and oppressed' her and she wrote a long letter to the author about it, containing criticisms which Theodore took seriously in making later revisions. Other correspondence followed, and in March 1922 Miss Warner went down to visit Stephen Tomlin and to meet Theodore. A few weeks later the two were putting their heads together to try to find Theodore a publisher; Tomlin suggested that Sylvia might call on David Garnett in London and take the typescript of 'Hester Dominy' with her. Tomlin knew Garnett slightly, but Sylvia Townsend Warner did not; however, she agreed to call at the bookshop Garnett was then running near the British Museum. After deliberation Garnett would seem to have suggested an approach to Chatto's, which as we have seen Theodore proceeded to make; for writing to Miss Warner some years later Charles Prentice of Chatto's records that just after the typescript of 'The Left Leg' arrived in the office he had lunch with Garnett, who warned him it might be on the way.

These three stories, although not the first written, were in some ways the best suited of T. F. Powys's early work to introduce him to the reading public; so new and individual and strange a talent was perhaps to be approached with circumspection, and taken in small measure. The world of 'The Left Leg' was like no world portrayed anywhere else in English literature, and no doubt it took a bit of getting used to; the reader had to adjust his own ideas to these new ones, as page succeeded page; and the adjustment was not easy. 'The Left Leg' made less than a hundred printed pages, and this brevity no doubt aided it in getting a hearing, just as by contrast their great length long stood in the way of recognition of John Cowper's vast novels. Because *The Left Leg* does not represent Theodore's final maturity it may well be the best beginning for a reader coming to his work for the first time, for there is here, as it were, a certain dilution of the dose, some watering to help it down; 'Hester Dominy' indeed is closer to a conventional plot and setting than any of Theodore's later stories

(significantly it is the weakest of the three in this book), and to pass
from this to 'The Left Leg' is to experience the same transition from
apprenticeship to mastery that the reader finds in turning from
Sketches by Boz to *Pickwick*, or from *A Portrait of the Artist* to *Ulysses*.
Both 'Hester Dominy' and 'Abraham Men' have a certain imprecision,
and they end loosely, with nothing done: Hester has tired of town life,
and gone to try life in the country, and she tires also of that. Luke Bird,
in 'Abraham Men', has given up his employment to be an evangelist
in the village of Dodder, and he has failed to influence a single soul;
so he goes back to his old job. But 'The Left Leg' moves surely and
triumphantly to a positive end—something 'determined, dared and
done'. Here there are no loose threads, no hesitations; in the other two
stories it is possible to suppose that the author is 'making them up as
he goes along', but the third marches inevitably forward; perhaps the
last two or three pages are a little abrupt, but this is not a serious fault;
few stories are the better for going on after the crisis has been reached.
'The Left Leg' has also the most 'Theodorian' plot of the three,
foreshadowing *Mr. Weston* and *Unclay*. It is a study in single-minded
corruption—'Farmer Mew's habit of life was to clutch all'. The farmer
owns virtually everything in the village—the land, the houses, the
people, even. The vicar is an amiable nonentity who never notices
what is going on, and most of the other inhabitants are indifferent,
some even admiring the farmer's ruthless ways. What he lacks, he
takes, whether it be another man's land or his stock or his wife. Only
the mysterious absentee Mr Jar is thought likely to be a curb on
Farmer Mew: 'There was an idea in Madder that if Mr Jar ever came
to the village again something would happen'. Finally, when several
people have been ruined, or crushed, or seduced, or done to death by
Mew's activities, Jar does return:

> At that moment they heard a voice calling by Madder well. It was
> Mad Button.
> 'Wold Jar be come, wold Jar be come,' the voice called.
> 'Who be wold Jar?' the voice asked itself.
> ''E be the leaf that do drift in the wind. 'E be the cloud that
> do cross the moon at night-time. 'E be the stone that a poor man
> do take up in road to throw at 'is dog. 'E be the pond weeds where
> do bide the wold toad. 'E be the bastard child before 'tis born.
> Wold Jar be come.'

Jar, who reappears in other stories, is a supernatural being whose exact identity is never established; he is less clearly 'God' than is Mr Weston, but his influence upon the villagers is of the same order; one might say 'Mew proposes, Jar disposes'. In 'The Left Leg' his return is decisive—the oppressed are relieved, the sinners are forgiven (all but one), the meek are exalted; 'curse God, and die', says the Scripture, and Farmer Mew does just that.

There is lacking here the subtlety of Theodore's later work, but it is a subtlety of execution rather than of conception that is to come; there is something crude still in the telling—Mew digging a hole under 'Jar's stone' and pouring in gunpowder before sitting on the top to apply the match . . . it is a little too detailed, too graphic; and the descent from the sky of his severed leg is close to farcical. Perhaps Theodore was working here to the same principles that lie behind some of Shakespeare's clowns, fools and naturals; and perhaps Tom Button is of their company in his reactions to events, just as he is of the company of Scott's witches and gipsies in his incantations. But Shakespeare's fools—and the fools elsewhere in the Jacobean drama—are not always successful; and there is something unconvincing in this last scene, as though it were written in to round the story off and in particular to provide a tag line for the tale—'I took him by the left leg', etc. When Mew disappears in a puff of smoke the end is—messy; later on, we find that Mr Weston departs in a similar way, without fuss and quite tidily. Theodore learned rapidly, and in less than five years, between the composition of 'The Left Leg' and *Mr. Weston*, he had taken a complete control of his medium.

To say this, however, is not to imply that these early stories are wholly 'prentice work by comparison with what came after. The superiority in conception of 'The Left Leg' is not accompanied by a marked superiority in the telling, although there are advances here also, especially over 'Hester Dominy'. 'Abraham Men' affords many striking passages and phrases, quite sufficient without the other stories to announce the appearance of an original stylist; and also this story best demonstrates of the three Theodore's awakening gift for striking and effective dialogue—for the dialogue in 'Hester Dominy' is conventional—'Good-bye, Mr. Dine,' she said, 'I've liked coming here',—and in 'The Left Leg' it is scanty and brief. There are splendid salty speeches in 'Abraham Men':

'They wold horses do know that spring be come.'
Mr. Dunell was looking over the gate at his two horses when

he made this remark; the horses were biting contentedly at the
sweet grass.

''Tis like this wi' they horses,' Mr. Dunell continued,—'they
do lie up in stable o' nights in winter an' do dream of buttercups,
and when the real spring do come they do think that all the world
be gone crazed wi' flowers. No, no, preacher, don't 'e tell I
nothing about Zachariah nor Timothy neither. I do know what
you would say, and so do they horses. They poor beasts haven't
lived so long without knowing what grass be made of.'

Again, this time with a group of speakers:

'Thik young man that do bide at your house, 'e do talk,' Mrs.
Topp was saying.

'Yes 'e do,' replied Betsy Pring, ''e do say all sorts of words.'

'So do squire,' Susan Dunell whispered mysteriously. 'Dark
Eliza do know what 'e do say.'

'That I do,' said Dark Eliza, pleased to be brought into the
talk. 'Squire did only say yesterday, when 'e saw I in mud—
"What a damned dirty pickle thee be in, Eliza. God 'Is woneself
wouldn't know thee."'

''Tis a world of wonder,' Mrs. Topp remarked. 'There's thik
half-penny be a-taken off sugar, there's wold Colley be dead in
workhouse, there's Rose Pring be lefted a £100, there's that
young Bird that be after she—there's Cobb the policeman,'—for
Mr. Cobb was seen to be riding down the lane upon his bicycle.

'True, Mrs. Topp,' said Dark Eliza, 'this world be a queer
place to live in. What with they carts and horses running over
folk in roads, and they falling stars in sky, 'tain't a safe place to
live in, this bain't.'

'I do mind George Pring saying a long time ago under they
blue skies,' remarked Betsy Pring, who loved nothing better than
her own family history, 'George did up an' say: "Betsy, 'tain't
worth our while to wait any longer, we may as well take an' do
en; we've fiddled about together Saturday nights and Sunday
nights enough, I do think", an' so to church we did go.'

Mary Bugg rubbed her nose with her finger. 'They clocks do
turn in day-time,' she said, 'an' maybe Bugg do want 'is dinner.
I did say to he only yesterday—"I wish that the young preacher
were here in house and did see 'ee eat, 'twould be a fine subject
for 'is next sermon on a gluttony sinner."'

This owes nothing to Hardy, just as Theodore's Dorset landscapes owe nothing to Hardy; it has an affinity with the dialogue in the plays and novels of Eden Phillpotts, but this may be accidental. These stories also exhibit the first incidental touches of humour which Theodore employs often enough even in the tragic tales, and here also it is of Phillpotts that one is occasionally reminded, as, for example, when Luke finds all the Whiffer family 'in dire consternation, not because their father was dead, but because the smoked ham ordered from Milverton had not come', or again reminiscent of Phillpotts the observation that the puzzled sheep hearing Luke Bird preach gathered around him under the impression that 'he was a new kind of forked turnip imported from Germany'.

Black Bryony was published in 1923 a few months after *The Left Leg*. In the chronological canon it precedes the three stories of *The Left Leg*, and is preceded only by *Mr. Tasker's Gods*. In Theodore's note on the composition of some of his stories *Black Bryony* is dated 1917 and described as 'a winter book'. After the horrors of *Mr. Tasker* those of *Black Bryony* seem muted and almost casual, and at first reading it might almost seem a rural comedy, except for the tragedy of the rectory fire; but reconsidered, the story is found to be sad indeed, with every character frustrated, or evil, or deprived, or brutish, or stupid, or ineffectual. There are many touches of humour in the telling, but they are *in the telling*, and not in the hearts of the people of the book.

The story centres upon Mary Crowle, a Salvation Army girl who comes to Norbury to preach the uncompromising gospel of her Church; but Mary is herself a sinner; she steals a rich farmer's wallet, and she gives birth secretly to an illegitimate child, which she deposits on the rectory doorstep; she also does everything she can to frustrate her aunt, whose harmless ambition is to marry the innkeeper from the next village. But if Mary's character and actions produce the central catastrophe, this is supported everywhere by the villagers, who are malicious and self-seeking and bigoted—a few minor comedy characters apart. Even when the vicar and baby Bryony are burned to death the people feel no horror, no sorrow, no remorse: '. . . in every face a secret pleasure glowed, lit up by the flames'. There is no attempt at rescue, no attempt to put out the flames. The servant Matilda has the grace to cry (she has carried out her best dress to safety, but had been too upset to pick up the baby) but when she asks Mr Potten to save the children Mr Potten 'discreetly' hands on the request to Mr Morsay, who does nothing. Even Mr Told, who is the bravest soul present, only goes near enough to the fire to get a burning brand from which to light his pipe. All this is told in simple, matter-of-fact terms, so that the reader is lulled into thinking the affair, after all, will turn out all right; and then, suddenly, '. . . a tall, burning figure appeared in the doorway coming out of the fire. The tall figure, burning like a torch, came out of the house and on to the lawn. Standing on the grass, Mr. Crossley took from under his cloak a little blackened and charred body. He laid the body tenderly down upon the ground.' He then raises his arms as if to send a prayer to heaven, and drops dead; it is melodramatic, but wonderfully effective after the played-down and almost comic pages that immediately precede it.

Much has been made of T. F. Powys's symbolism, and it is of course a strong element in his work; but it can be made too much of, in my opinion. Here in *Black Bryony*, for example, Mary's plucking of the spray of this poisonous plant right at the beginning seems to spark off the whole explosive train of events which leads to the final conflagration; and the plant is linked with little Bryony by the leaf-shaped birth-mark on his brow, and his given name; elsewhere in the book the beautiful and deadly plant is mentioned as though to direct attention to it as integral to the narrative, and no doubt it could be argued that Mary too is poisonous and beautiful. But why bother? If every reference to Black Bryony were omitted, and if the baby were called Sam, the story would be as artistic, as effective and as moving. Furthermore, Mr David Garnett tells us that the plant Theodore really had in mind was the White Bryony . . . but I leave readers of Culpeper's *Herbal* to determine the rights of that.

───── 10 ─────

In September 1925 the *Century Magazine* published an article by John Cowper Powys called 'Four Brothers: A Family Confession', in which he surveyed the writings of the family up till that time. The fourth brother was A. R. Powys. This brother, often called 'A.R.P.', and sometimes Bertie—'Brother Positive', Llewelyn had once dubbed him—had become Secretary to the Society for the Protection of Ancient Buildings, and to this work he gave his whole attention. His writings are in the main incidental to his work, consisting chiefly of detached articles on architectural subjects, some of them controversial in character. He writes in a plain, forthright and lucid style, and the reader of his essays may feel a regret that they are specialized and occasional, for this man's thoughts on any subject would be arresting; the student of his brothers' writings will be interested to see how completely different his work is from theirs—quite as different as they are from one another. He writes squarely in the tradition of inornate English prose of the order of Dryden's and Southey's: an honest use of language solely for the purpose of conveying ideas as accurately and as effectively as the writer can manage. Here is an example:

> It is unnecessary again to describe the beauty and value of the bridge. It is, however, desirable to write a word or two in answer to those who, while they appreciate the fine qualities of the bridge, have somehow come by the idea that the societies which are opposing its demolition are die-hard obstructionists. That suggestion must be dismissed at once. It is not the work of an obstructionist to attempt to preserve a building which adds so much grace, dignity, and mystery to a view of London that is so fine. It is not the work of an obstructionist to stand for the protection of a comparatively narrow bridge at a crossing of the river where

no one now would propose to build newly, had the present bridge never been built. It is not the work of an obstructionist to urge that the right place for a new bridge is at that crossing of the river where converging traffic most requires it, namely, at some place not far from the present Charing Cross railway station. On the other hand, it is the work of an obstructionist to lead to the present rather awkward crossing of the river an increasing quantity of traffic, and still to draw thither daily all that which already overcrowds the roadway. It is also his work to hinder the fulfilment of a piece of town planning which will ease the life of the citizens of London and at the same time preserve for their proud enjoyment a building which may justly be numbered among the wonders of the world.

A. R. Powys was far too busy with his work for the Society to be a man of letters; he wrote various papers which were collected in part after his death in *From The Ground Up* (from which the quotation above is taken—it concerns, of course, the unsuccessful crusade to save Rennie's Waterloo Bridge) and two or three pamphlets; his only books of any size are *The English Parish Church* (1930) in Longmans' 'English Heritage' series, and *The Repair of Ancient Buildings* (Dent, 1929). *The English Parish Church* is a survey of the growth and use of the church in England, with special emphasis on the fabric and furnishings, full of unusual detail and out-of-the-way information; it suffers, I think, from lack of comprehensive illustration. If reissued with a large supporting provision of photographs it might well establish itself as a standard work, and the companion pocket survey of *The English House* (1929, in Benn's 'Sixpenny Library') would make an admirable appendix. I give myself the pleasure of making one more quotation from A. R. Powys, in the hope that the reader may be encouraged to seek out this least known of the writing brothers; it is from *The English Parish Church*:

That the parish priest, who was also rural dean, had some difficult duties to perform is seen by the story of him who held that office in 1315 in the deanery of Crewkerne. He was sent to reprimand Sir Allan Plucknet for not carrying out the instructions of his mother's will, by which she ordered her burial in the Abbey Church at Sherborne. Sir Allan, when the good dean called on him, caught him by the throat, twisted his hood, and caused him to bleed, at which the dean with difficulty fled away. Later, when the dean and his men came upon Sir Allan at Haselbury, the knight had the better of him again, making the poor priest eat the bishop's letter, together with the great wax seal. Yet in the end Sir Allan was forced to submission, but I imagine that he had already had his money's worth out of the affair.

In 'Four Brothers' John makes shrewd observations on the respective merits and capabilities of his brothers and himself, and the article is of particular interest because of its early date; it was written before any of the brothers had published works of full maturity. Of Llewelyn John says:

Among these various forms through which my brother has chosen to express himself, it seems to me that it is the first, the diaristic or autobiographical one, that lends itself most naturally to his peculiar turn of mind and becomes the most fully impregnated with the essence of his personality. It is indeed inevitable that this should be the case, since the most characteristic quality in Llewelyn's temperament is his power of registering an integrated, banked-up, and massively simple response to every actual situation in which he finds himself.

One might say that the characteristic yeast of this writer's 'whole-wheat' bake-shop, even in the cases where he uses the biographical, discursive, or short-story formula, always springs from the same integral response to the same quite definite and quite special stimulus. For it is only a certain kind of human situation—a kind purged and winnowed of everything not basically rooted in our common earth-life—that really stirs his interest; and his heart-whole, compact reaction, when his interest *is* stirred, is as reiterated and undeviating as it is idiosyncratic, exclusive, empiric. It goes very deep, this response of his; it goes as deep as life. But it always remains obstinately unporous to certain overtones and undertones, to certain shadowy intimations, which must be admitted, in a more objective synthesis, to have their place in the world's complicated orchestra.

Llewelyn, in plain words, is a poetical materialist with an unconquerable zest for life—for life on any terms. . . .

John speaks in this essay of Llewelyn's four ways of writing, the autobiographical, the 'straight' essay, the biographical essay and the short story, and he places them in that order of importance. Nothing in Llewelyn's later work (although in bulk it greatly exceeds what was before John as he wrote this) in any way upsets this judgment, and the last and least important division—fiction—Llewelyn virtually abandoned. *Love and Death* reads like a novel, but it is not a novel; and *Apples be Ripe*, although more nearly a conventional novel, has so much autobiography mixed with it that it cannot be claimed that it affords an example of creative fiction writing. John detects as main influences in Llewelyn four writers: Lamb, Pater, Maupassant and Lytton Strachey, and of these he finds Lamb the strongest; but he goes on to say that in Llewelyn's best and most characteristic work the influences are least to be detected, and this, it may be added, is what ultimately marks the great writer: it is by how much he is himself first that he must be assessed, and only afterwards is it of interest to trace those influences that went into his making.

In Theodore John notes the originality of his 'super-sophisticated, elusive, provocative, bewildering art . . . the darkly muttered mystical resentments, low-voiced out of supernatural clairvoyance, of some Druidic captive'. He is, John notes, the most original of the brothers, both in subject-matter and style; his humour has a 'deep, sweet-bitter subterranean malice', and the religion that enters profoundly into the texture of Theodore's stories does not bring reassurance or comfort.

Theodore Powys's world is indeed a world projected whole and entire out of the shadowy recesses of his own unusual sub-consciousness. So original is his extraordinary vision of things, so saturated with his extraordinary personality is every word he writes, that one feels certain that these strange tales are assured, if anything is assured, of a lasting hold upon certain troubled minds. The passages that are least affected by this unceasing and remorseless pursuit of the weak by the strong, this dark hunt that we follow with such mingled emotions—for the human heart is a colosseum of contradictions—are the passages in which the rambling choruses of old men and old women exchange their comments upon it all. In 'The Left Leg' the women meet in the village shop. In 'Hester Dominy' the men meet in the pound, in *Mark Only* in Mark's stable. While in *Black Bryony* the meeting-place of men and women alike is the motor-van of the carrier. In all these scenes, where the gloom of the plot is relieved by a unique and elfish humour, one is aware of something mysteriously simple and yet mysteriously profound in the writer's philosophy —a philosophy to which door-handles and loaves of bread and wooden settles and church-porch-biers and spades and mugs and platters and pitchforks and horse-dung all contribute their quota of mystic intimation.

Of his own writings John remarks that they are 'indolent, careless, *occasional*' beside the 'concentrated and premeditated art' of his brothers; and yet he feels that his interests, his scope, extend beyond theirs. It is because he is a talker, and not a writer by instinct, that his style is so often open to criticism, he says—that he so often writes clumsily, imitatively, indolently, carelessly, 'dropping, as I go, so many "bricks", as we say in England, and uttering so many platitudes and banalities', but he adds:

> Now and then, however, so I allow myself to imagine, the high gods in their capriciousness select just such a wind-shaken reed as I am through which to whisper their translunar secrets. And I would finally say that just as A. R. Powys has the most definite art-sense, just as T. F. Powys has the most original sensibility, and Llewelyn Powys the most idiosyncratic and winning style, among us, my own quality, when it *is* allowed to appear through the slag and rubble, is neither displayed in art nor originality nor style, but in a breath, a touch, a tremor, a hint, of that mysterious and hardly human phenomenon which civilization has done so much to obliterate from among men, and which in every age has excited suspicion, hostility, and misunderstanding. I refer to the ambiguous phenomenon known loosely and vaguely as *in-spiration*.

These brief judgments stand up well forty years after they were first written, even though all the brothers so materially increased the body of work upon which each must ultimately be assessed.

The years 1923–25 were significant in the biographical sequence for a number of reasons; they saw Theodore's definitive launching as a writer, and the appearance of two of Llewelyn's significant works of autobiography and also his marriage and return to England. But first must be recorded the death of the Rev. C. F. Powys, on 5 August 1923, at Weymouth. The old man had been failing for some time in his house in Greenhill Terrace, facing the sea, under the devoted care of his daughter Gertrude. His death released her at last from her freely given years of service, and she was able to go to Paris to study art. A large fortune—£40,000, at that time of course worth considerably more in purchasing power than it would be today—was to be divided among the children, and although so large a family necessarily meant a comparatively small share to each, the frugal-minded brothers were all able to make good use of it in ordering their lives; to Theodore, for one, something in the region of four thousand pounds must have represented wealth. The last glimpse we have of the formidable old vicar comes in Llewelyn's moving essay, 'Out of the Past', which may be found in *Earth Memories*. One day in his last years he set out without revealing his intention to go from Weymouth to the ancient Dorset village of Stalbridge, where he was born. Llewelyn evokes a picture of him, trudging doggedly along the dusty lanes, driven or guided by some deep-rooted impulse to revisit the house of his father: 'What manner of call had he received, imperative and not to be denied, to return unto that place from whence he came? Far away over the seas as I was at the time, I have often wondered whether I could have borne to have found him, this old man, my father, advancing with deliberate intention, with intellectual intention, along the green leafy lanes of Dorset. Should I have had the temerity to divert him from his dedicated pilgrimage with the cry of "Father!" as he went forward, this octogenarian who was lost and yet who knew every stile, every ditch, every shard, along the way he was taking?' In another essay, 'Stalbridge Rectory', in *Dorset Essays*, Llewelyn returns to the theme; he recalls that on leaving home the old man had taken leave of Gertrude with 'unusual formality' when setting out (as she supposed) for his usual morning walk. In fact, he took train to Templecombe and then walked to Stalbridge, where at the rectory he was given tea and 'settled himself in the parlour looking about him with a benevolent expression but spoke no word'. Then he returned to Templecombe and sat quietly on the station platform, perfectly happy, while puzzled officials tried to find out his identity, and get him safely on his way home. There is a Homeric simplicity in this small incident in the life of an old man come close to death and using his last reserves of strength and determination to make a pilgrimage to the place of his boyhood.

In New York the Powys colony, round its nucleus of Marian and Llewelyn, with frequent sojourns by John Cowper Powys, was constantly augmented by other visitors; Philippa and Bertie both made visits at this time, Philippa soon after their father's death, and Bertie in the winter of 1924–25. Philippa was beginning to write, although 'something flew between her and the sun' when she attempted to put her poetical and original ideas into words, and her published work of one novel and one pamphlet of verses does not do her complete justice. Llewelyn was her constant encourager, and it was after his return to England and while they lived as near neighbours that she wrote and published her novel *The Blackthorn Winter*, to which I shall return. It was also in 1924–25 that Bertie's occasional writings began to appear more regularly, for J. C. Squire, then editing *The London Mercury*, opened the columns of that journal for his architectural notes; and it may be that Bertie's presence in America prompted John to include him in the article, 'Four Brothers', to be published at that time. Llewelyn, writing to Lucy Powys in February 1925, records a 'wonderful new year' with John and Bertie gathered round a wood fire 'which Bertie would build with extreme care and deliberation'. This was at Montoma, in upper New York State, to which Llewelyn, now married to Alyse Gregory, had retired after a return of his disease.

We must take here a backward glance. From the time of his meeting with Alyse Llewelyn had been busy and happy, and the results of his labours were published first in various journals, and later collected in the several books I have already mentioned above. In June 1924 he went with Dr Watson of *The Dial* on a trip to the Rocky Mountains— that part of the great range which lies in Wyoming. While the doctor was off hunting the grizzly bear Llewelyn would explore the forest, and climb the silent snow-clad slopes of the mountains, going, it would seem, farther than his strength warranted, just as he had done years before in Switzerland. At all events, it was during the journey back to New York that he became convinced of the return of his sickness, and for the next few weeks he was beset by anxiety as the signs multiplied. Alyse felt that he would be better out of New York, and she arranged for him to visit her parents at Norwalk, Connecticut; it was here that he arrived already suffering from a haemorrhage, and here Dr Gregory cared for him for six weeks; and from here, instead of venturing back to New York, he went with Alyse to the farmhouse they found at Montoma, in the Catskill Mountains, not far from the home of their friend Le Gallienne. At the small town of Kingston, New York, they were married on 30 September 1924, by Father Hamilton Cowper

Johnson, a cousin of the Powyses, who was then living at Boston. Many readers will recall the publication of Father Johnson's correspondence with Rose Macaulay some years ago. He was a man of great character and charm who makes his appearances in the Powys story for 'births and deaths and bridal nights'; it was he, three years later, who officiated at the burial of Walter Franzen at East Chaldon, when that friend of the Powyses fell accidentally to his death on the cliffs of White Nose. The tragic story is told in Llewelyn's essay, 'A Grave in Dorset' in *Earth Memories*, and the visitor to Chaldon may find his grave today, 'a little too near the churchyard gate'.

At Montoma Llewelyn's health improved. Miss Gregory gives a wistful vignette of their life here in her introduction to the *Letters of Llewelyn Powys*:

> We were happy in our small wooden house, with its enormous fireplace filled with crackling pine logs, and its small porch where we slept through the freezing nights, while the winter snows banked themselves higher and higher about us. I was at this time acting as Managing Editor of *The Dial* magazine, which necessitated my dividing my time between the country and the city. It was always an anxiety to me to leave Llewelyn alone, as he was only just recovering from a haemorrhage brought on by a trip to the Rocky Mountains, and after our servant left in the afternoon we were cut off from communication with the outside world. I can remember particularly, one late afternoon, as the moment drew near for us to part, seeing a pale shaft of sunlight on the yellow wall of our small study, and in this flickering transient reflection seeming to read, as in a magic mirror, the whole drama of human hearts—swept together by love, isolated and dependent, entranced and desperate, and in the end doomed to eternal separation.

Llewelyn's remarks about the house are more down to earth: he tells Lucy how the winter temperature fell to twenty degrees below zero: 'Our eggs froze, our ham froze, our water froze even in a room with a coal stove burning. For days my beard was stiff with frost, stiff as the hairs on the elephant's tail in Father's study.'

Away from the noise and distraction of New York Llewelyn spent the autumn and winter writing his most ambitious work to date, the series of autobiographical chapters published as *Skin for Skin*. In the meantime another autobiographical book was published in New York, the English edition following some months later. This was *Black Laughter*, the second of the books with an African theme.

Black Laughter has a maturity and assurance not present in the unequal and disconnected essays of *Ebony and Ivory*. It is a full-length connected autobiographical narrative, as published in book form, although detached chapters had appeared separately as articles in the press. In a brief preface the author explains that whereas in *Ebony and Ivory* his aim had been 'literary and aesthetic rather than personal' in *Black Laughter* he had sought to reproduce more intimately the 'casual diurnal occurrences in an alien environment as they impinged upon a receptive nature'. He succeeds in this, but without sacrifice of the 'literary and aesthetic', and the book is the only one of his first six titles which reads as if it were written *as a book*; the only one which is not a miscellaneous collection of shorter pieces. This point is of some importance, because in fact *Black Laughter* is such a collection, and accordingly it marks an advance in Llewelyn's practice as a writer, that the joins are concealed and the narrative continuous. Very many writers at the beginning of their career are daunted by mere *length*— by the thought that the book they are engaged on cannot be completed at a sitting, as an essay or short story often can; and that the same work may be occupying their time and thought six weeks and six months ahead. This may well have been so with Llewelyn, even if only subconsciously. We have seen that he found difficulty in completing his early attempt at a novel. The solid 'feel' of *Black Laughter* was doubtless an encouragement when he sat down to write *Skin for Skin*. As for *Black Laughter*, Negley Farson (a man who knew Africa intimately) wrote in his introduction to the 1953 reprint that it was far more than just a book about Africa, although the strictly African landscape and observation were all true; he says he reviewed it on first publication, carried it along on two African trips, and has 'packed a copy around the world ever since'. Such a traveller as Negley Farson carries no unnecessary luggage, and this is about as convincing a tribute as *Black Laughter* or any book could look for. And because of its greater length there is a cumulative effect which no short essay could expect to produce.

By the beginning of 1925 Llewelyn had been absent from England almost continuously for ten years; he felt the urge to return home, and the state of his health suggested that such a return might be wise. It was not an easy decision, for Alyse was now Managing Editor of *The Dial*, and for a variety of reasons a severance would be a pity; but her husband counted for more than the attractions and distractions of literary New York, and if either of them doubted the decision it was Llewelyn. Early in May they sailed from New York, and by the middle of the month they were settled in Dorset; the ten years of 'exile' were over for Llewelyn. He was now to begin ten years of happy production, the most productive of his life.

I I

For the five years of Llewelyn's residence in and around New York John Cowper published no major work. During all that time he was very busy with his lecturing, and although this would not be an impediment to writing if a man were solidly based in one place, it made a difference when most of his time was passed in making long journeys from city to city and state to state, travelling in trains and staying in hotels and (occasionally) private houses, even though he did some writing while in transit. Comparatively few Americans can have seen as much of their vast country as John Cowper saw in those itinerant years, and it is to be regretted that he didn't give us at least one large American novel on the scale of *Glastonbury*, with a full cast of the extraordinary people he writes of in the *Autobiography*—the Jews and the nuns and the railroad conductors and the drug-store attendants and the hotel receptionists behind wooden counters with their hats on, and the grinding street cars of San Francisco and the roar of the Chicago elevated railway and the press of humanity in New Orleans' Canal Street, and the deep Maine woods and the open vastness of Oklahoma. But a great deal of the insight and observation which went into the novels must have been developed and sharpened by his day to day contacts over thirty years with the people of America; he saw violence and humility and greed and poverty and pride and eccentricity enough to fill a dozen books, whether American or English; for human nature is a subject that is not confined by frontiers.

But if between *The Complex Vision* of 1920 and *Ducdame* in 1925 there was no large book, this is not to say that John stood still as a writer. He wrote a good many periodical essays, some of them long and weighty, and contributed regularly to such journals as *The Freeman*, *The Dial* and the *North American*; in these years, too, his poems appeared regularly in magazines.

94

Malcolm Elwin has spoken of *Ducdame* as 'the most condensed and least digressive' of John's novels—which indeed it is—and attributes this to Llewelyn's influence. It may well be so, but it is also the only one of John's novels set in what might be termed the 'T. F. Powys country', for the old manor of Ashover lies (or seems to lie, for the topography is not so precise as in other J.C.P. novels) in the same stretch of Dorset as Dodder and Madder and Norbury and Shelton, though perhaps a little to the north and west; I think of it as lying in the neighbourhood of Poxwell (as to the village) but being (as to the house) somewhat like the manor of Galton—both of these small places lie on the Wareham–Weymouth road. Is it not possible that in the writing some part of John's unwonted brevity may be traced to his reading, at that time, of the T. F. Powys novels, themselves so marvellously 'condensed'? It is also true of *Ducdame* that the plot is as condensed as the telling: there is but a single theme, centred upon a handful of principal characters all of whom are directly concerned in the single story, whereas in the other novels a much larger *dramatis personae* plays out a much more complex set of interlocking but not necessarily interrelated events.

The ancient house of Ashover—rather like another Usher—is declining and faces extinction; last of the line are the brothers Rook and Lexie. Rook is unmarried and lives with a girl by whom he has no children; his mother in her fierce family pride works to make him marry a cousin who will give the house an heir, but he nervously and obstinately resists; nor will he marry Netta, who in any case cannot give him a son. The younger son, Lexie, is already close to death from consumption; he has never married, and is unlikely to do so—indeed, the doctors do not recommend it; his love, moreover, is given to a girl already married. From the first page, we see that this is a tragedy to which there can be no happy ending; that Rook does finally marry the Lady Ann and that she does indeed give him a son makes no difference, for the ill done to all the people closely concerned is far greater than the good this new birth produces. The house of Ashover may go on, after all, but the brothers and the luckless women they have loved are destroyed.

'I *did* read *Ducdame* chapter by chapter to Lulu,' John Cowper wrote in a letter years afterwards to Louis Wilkinson. '. . . I clearly recall his making me change the end of the book completely. . . .' But he may have had reservations, even as he revised, for he goes on to speak of Llewelyn's dictum, 'Everything cut out increases the value of what's left' as in direct opposition to his own 'grand writing motto, which is: *The More the Better*'. There is in fact a sure instinct here: John's genius called for prolixity, space, room, as did that of Rabelais and Dumas and Dickens and the great Russians; he spoke to me once of 'the abominable art of the short story', and his one essay in this field, 'The Owl, The Duck, and Miss Rowe! Miss Rowe!' is itself far from 'short' compared with many of Theodore's, or with the stories of admired practitioners in this form from Katherine Mansfield to Coppard and Bates. If it was indeed Llewelyn's insistence that reduced *Ducdame* to conventional novel length, then I think that in this instance his advice was misdirected; the huge scope of John's imagination could not be prisoned and confined. Brevity in Theodore was often a necessity, and always a merit; and in Llewelyn it arose naturally from the nature of his subjects in a score of essays, where needless embroidery would be a mere decoration. The sprawl and diffusion of John's novels is often more apparent than real: when it comes to deciding what might properly be cut, an abridging editor might find, after all, that every word has an integral value whose removal would leave the book the poorer; perhaps among eleven hundred pages of *Glastonbury* some might be omitted—I don't know; I only know I would not care to have the task of choosing them. So far as *Ducdame* goes, I have always thought it the best of the early novels, which might seem to be an admission in favour of the cutting Llewelyn imposed; but I have always wished it longer. Its successor, *Wolf Solent*—the first of the major novels—is of course very much longer than *Ducdame*, and it is a good deal better. I sometimes wonder how much was lost when *Ducdame* was subjected to revision.

The ten years from 1923, when *The Left Leg* appeared, to 1932, which saw the publication of *A Glastonbury Romance*, produced nearly forty books from the Powys family. This large output was made possible in part by the accumulation of work previously written and not published: Theodore's earlier books now published in succession, and by Llewelyn's gathering into volumes of material contributed to magazines; and also because Llewelyn and Theodore lived retired lives with little outside distraction, and were able to work steadily at their writing (for even during his attacks of illness Llewelyn was never idle for long). But of all this work the greatest bulk was contributed by John Cowper, and it is a remarkable thing that two vast novels and two solid books of philosophical commentary, as well as a respectable

quantity of other writing, could have been written by a man constantly
on the move, as he was.

Speaking of *Wolf Solent*—but it is true of all his work in the twenties
—he says it was written while travelling 'through all the states of the
United States except two' and as he habitually went by train we may
conjure up a picture of him, pad on knee, writing, writing, writing, as
the long train pulled across the flat land of Kansas towards the distant
Rockies, or jolted over the endless points and sidings of Chicago, or
skirted the broad Hudson, mile after mile, between Albany and New
York, or edged round the long curve into the Union Station at St
Louis; writing, as he says, 'in a foreign country with the pen of a
traveller and the ink-blood of his home'. Those were lonely years for
John Cowper, for a man always on the move can hardly put down
roots, and he was cut off from his family and friends for long periods.
No wonder *Wolf Solent* was 'a book of Nostalgia'.

But this decade—the last in which he was employed full time as a
lecturer—was also the period of his greatest celebrity on the platform.
Comparatively few English readers of this book will have heard John
Cowper lecture, and perhaps most of those heard him only at the close
of his life—for he made a few appearances in his seventies and eighties
—but in America there are still thousands who were lucky enough to
hear him at the height of his powers and eloquence, and this ought to
be remembered, for he undoubtedly exerted a great influence as an
interpreter and propagandist for the world's most significant writers.
No one who ever heard him speak would be likely ever to forget him;
he was more than an actor, more than an orator. As he has said, he
'became the person he was lecturing on'. Every lecture he gave was
unique: it was never a mere 'repeat' of what he said on Dickens or
Keats last month, or last week. He lectured without notes, impromptu.
He acted, moved about the platform, made great use of gesture. I have
seen him go almost on his knees and rise with uplifted arms for
emphasis: to hear him was exciting, thrilling, stimulating, exhilarating;
he carried you away, like certain great music, so that as he spoke there
was a temptation to shout with him, like the sons of God shouting for
joy. He took his golden-tongued enthusiasm up and down the States
like a revivalist and the crowds flocked to hear him.

This is hardly an exaggeration; let me give an example. He says in
his *Autobiography* that he visited scores of smaller universities and
colleges, and one such was Colgate University, in upper New York, a
foundation of considerable antiquity, but never large. When John

Cowper was there in 1929 the student enrolment was approximately a thousand; he had an audience of nine hundred. Making allowances for absences, students sick and similar impediments, this really represents a turnout of almost a hundred per cent. It may be doubted if any speaker living could command such an audience today, even at a university ten times as large as Colgate, for a 'routine' lecture on a literary subject; to attract an audience of such proportions the speaker would have to be a figure of world stature, a Sir Winston Churchill, whom the audience would be drawn to for his reputation and, as it were, for his 'curiosity value'. Perhaps the closest parallel to John Cowper's achievement would be the nineteenth-century audiences who crowded to hear readings by Charles Dickens, Artemus Ward and Mark Twain. It is amusing to speculate how he would have replied to the famous telegram, 'What will you take for fourteen days in California?' to which Artemus Ward made answer, 'Brandy and water!'

As soon as Theodore Powys published his first novel he began to find a market for his short stories, notably in the *New Leader* and the *Nation*; between them these two journals published sixteen stories in the three years 1923–25, and these regular appearances served to bring his name forward as a short-story writer of humour and originality. Most of these early stories, with a few others, are collected in *The House with the Echo* (1928) and they make an interesting contrast with the maturer later stories. The early stories were nearly all anecdotes, without complexity of plot—typical of these would be 'Nor Iron Bars' in which a man formerly quite obscure is sent to prison, and on his return to the village becomes for a time a person of some consequence because of the experiences he has undergone; but the nine days' wonder wears off, and also Christmas is approaching. He remembers the warmth and good food, and sets fire to a corn stack in order to get back to prison in time for the festivities. This is hardly a 'plot', and it is of course quite unoriginal. In 'The Lonely Lady' James Candy wishes to benefit the village, so he arranges for a new graveyard to be opened; his own wife is the first person to be buried there; the point here is not the irony of her death just at that time, although that also is implied, but the fact that she was a gregarious soul and they bury her in the middle of this otherwise empty field. These stories and many of the others are very slight, but they are not to be dismissed. They contain many felicities of thought and language; they are sketches for the more finished portraits in the novels (and indeed many characters reappear time and again—Mr Dottery, for example, and Mr Balliboy and Mr Truggin) but they are more even than this. I think the same may be said of these stories in relation to the whole body of Theodore's work as was said by Wordsworth of his minor poems—that they are the side chapels and chantries to the greater fabric of the cathedral which here would be represented by *Mr. Weston* and the major stories and novels.

Certainly the publication of Theodore's short stories during these early years must have been helpful in several ways: as an encouragement to continue, after many years in which he had small encouragement; as a source of income, perhaps not large, but certainly useful; and as a means of making his books known to a wider public. He also was able to share in the rewards of the growing fashion for 'limited editions' which was so prominent a feature of the book trade in the twenties and early thirties; not only were many of his books offered in 'signed, limited editions', either separately or simultaneously with the publication of a 'trade' edition, but various individual stories were published separately in limited editions, over the years 1926–36; and even these were sometimes 'limited' still further—for example, Douglas Cleverdon's edition of 'Uncle Dottery' (Bristol, 1930) consists of 350 signed and numbered copies; but numbers 1–50 contain extra proofs of the two Eric Gill engravings, and are more expensively bound, and reasons of this kind are responsible for the large bulk a collection of Theodore's works will make if assembled complete in all editions. But the 'limited editions' craze among collectors had two useful results. First, it put extra money into the pockets of many writers who were not well off, and next it stimulated the production of many beautiful books. It also provided a useful stimulus for book illustrators, and was reflected back in improved production for the ordinary unlimited or 'trade' edition. Llewelyn benefited also from the fashion, and it resulted in several of his books being physically among the most attractive of their time—*The Twelve Months*, for example, which was not an expensive book; or among those that were, the fine Golden Cockerel Press edition of *Glory of Life*. John's works did not lend themselves so readily to this treatment, because of their great length. There was a numbered and signed edition of *A Glastonbury Romance*, consisting of 204 copies bound in quarter leather and issued before the regular trade edition, but slight details apart the book does not differ from the ordinary edition; the vigilant reader might note that in the limited edition the title-page wording

'A Glastonbury Romance' is printed in green, and in the other it is in black, but this represents rather a cashing-in on the fashion than a fine book in its own right; and the collector of private press books will not find many items by John Cowper Powys on his shelves. A further explanation of this may lie in the fact of his absence in America, for although private presses were operating there, the great collecting boom of the twenties centred mainly upon certain English presses— the Golden Cockerel, the Nonesuch, the Beaumont, the Corvinus; and the publications of the Limited Editions Club. These publishers—and others less prominent—worked along two broad lines of policy; they printed fine editions of the classics, and they printed contemporary authors. But their interest in contemporaries was—very commendably —centred on the younger generation, or (for certainly Theodore and Llewelyn were not young) on new names; prominent among their authors we find the names of writers then at the threshold of their careers—A. E. Coppard, H. E. Bates, Aldous Huxley, Liam O'Flaherty, and in general absent from the lists names from an older generation: no Walpole, or Kipling, or Galsworthy, or Bennett. These and similar writers made an occasional appearance with the private presses, but they lay outside the main stream, and in passing them by the presses passed John Cowper also. He was an older man; he was abroad; his books did not lend themselves readily to the treatment of fine paper, lavish illustration and thin quarto or folio format. Indeed, one may reflect that he was never a 'promising young author' in the sense that writers like Huxley and Aldington and David Garnett were. He published his earlier books largely unnoticed, and then with *Wolf Solent* he was suddenly alongside Hardy and other masters who had long since taken their place in the literary scene.

— 12 —

THERE were no links with Montacute now, and it was natural for Llewelyn on returning to England to settle near his other writing brother, at East Chaldon. This was close to Weymouth and Dorchester, towns rich in associations for him—and Llewelyn was always loyal to such things—and it was of course his native county, Dorset. The alternative, apart from settling somewhere quite new, would have been Sherborne; but Llewelyn had no great desire, we may suppose, to be back in the atmosphere of schoolmastering, even if it did not again engulf him, and moreover, despite their affection for one another, Llewelyn and his schoolmaster brother had little in common. Littleton was indeed the least typical of the Powys brothers, and the most conventional. He was content with the Christianity he had been taught as a child, and his decorous and conventional outlook on matters of politics, morals and behaviour would not engage Llewelyn's sympathy. There was no originality in Littleton. He looks out from his photographs with a slightly puzzled, slightly worried air, as if he suspected life was somehow not so safe, nor yet so dull, as his own experience of it suggested.

Llewelyn at first appears to be unsure of his address. He dates letters from 'The White Nose, Owermoigne' and occasionally from 'The White Nose, Warmwell'; there was also the problem of the spelling—was it perhaps 'White Nore' or even 'White Nothe'—which is what the Ordnance maps say. As to that, Thomas Hardy was able to help: it was 'Nose', he told Llewelyn, adding that it looked in profile like the nose of the Iron Duke, which indeed it does.[1]

The great headland itself lies a few miles east of Weymouth, and

[1] At the beginning of *Wolf Solent* John Cowper refers to 'White Nore'. The Powyses apparently only learned the local name when they came to live in the vicinity.

forms the western seaward boundary of the line of chalk cliffs which runs eastwards to Old Harry, the farthest tip of Dorset. On the Weymouth side the nature of the coastline changes; the chalk turns inland, and instead we find the flatter country and the gravel of Redcliff and Ringstead Bays. White Nose itself is an ideal place to live if one enjoys fresh air and solitude. The row of old coastguard cottages lies just back from the cliff edge, six hundred feet above the water; the view along the coast, and across the bay to Portland, is magnificent; inland, fold after fold of the downs cuts the place off from the villages, Chaldon, Poxwell, Warmwell and the rest. Along the cliff edge, mile after mile, runs the old track, locally known as the Roman road, deserted in winter, almost deserted in summer. Llewelyn's actual residence at White Nose was not of long duration—about two years, taking into account long absences—and it is understandable to associate him more particularly with the house he removed to later, Chydyok, which is a mile or so nearer the village of Chaldon; but how deeply the spirit of the White Nose entered into his own may be seen again and again in his writing, and most of all in the three major expressions of his personal philosophy, *Glory of Life*, *Now that the Gods are Dead* and *Impassioned Clay*.

These essays were to come later. His first work after settling at White Nose was *The Verdict of Bridlegoose*, and his first publication *Skin for Skin*, which he had sent to press shortly before leaving America. These two books present a considerable contrast, but it is convenient to consider them together, and indeed many readers will have the 1948 uniform edition which combines them in a single volume.

Skin for Skin is a work of great significance in the Llewelyn Powys canon, his best book at the date of first publication, and one of the two or three best in the overall list. I would say that *Love and Death*, *Skin for Skin*, *Impassioned Clay*, are the single works by which his reputation will endure, plus a group of individual essays drawn from half a dozen volumes—I am thinking now, not of a current reputation, but of his reputation as it may stand a hundred and two hundred years from now; that he will be read and highly regarded then and later I have no doubt, but with the passage of time every writer's work is winnowed and diminished in bulk, except for the student; few people read the whole of De Quincey or Hazlitt now, fewer the whole of Johnson and Swift.

Skin for Skin was written in the quiet of the Montoma cottage, and this quiet is distilled into the book; here indeed is 'emotion recollected in tranquillity'. There are no joins, no hesitations: the book is whole and balanced. For the first time we find in Llewelyn the assurance and authority of a master, and for the first time we have a book of his as nearly without flaw as a book may be; the most that can be said is that the style is occasionally a little self-conscious, as though a word were introduced artificially and for effect, instead of falling into place inevitably because it alone would serve and no other: as when he speaks of the sanatorium as a 'dolorous citadel'. But not every reader will think these are blemishes, and those who do will agree that they are small.

The book begins with Llewelyn's discovery that he is suffering from consumption. It describes his reaction, the family's reaction, the measures taken to arrest the disease and if possible effect a cure. There are descriptions of the sanatorium at Davos, and of its patients; observations on life and death, reflections on manners and religion and ethics; and through all a thread of events, covering about two and a half years, so that the book is true autobiography, and the autobiography is not merely a peg to hang the essay on. We learn what happened to Llewelyn between November 1909 and March 1912—where he went, what he did—but much more than this, we see his character developing under his hand as he writes, from the first shock of a fatal illness threatening to the strengthening philosophy he learned in Switzerland from fellow sufferers and from the nurses and doctors. But the book is not all sickness, or all philosophy. There is an interlude of idyllic enchantment in the spring and summer of 1911, when after his first and seemingly complete cure he was back in England and enjoying the company of his friends and brothers—walking the Montacute lanes with John, exploring Somerset with Bernie O'Neill, spending the long autumn evenings with Theodore; in themselves trivial things enough, these walks, talks, encounters in pubs, but Llewelyn's prose makes them seem the last enchantments of the Edwardian age—that age already over—and the younger reader turns these pages with feelings of nostalgia for a world and a way of life he can never know: a world of hinds who pulled their forelocks, of dusty, unmetalled roads, of great farm wagons and teams of horses at plough, a world in which every manor house was lived in by a squire, and income tax was ninepence in the pound. How unforgettable is his picture of himself and Theodore praying with the two daughters of a local vicar on a late-night Christmas Eve, after Theodore has read a chapter of the Bible! The iron kettle on the fire, the supper of bread and butter and goose eggs, the 'garments they were making for the poor of the parish' laid aside, and Theodore's new sledge-hammer propped against the wall on the uncarpeted kitchen floor.

Once my eye rested on the figure of Joan, who knelt before me in rudely cobbled boots, with clasped hands raised above her head. And I suppose, until I am dead, the august, admonitory words that came to my ears will be associated with a little, frolicsome Christmas mouse, with a bespattered window as seen under a coarse calico blind, with the ecstatic look on a praying woman's face.

Here, and in a score of passages, a reader with a sense of the past may be moved to say, 'Ailinon!' as John was wont to do, and to reflect how much life is diminished and impoverished by the passage of time, no matter what new experiences it brings; and how much of a debt we owe to writers such as Llewelyn Powys who can bring a moment out of the past and fix it like a moth on a board, for ever.

The contrast between *Skin for Skin* and *The Verdict of Bridlegoose* is worth exploring. The two books came together: the first was finished early in 1925, and the second commenced later in the same year, no other sustained work intervening. But they are concerned with dissociated events. In the quiet of Montoma Llewelyn took his thoughts back more than a dozen years to a time which must indeed have seemed remote, with all that had happened since, the war, the deaths of his father and mother, the years in Africa, the years in America, his marriage, his progress as a writer; the young, stricken Llewelyn of 1909 must have seemed another man, although no stranger. But the scenes and persons of *Bridlegoose* were distant only in miles, an easier obstacle for memory to cross than time. In his up-state cottage he had set himself to re-create days and scenes already a part of history, whether personal or of wider application; but now on his Dorset headland he was concerned rather to record something only of yesterday, something he was still actively concerned in, though temporarily withdrawn. And so *Bridlegoose* is much more nearly a piece of reporting, and this is reflected in the prose, which is more colloquial, being concerned often enough with matters of smaller moment.

As with *Skin for Skin*, the book begins with a crisis: Llewelyn's return from Africa, and his sense of being 'back where he started from' with the years of his life slipping away, and nothing done. He tells how John persuaded him to return that autumn to America, and then he goes on to describe his five years' residence, the places he visited, the people he met, the work he did, ending with his marriage and return to England. Like *Skin for Skin*, the book is a satisfying whole—it begins naturally, and comes to a natural end. It is not a 'travel book' in the usual sense, nor even in the sense that Llewelyn's own *A Pagan's Pilgrimage* or 'A Voyage to the West Indies' are; but the visitor to America—and especially to New York—will find it, forty years after first publication, a most agreeable introduction to the United States, just the thing to read on the ship or plane going over. Again and again a few sentences catch the very essence of the basically different way of life to which the traveller is being carried. Malcolm Elwin tells us that the book was received with reserve by reviewers, who saw in it something inferior to *Skin for Skin*, but it is always a mistake to judge one book by another. The heightened poetical effect attempted and attained in *Skin for Skin* would have been inappropriate in its successor; in a few passages where it is appropriate, there it may be found, but the author was by now far too experienced in his craft to harp on a single string, and there is a wide variety of effect—wider than in *Skin for Skin*—in *Bridlegoose*. But he is never deceived, never once. He remains the countryman, with a countryman's reactions and seeing eye, and time and again a flash of illumination brings the great city of New York out of the page almost in three dimensions, this 'modern Babylon, with its proud, hard, dog-tooth outlines'. In that 'asphalt jungle' he goes daily with John to watch the progress of a dock plant which has pushed its way up through some railings. 'We both of us felt strangely restored by daily observing the broad leaves of this simple plant widen and widen, those same leaves that had cured our nettle-stings as children, and that had been used by the yeoman in the *Canterbury Tales* for keeping away from his sweating forehead the hot yellow sunshine of the Kentish highroad.'

While John and Llewelyn were producing work of great variety, Theodore was concentrating on a single objective: perhaps consciously, very possibly unconsciously, he was creating and populating a world. His villages and towns have a close resemblance physically to East Chaldon, Weymouth and Dorchester, but it is not a photographic likeness or even one produced by paints or pencil; the scene has a plastic, pasteboard quality, the buildings seem made of lath and canvas, like a stage set, or even more, like a film set. One feels that

Dodder and Sheldon are authentic and realistic, *from the front*, but that behind and beyond them there is nothing. Theodore's world is like that of the ancient cartographers, shading off at the unknown edges in clouds, and water, and conjecture; nor does it matter, for we are not concerned with matters beyond these marvellously tinted confines. In no modern writer is a willing suspension of disbelief in the reader more immediately called for—nor, one may think, more readily given. To open one of Theodore's books is like taking a seat in a theatre at the rise of the curtain, and this parallel may be extended in pointing the contrast between this writer and his brother John. In Theodore there is constant action, and it is always dramatic action—'dramatic' strictly in the sense of 'theatrical'; how excellent, for example, is the opening tableau in *Mark Only*—the vicar, the clerk, the parents and the child grouped around the font of Dodderdown church, with the heavy clouds massing outside to darken the scene and suggest that this child's destiny will be heavy and dark; and so it is. By contrast, *Unclay* opens with an empty stage: a narrow, deserted lane. And then a fox appears, slinking through the hedge to run up the lane. And then the hounds in full cry: again, a bold, dramatic beginning. In *Black Bryony* we plunge at once into action, with Mr Balliboy furiously cranking his broken-down car, filling the stage with bustle and noise. Perhaps Theodore was conscious of this affinity between his stories and the theatre, for *Innocent Birds* begins with a reflection along these lines: 'A village is like a stage that retains the same scenery throughout all the acts of the play. The actors come and go, and walk to and fro, with gestures that their passions fair and foul use them to.' Equally, Theodore's stories may be likened to plays in their brevity and discipline. The theatre bows to certain conventions—I am not thinking so much of the unities, as of practical considerations: too many people on stage at a time is confusing, too many threads of plot in a single act are confusing; and the show has to be over in time for people to catch the last bus home.

On the other hand, John Cowper does not shape his novels along such lines as these. It is true he has his moments of high drama, and certain scenes which are effective 'theatre' out of context. But his novels are epic in conception, and the epic proceeds by rules quite different from those controlling the drama. It is not a question of the one being bigger or better than the other; here that does not arise. It is simply a matter of each writer with an instinctive tact taking the way best suited to his talents.

In Theodore there are constant movement and action; in John there
are sometimes a dozen big pages in which the story is not advanced
an inch. He tells us what people do, and what happens as a result;
but he is often enough more concerned to tell us why they do it, and
how they react to the result, whereas Theodore's characters sometimes
do the most dramatic actions without a word of explanation before or
after. This is because of the quite different natures of the two sets of
characters. John's characters are subjective, projections of himself and
his own extraordinarily complex personality; but Theodore's are
objective. He is nowhere personally committed, but he is a puppet
master manipulating strings. It is a commonplace, perhaps, to talk so
of his people; to call them puppets, to speak of them as cut-out figures
without depth, all black or all white. It has been said of them that they
are like carvings: caricatures in stone from medieval churches, hard in
outline, grotesque: saints, or fools, or villains, without gradation. If
these are critical commonplaces it is because they are true. Theodore
has pretty girls in plenty, but hardly one a man can feel moved to take
in his arms, as he might feel moved to take Gerda, in *Wolf Solent*.
Theodore's people are 'in a book' or 'in a play' all the time, but a
score of John's might even now be at the reader's elbow, or in the next
room. Gerda, to take again the same example, seems like a real girl
who has been written about in a book; she does not 'step out of the pages',
but she appears to have just stepped into them. Perhaps some of John's
people are grotesque enough, but theirs is not the Gothic grotesque-
ness of Theodore's, cut in stone. The most unlikely of them is warm
to the touch and seems to have a life outside the book: to have been
there before the writing began, and to continue after it is finished. They
are deformed, but they are not inanimate. So too are many of Theodore's subordinate characters, and a handful of his major ones: Mr
Dottery, for example, is round and life-size and human, lovable and
credible. But with many—most—of the others we are in a world which
keeps its own conventions and does not ape actuality. Mr Tasker is a
figure in a nightmare, Mrs Vosper belongs in a canvas by Arcimboldi,
Farmer Mew comes from a morality. Perhaps this is the clue: none of
Theodore's people is of our time, even though they take railway
tickets or ride in motor-cars. These are stage props like any others.
These people are of no time, and of all times. Sexton Truggin is an
Elizabethan, Squire Kennard is a man of the eighteenth century, Mrs
Fancy is Edwardian. There are characters in these tales from Chaucer,
from Shakespeare, from Dickens. They mix without incongruity,

because they display only the basic and unchanging qualities of greed, lust, hate, love, pride, humility. They are surely the most consistent characters in English fiction; when they are good they are very very good and when they are bad they are horrid. The leopard will change his spots before Charlie Tulk will do a generous action or Mr Hayhoe a mean one. They are as predictable as night and day in their impulses and actions. Moreover, each carries his nature, be it good or bad, to its limits; one who is meek—James Gillet, say—is meekness personified; one who is vindictive—Miss Pettifer, say—will make vindictiveness a religion and a way of life.

13

IT IS convenient to divide the work of T. F. Powys into roughly equal halves, consisting of the books published before 1927, which saw the appearance of *Mr. Weston's Good Wine*, and those which followed. That *Mr. Weston* is his greatest achievement has never been questioned, and this, with a small group of short stories, would be the basis of any claim to rank him with the most important English writers of the twentieth century—nor would such a claim be easy to set aside. All the work written after *Mr. Weston* bears the stamp of that book's authority—even such a book as *Kindness in a Corner*, admittedly a lightweight by comparison; and all the work written before *Mr. Weston* in one way or another betrays marks of apprenticeship or immaturity, although isolated passages anticipate and prepare the way for Theodore's masterpiece. The work which followed *Mr. Weston* nowhere advances—unless perhaps in a few short stories—but neither does it notably decline; T. F. Powys came from his beginning as a writer to full maturity in the short space of ten years, from *Mr. Tasker*, begun in 1915, to *Mr. Weston*, completed in 1925; and he continued to write for approximately ten years more in full command of his powers; he then, it would seem deliberately, went 'out of business' and remained silent, or virtually so, for nearly twenty years more, until his death in 1953.

Theodore's working life as a writer was thus concentrated into some twenty years—leaving out of account the tentative beginnings whose only published result was the little *Genesis* essay. They were initially also years of concentrated publishing activity, as the accumulated unpublished stories were put into print—four in 1923, one in 1924, two in 1925 and one in 1926, not counting four short stories published separately in book form in the same year—'A Stubborn Tree', 'Feed My Swine', and 'A Strong Girl' and 'The Bride' bound together. In the same four years 1923–26 Theodore published twenty short stories, mostly in *The Nation* and *The New Leader*; in the main, these represented 'work in progress', for there was not the same accumulation of unpublished short stories as of novels and longer stories. It would seem that Theodore discovered and began to exploit his bent for the short story when he found that there were journals ready to publish his work in this form; but here too there is a development over the years, for such a story as 'Squire Duffy', first published in *The Nation* in January 1924, is a very different affair from 'Darkness and Nathaniel', five years later. The early short stories do not call for extended comment; the humorous ones are the most rewarding, but even these must give way before the later work. 'The Lost Proofs' is a pleasant enough trifle to find in a file of *The Nation* for 1925, but 'Archdeacon Truggin' and some of its later companion pieces are unique in English humour, with qualities paralleled only in the masters—in Chaucer, Shakespeare, and Dickens.

Because the novels preceding *Mr. Weston* are but stepping stones to that firm shore, it is not to be supposed that they are individually negligible; *Mark Only* is a very moving book, the most 'Shakespearean' of the novels, full of pity and sadness; and *Mr. Tasker's Gods* 'invokes great beauty and great horror', as Liam O'Flaherty said; within their lesser scale *Mockery Gap* and *Innocent Birds* are keystones upon which the greater weight to be added may bear.

Mark Only begins with Mark's christening and ends with his death; Mark, the poor farmhand, for whom nothing goes right. There is no 'Wold Jar', no Mr Weston, no John Death to whom Mark Only can turn; he is puzzled, hurt, alone, throughout, a sad figure too uncomfortably true to life whose futile career might prompt to 'angry prayers' any reader who believed prayer to be effective. How many folk go through life with no better fortune than Mark! In contrast we are given the highly successful Charlie Tulk, mean, evil, cunning, a man who leaves a blight on everything he touches; whose accidental death hardly brings the reader satisfaction, for it comes too late to undo the harm the man has done. Between these two, Tulk and Mark, there is no chance of happiness for Nellie Holland, nor does she find any, unless for an hour perhaps on her wedding night, and we may feel some doubt of that. Behind these three, standing as chorus, there are the village gossips and cronies; they may not actively participate, but if they can give a young girl a shove towards disaster, they will; those who are not malicious are stupid, and those who are not stupid are selfish, and those who are not selfish are blind. Yet, in *Mark Only*, there is a compassion under all which is entirely lacking in *Mr. Tasker*. Mark is a figure of true tragic proportions, the victim of man's inhumanity to man, but his story brings the note of sadness in; whereas Tasker is everywhere contemptible and loathsome, a monster and a beast.

The evil in *Mark Only* is more subtly conveyed than in *Mr. Tasker*, and whereas the killing of old Tasker by the pigs arouses only feelings of disgust, in such a passage as this, from *Mark Only*, there is an inescapable pathos:

Emmie followed James into the parlour. 'I've brought something from Charlie,' she said by way of explaining her presence. Emmie handed to James a little tin that had once contained a brand of tobacco called 'Bishop's Sermon.'

James opened the tin.

''Tis medicine,' he said, 'for mother's cough.'

Kate Tolly took the tin and looked at the powder inside. ''Tis the same kind,' she remarked, 'that Charlie Tulk do cure Mrs. Begwell's fowls with when they be moulting.'

'Charlie do say,' explained Emmie, 'that you do shake a little on old woman's buttered bread and put strawberry jam on top.'

'That's me,' said Mrs. Andrews, all at once waking up to what was going on. 'That's me they be telling of. I be the wold 'oman who have caught a cold.'

Susan Peach took the tin. ''Tis a pity for poor mother to cough so bad,' she said. ''Tis a nice powder to look at, this be, an' 'tis best to give she some at tea-time.'

'Mother be always coughing at night,' said James. 'An' I do bide awake and listen to she.'

'Charlie did say,' repeated Emmie, as though she had been told to be sure to give her message correctly, 'that 'tis to be taken at tea-time, covered with strawberry jam so as she don't taste en.'

Old Mrs. Andrews nodded her approval; she liked strawberry jam.

Again, the merest touch, but wonderfully effective:

'Poor father do lie upstairs dead on's bed in darkness,' Susan sobbed, slowly swaying from side to side, 'and down here mother be a-talking and Mark be laughing, and no one don't know who furniture do belong to.'

Kate Tolly began to look with a new interest at a vase of flowers that was upon the table. ''Tisn't much that I've got at home,' she said sharply, 'and when mother 'ave stopped talking and do die, that be mine.'

Mr. Tasker's Gods, which was published next after *Mark Only*, is more violent, more crude, more melodramatic; a book of great power, certainly, but of undisciplined power, power not under complete control. It was Theodore's first novel, and apart from the fact that he was still seeking his way as a writer, still moving with some hesitation towards the style which was later to become such a precise and marvellous instrument, it may be that he was as yet unclear about the nature of his gifts. Writing to Louis Wilkinson in February 1916, when it was already finished and in Louis's hands for revision, Theodore says that with 'a little sorting out' the book will make a decent picture of country life. He can hardly have meant that; yet, a few months later, he tells Louis that Tasker is extremely modest and innocent. Here indeed is the irony for which he is famous carried as far as irony will go.

This novel, more than any of the others, is painted in the plainest blacks and whites; innocence here is such as never was on sea or land, evil as absolute as the pit, gentleness wonderfully gentle and wholly ineffective. Tasker himself, the grasping farmer, prospers till the end, setting his heel on all opposition, and although Mr Turnbull, the selfish and worldly vicar, comes to an untimely death he meets with it painlessly, by a stroke while pursuing a naked girl up the stairs of a brothel, and in the world of T. F. Powys there are stickier deaths than that. In the vicar's sons, the Rev. John and Dr George, we have two sketches out of Trollope, motivated by the hard self-interest of Archdeacon Grantly; in the meek and dying Neville, in Rose Netley, in Molly Neville, in Henry Turnbull, we find decent people who are given no chance, offered no hope. *Mark Only* leaves the reader saddened; *Mr. Tasker* leaves him depressed. The humour of the book—and it is full of delicious asides and comments—does not relieve the gloom so much as highlight and underline it, darkening it by contrast. Another difference between the later book and this first one lies in the prose; in *Mr. Tasker* a sentence or a paragraph sometimes suggests that here may be a great writer in the making, but there are no lengthy passages to support the occasional flashes; whereas in *Mark Only* such passages are frequent and sustained. The dialogue in *Mark Only* may be compared with Shakespeare and Hardy and not be shamed. *Mr. Tasker* is an unpleasant book, but a necessary forerunner to *Mr. Weston* and *Unclay*; its most nearly successful element is its humour, and here, it would seem, T. F. Powys needed to serve no apprenticeship.

Mockery Gap was written in the spring and summer of 1923, and *Innocent Birds* immediately after, in the winter of 1923–24. The two books have points in common; there are some happy people, and the evil in life doesn't have all its own way; there is at least hope offered, and a promise implied that evil may be confined, if not conquered. There is not so much meanness, frustration, deceit. In these two novels the country scene is painted in more fully than in the former two, and there are hills and fields that are identifiably Dorset, although Mockery Gap is a village we do not meet with again—it lies closer to the sea than Shelton or Dodder or Madder, as in real life Osmington Mills lies closer to the sea than East Chaldon and, as it were, just outside the border of Powysland proper. With *Innocent Birds* we are back in Madder, and the careful delineation of that village begun in *The Left Leg* is continued.

The plot in *Mockery Gap* is more sketchy than in either of the two previous full-length novels, and is hardly weightier than the anecdotes —for they are little more—making the content of *The Left Leg* and its companion pieces. An early critic, Mr William Hunter, calls *Mockery Gap* 'an ironic allegory, a dream fantasy', and Mr H. Coombes has spoken of the 'sense of expectancy' in this novel. The two comments merge and combine excellently, for the events in *Mockery Gap* happen as in a dream, irrationally, unexpectedly, capriciously, and they are accepted by the characters, and by the reader, without surprise, almost indeed without emotion. When Mr Pink walks into the sea and is drowned we feel no pity and no regret; nobody in the village remarks on his absence, and his sister accepts it as a matter of course, merely telling herself that he has gone for a sail: he vanishes from the story without trace, and even his body is never washed ashore. In the same manner, the death of Mrs Pottle is contrived by Caddy and accepted by all as fair and reasonable; he explains quite frankly that she has, in effect, been murdered, but nobody protests or exclaims. It is as though conventional standards of behaviour have no currency in Mockery Gap—for example, Simon, the lecherous farmer's son, complains to the vicar that he can't get enough girls any more, and the vicar is sympathetic rather than censorious (though harsh enough upon himself for much more innocent carnal desires—he only desires his own wife). The sense of expectancy noted by Mr Coombes is indeed the strongest element in the book: throughout, we are waiting for something to happen, and the sense of foreboding is the more remarkable because the Christ-figure of the Fisherman, upon whom all this expectancy centres, is a benevolent and beneficent figure, bringing chiefly good to the village, whereas the feeling everywhere is of the imminence of something evil—of a monster, an unknown, frightening 'nellie-bird', something dreadful from the sea. The Fisherman himself is more human—though supernatural too—than most of Theodore's supernatural beings. He goes with the girls almost as much as Simon does— and he gives them a greater measure of happiness by his ministrations —and he bathes and fishes and sails. He is happy and self-sufficient, but at the end, at his departure, we feel that the village will drop back into its old ways: he has not been a permanent influence for good. As he departs over the hill—never looking back—the Pottles and Prings, village Montagues and Capulets, are already at their strife again, and already the village children are returning to their sadistic persecution of anything poor or ill or innocent. The reader is left with the feeling that even those villagers who have got what they wanted have somehow been cheated. Mrs Moggs has never seen the sea; the first day she visits it, it drowns her. Mr Dobbin seeks quiet, and he finds it in a grave. Mr Cheney succeeds in tunnelling into the tumulus and he uncovers ancient relics; but the roof collapses on him. Perhaps two or three people are left happier than they were when the book began: the 'other Mary', nursing her illegitimate child, and Mr Pattimore in bed with his wife. The symbolism of this story contributes little to the final effect; it is somehow elementary and obvious. Perhaps the Fisherman is principally a 'fisher of men'; perhaps Dobbin does, Judas-like, deny his friend the monkey; perhaps the monkey, naked and garlanded with flowers, does represent carnal and wanton delight; it seems hardly to matter. Again, something of which T. F. Powys became a master is here not yet mastered.

There is an element of the supernatural in *Innocent Birds*, when from time to time a great black bird of evil portent hovers or settles momentarily in Madder, as innocence is outraged, or death comes for some wronged maiden; but the story itself proceeds without further recourse to the supernatural, and is essentially earthy of the earth. The

'innocent birds' are the village maidens, whom Mr Bugby the innkeeper rapes, one by one. Here, as elsewhere, we have the peculiar
morality of T. F. Powys's world: it is an open secret that Mr Bugby
will rape any young woman he can lay his hands on, but nobody makes
any protest, mothers do not warn their daughters against him, the
parson merely goes on reading his interesting story book, and we
seldom hear in any of the stories of a village policeman—who, if he
does happen along, will probably look the other way, or say a few
irrelevant words about the weather.

The 'innocents' in this book include most of the male characters
too: indeed, it might be argued that the entire population of Madder is
weak in the head; Mr Pim has a son, but he spends a great deal of time
asking how babies are made—and it is rather odd that nobody seems
able to tell him. Farmer Barfoot has a wooden leg called Betty which is
the village oracle whose advice is sought and acted upon by all. Mr
Tucker, the vicar, essentially a good man, is the least effectual of any,
living in a dream world, oblivious to what is really going on in his
parish. Mr Solly lives in 'Gift Cottage' and waits to see what the gift
will be which is to bless someone in the village—characteristically
Powysian, it is the gift of death for Polly after she has been raped, and
for Fred, her true lover. Mr Solly also orders his life by frequent
reference to a *History of America*, in whose pages he finds parallels with
his own experience, and lessons by which to enlarge it. When, at the
end, the Americans have, as he feels, come to the conclusion of their
history and have settled down to manufacture iron, Mr Solly buries
the two books in his garden, as Augustine Birrell did once with the
Works of Hannah More (but there were nineteen volumes of that).

All in all, the characters of *Innocent Birds* are indeed innocent,
simple—almost, as country people might say, 'natural'. The practical
element of evil is furnished by Mr Bugby; the theoretical, by Miss
Pettifer, selfish, narrow, vindictive, plotting continually to prevent or
destroy the happiness of others, always from high motives. The
'perfect gift' for which Solly was looking and waiting, which is death,
is an anticipation, again, of *Mr. Weston*: as though in this, as in all the
earlier works, Theodore was trying out ideas and situations—unconsciously, no doubt—for the consummate novel which was to come.
Innocent Birds is not completely satisfying, but it is an advance on
Mockery Gap. The life of Madder and its physical delineation, although
seen by the reader through a distorting mirror, are consistent and
rounded, much more a portrait of a community than that of Mockery,

where many of the people are little more than puppets. The folk of
Madder are flesh and blood, although one would not much relish
meeting most of them in real life—perhaps because they are so uncomfortably true to life, though exaggeratedly true. It is, after all, not only
within the pages of a book that we may find laziness, and stupidity, and
malice, and cruelty, and lust; and not only in the pages of a book that
evil is triumphant.

14

THE final chapter of Louis Marlow's *Welsh Ambassadors* is called 'Llewelyn Itinerant', and it covers principally the years 1909–25; but 'itinerant' might be used of his life until the end, and for a man so gravely stricken in health he made an astonishing number of lengthy journeys—not all only in search of better health. In Chapter 12 above we left him settled in Dorset, and it might be supposed that for a time at least he would remain there: but in fact, although Dorset was his base thereafter until his final departure for Switzerland (and even then it was his intention ultimately to return), in the years between 1925 (when he first arrived in Dorset) and 1931 he was constantly on the move, perhaps prompted in some degree by a restlessness born of his illness—we may note the wanderings of Stevenson and Lawrence, to name but two similarly situated. In 1926 Llewelyn and his wife were in France and Austria; in 1927 they returned to New York for Llewelyn to serve as 'visiting critic' for the *Herald-Tribune*; in 1928 they were in Holland, France, Italy and Palestine, and they moved on to Anacapri and Capri until the spring of 1929; in 1930 they were again in America, and in 1931 they made their visit to the West Indies. Very justly could he say to me, as he did once, 'I am like Ulysses, I have seen many cities'.

In all of these places he found material for his writing, and there are essays and passages owing their origin to scenes of travel and travel experiences; but they make a comparatively small part of his total output in the years from 1925 until his death in 1939. There is one long essay on his trip to the West Indies, and one travel book cut to the conventional pattern, *A Pagan's Pilgrimage*; and of course in his last few years he wrote eloquently of the Swiss scene, as he had formerly of Dorset and Somerset. But there is no large series of traveller's tales to set beside such books as Stevenson's *Silverado Squatters* and *In The*

South Seas, or Lawrence's *Sea and Sardinia* and *Mornings in Mexico*. Although Llewelyn Powys travelled with an eye lifted to every strange scene, and every oddity of human behaviour, he was not to be diverted in his writing from the main purpose of being a teacher and a preacher: 'By day and by night no sight that we see, no sound that we hear, but has its own poetical burden.' It was not the sight, but the burden it carried that was significant to Llewelyn. Certainly, Lawrence had his message to be conveyed, and a strong urge to convey it, but he was not so single-minded or so determined as Llewelyn, who was always conscious, no matter what he was writing, of the need to influence and persuade.

His first book after completing *The Verdict of Bridlegoose*, which has been discussed above, represented a new departure for Llewelyn. It was a work of historical biography, the life of Henry Hudson, designed as one of the 'Golden Hind' Series of lives of great—and in the main, Elizabethan—explorers. The work entailed research in the British Museum, and he and Alyse stayed for some time in London. The book progressed slowly, doubtless because any such work takes more time in the reading and preparation than in the actual writing, and Llewelyn told his sister-in-law that he had never worked so hard before. It was also necessary to consult various authorities in Dutch, which Llewelyn could not read, and this entailed arranging for translations—time consuming and teasing extra labour. Perhaps the book proceeded slowly also because the author was not altogether at home with a work of this kind, calling for the examination and sifting and selecting of a great mass of material—for although the complete facts of Henry Hudson's life as now known are somewhat meagre, none the less much reading must be done in original sources to come upon them. Mr Elwin—himself a master of biography—has spoken of Llewelyn's qualities as those which 'stamp the master of biography', and suggests that the lack of response to *Henry Hudson* on publication 'undoubtedly lost to English literature more than one biographical masterpiece'. This seems to me to be going too far, for I cannot feel that Llewelyn was even potentially a biographer of many books; the biographical essay, yes: in which, using facts already established, he is able to portray the essence of a man's life and work as he himself sees it—that is, an idiosyncratic vision whose value for readers lies just in this, that it is Coryate, or Burton, or Bewick, *as he strikes Llewelyn Powys*.

This method served well with Hudson, although as Llewelyn

himself noted it produced a comparatively short book, shorter than the average of the series in which it appeared, and shorter than the contract called for. But for the writing of a full-scale biography—like, say, Leslie Marchand's *Byron*, or Leon Edel's *Henry James*, or Sir Arthur Bryant's *Pepys*, I don't think Llewelyn Powys had the temperament or the equipment. Such works call for specialized study in fields comparatively restricted, and Llewelyn's studies were discursive and far-ranging. Marchand's *Byron* was six years in the writing, and I know not how many more in preliminary research, reading and preparing. Llewelyn Powys was too much of an original creative writer to wish to impose upon himself this kind of discipline for so long. Indeed, it is because he was an original creative writer that the Hudson book failed —failed, that is, as a biography compared with other biographies. It is essentially a personal book, and Llewelyn Powys is always present in its pages, speaking in his own voice. This is Henry Hudson as Llewelyn Powys found him: in effect, Llewelyn's creation, his interpretation, his impression of the man. That is not to say there is distortion, omission, suppression: this is not a portrait by Macaulay or Lytton Strachey. But, with all the known facts given, there is yet imposed upon the book another personality, Llewelyn's, through which the subject is seen. Such a book may certainly be a masterpiece of biography (in the sense that Izaak Walton's biographies are masterpieces), and in this sense I have no quarrel with Mr Elwin's words. I differ from him only in believing that Llewelyn would not have wished often to engage in work of this nature because of the mechanical initial labour it inevitably involves.

It may be pertinent here to glance at his other excursion in this field, the abridgment of Andrew Clark's *Life and Times of Anthony Wood*. Wood was a man after Llewelyn's own heart, 'whimsical, wise and wanton', and Llewelyn produced a notable work in making his abridgment, retaining—with the sure eye Elwin mentions—every essence of the original; but the mechanical work had been done for him by another; and I cannot feel that he had the kind of specialized tenacity and application called for and employed by Andrew Clark in producing the original five volumes which Llewelyn so admirably reduced to one. Llewelyn's strength did not lie in finding and evaluating new material—there is virtually nothing new, in the way of facts, in any of his biographical essays.[1] He is an interpreter, an

---

[1] But in *Henry Hudson* he did publish a document previously unnoticed, the lost verdict on the mutineers.

appreciator, a commentator, almost always subjective: and he makes us see the subject of his essay more abundantly. In this, in his different way, he has his brother John's capacity for illuminating his subject from a new angle, in an unfamiliar light; and he does this (as John does) not by finding new material, but by a new vision of the material already known.

It is incidentally of significance in this context that John's sole essay in biography—the *Rabelais*—is among the shortest of his works (the *Dostoievsky* having no biographical chapters) and the 'Life' in John's book makes less than fifty out of four hundred pages. Neither of these brothers was primarily interested in the biographical details of a man's life, but rather in what he made of his life and how his personality, his deeds and his writings are of importance to us. John's own feeling is humorously summed up by a comment scrawled upon my copy of the advance announcement of his *Rabelais*, a leaflet circulated in advance of publication. The publisher says the book has 'a remarkable breadth and depth of scholarship' and John interpolates, 'and wondrous little *exactness*!' Certainly, he does himself an injustice; but it is also certain that neither he nor Llewelyn would think it necessary to spend weeks of labour to determine whether Rabelais was born at two, or twenty past two, in the morning. This kind of biographical exactness has its place and its value, but they would see it in a perspective bounded by considerations of greater relevance.

Henry Hudson finished, Llewelyn returned for a few months to White Nose, and it was here that the tragedy occurred which Llewelyn writes of in his essay 'A Grave in Dorset'. An American friend, Walter Franzen—their first guest at White Nose—went out to swim before lunch, and slipped on the cliff while climbing back. Those cliffs of chalk are always treacherous, there is much loose and decayed rock, and dry or wet they are slippery, and almost everywhere precipitous. Franzen fell to the beach and was killed instantly. Perhaps no English writer of our time, or of any other, could have written an essay on this event so entirely fitting and right. For Llewelyn Powys the familiar text, 'In the midst of life we are in death', had an everyday significance; he was always conscious of it for its ever-present possible application to himself, and for the occasions when he had seen death come unexpectedly and prematurely for his friends. There is a group of essays in which he tells of the coming of death in such circumstances: 'A Grave in Dorset' has a companion piece, 'On the other side of the

Quantocks', in the same volume, *Earth Memories*, where he writes of the early death of Louis Wilkinson's second wife, Ann Reid, and among others the essays on Albert Reginald Powys (in *Somerset Essays*) and on Ernst Ludwig Kirchner (in *Swiss Essays*) come readily to mind. Such an essay as 'A Grave in Dorset' is more moving than a funeral sermon, and one may say soberly and seriously that it will keep the name of Walter Franzen in memory when the headstone in Chaldon churchyard is obliterated.

The winter of 1927–28 was passed in New York, where Llewelyn served as 'visiting critic' for the *Herald-Tribune*; only a handful of letters of this period have been published, but he writes of the pleasure of seeing old friends again, and he made a visit to Steepletop, Edna Millay's home, where he was later to make an extended stay and write some of his finest pages. In April he and Alyse returned to England, but within a few weeks they were packing again, this time for a visit to Europe which would take them through several countries and bring them at last to Palestine. But first they went to Holland, where Llewelyn wanted to see relics of William Barents, about whom he had written in the preliminary chapters of *Henry Hudson*. Barents had suffered a fate not dissimilar to Henry Hudson's and Llewelyn's imagination was fired by reading of the discovery of the hut in which Barents had wintered in 1597, removed, with many of its contents, from Novaya Zemlya to Amsterdam in 1871. In Holland they also saw Rubens's house, and Rembrandt's, but Llewelyn told his friend Rivers Pollock that they 'did not care much for Holland. It seemed gross and prosperous'. 'Prosperity' never evoked his sympathy: I recall his reference to the 'prosperous modernity' of Bournemouth as the last place in which one would look for a poet, but '"where you least look for it, there starts the hare"'.

The progress towards Palestine was leisurely. After the side trip to Holland Llewelyn and Alyse settled for ten weeks or so at Belley, a small and ancient town about midway between Lyons and Geneva, though somewhat south of both. Here 'too quickly and too carelessly', as he afterwards said, Llewelyn wrote *Apples be Ripe*. Once before, years earlier, he had worked at a novel, with doubt and difficulty, at last laying it aside; and now again, as he sat at his writing table, he felt that he could not do it. He wrote to John in despondency, but this time he kept at it and the first draft was quickly finished. It was rejected by Cape, who had been the English publisher of *Bridlegoose* and *Skin for Skin*, and taken by Longmans, but not immediately; in the event, it was one of the most successful from a sales point of view of all his books, and he wrote on publication that he was 'not ashamed of it', that the story was simple, but with something in it 'wild and challenging'.

Apples be Ripe is indeed simple enough. It tells of the life of Chris Holbech from his birth in a country vicarage, through his school and university years, until he becomes a schoolmaster and marries the headmaster's niece. Their marriage is a failure, for she is narrowly conventional, he impulsive and impatient. He chafes in the suburban atmosphere of his home and of the dingy boarding-school, and finally throws it all up and goes off with a servant who has been seduced, letting his wife suppose him responsible for the girl's condition. He wanders aimlessly, looking for casual work, and stays some time with a west country farmer; he finds something nearer to the love he has looked for with the farmer's daughter Eleanor; but his true love, he thinks, is a girl known briefly in his childhood, and it is with her that he finds a fleeting ecstasy at the end.

Apples be Ripe is not a satisfying book, and its hero is not a satisfying character. He is weak and ineffectual, not filled out or made complete: he is a mouthpiece for some of Llewelyn's ideas on morality, religion, the conventions of middle-class life and others of the sort he held all his life; but Llewelyn expresses these much more forcibly, in his own voice, in his essays. Something of the distress and frustration of Llewelyn's own schoolmastering experiences is conveyed in the account of life at the Eastbourne school, and indeed the chief value of the book to the student lies in its autobiographical element. With incidental differences the early chapters may be considered almost wholly autobiographical, and how closely it adheres to fact may be seen in the very first pages: here, for example, in the description of Chris Holbech's father, it is impossible not to recognize the Rev. C. F. Powys:

> The Rev. Thomas Holbech was a proud and reserved man. He had inherited from an ancestry largely Celtic a deep inarticulate love of nature. Although he cared nothing for poetry, his temperament was essentially a poetic one. His surface mind believed what his fathers before him had believed, but the physical constitution of his whole being could tremble with a purely animal gusto for life that it would have been difficult to reconcile with the propriety of conventional religion. This lust for

existence did not display itself in personal waywardness; the inhibitions of his traditional upbringing lay too heavily upon him for anything of that kind. It showed itself, however, in a naïve exultation at the mere fact of his own consciousness, in a kind of strange jubilation that he, the Rev. Thomas Holbech, the son of Davis Holbech, had been born at all . . .

As soon as the novel was finished Llewelyn and Alyse set out for Venice, *en route* once more for Palestine.

Mr. Weston's Good Wine would seem to be the book into which T. F. Powys put the greatest care—or the one which gave him the greatest trouble. It was begun in January 1924 and completed in the autumn of 1925. Mr Francis Powys says his father wrote for two or three hours daily, 'year in, year out'; and Louis Marlow tells us that Theodore would be well satisfied with two or three hundred words written in a day, say something under two thousand words a week. At about 85,000 words, this would have meant forty to fifty weeks' work, but Theodore took nearly twice as long as that. Just why, the manuscript might reveal if it became available for study; without it, the commentator must speculate, using inferential evidence. Perhaps *Mr. Weston* did give the author some extra trouble, some call for second thoughts and modification or revision; but, in general, the book does not support this view; rather, it suggests that the seemingly effortless mastery of matter and manner was achieved and sustained from the first page onwards. The book may have been written slowly, every sentence and paragraph long meditated upon before being set down. But it has a coherence and continuity. It could not be said here, as it was said earlier of *Mr. Tasker*—and by Theodore himself—that the chapters could be shuffled and rearranged however suited best. *Mr. Weston* has the verbal exactness of a passage in *Paradise Lost*, where not a word may be altered without lessening the structure of the whole.

Mr. Weston was completed, then, in autumn 1925; but it was not published until nearly two years later, and then in an edition limited to six hundred copies (the American first edition, in the same year, was 'unlimited'). It may be that the publishers were uncertain what reception the book might get, for allegory is not the most popular literary fare in the twentieth century, and indeed little had been offered in the century's first quarter. The fact that later years have seen some increase in the use of allegory by dramatists and novelists may be attributable in part at least to the impact of *Mr. Weston*; the book may have shown the way not only to the writers of such tales as *Animal Farm*, but also to the readers. And readers, it seems, need some stimulation before they will give themselves willingly to this literary form, for allegory appears somehow alien to the English temper. It occurs rather sparingly in our literature (except in the earliest times) and has given us few indubitably great works, perhaps only *The Faerie Queene* and *The Pilgrim's Progress*, with the first two books of *Gulliver's Travels*. The first is great despite and not because of the allegory, and generations of readers have enjoyed the other two for their stories, without giving the implications a second thought. This is one of the dangers the allegorical writer must encounter, the danger that 'the story' will submerge the message, and this has largely been the fate of *Gulliver*. It may be that this threatens *Mr. Weston*, but at least there is no danger that the under-lying element of allegory will not be understood, for its basic proposi-tions are plain from the start: Mr Weston is really God, and his two vintages are the wines of Love and Death; these he sells to suitable recipients, and the greater of them is the second. This understood, the reader may go on to enjoy 'the story' and suppose that he has under-stood all; but in fact there are subtleties in this book which are not all yielded up at a first reading, no matter how attentively they may be looked for. It is a book that must be lived with and pondered over. Certainly, we may say of *Mr. Weston*, as Hazlitt said of *The Faerie Queene*, that the allegory doesn't bite, and therefore need not frighten the reader away; and we may expect any reader with a feeling for beauty in style to read on, once started, allegory or no, just as such a reader will be led insensibly on into *The Faerie Queene*. But the allegory in *Mr. Weston* is more intrinsically essential to the work, and the reader who will not follow it is depriving himself of a rare added pleasure; whereas, to the twentieth-century mind, the allegory in Spenser's great poem is at best a little strained, and is nowhere of anything but an academic application.

The story—it is hardly complicated enough to be called a 'plot'—can be summarized in a paragraph. Mr Weston is a wine merchant, acting in the present case as his own travelling salesman, and the Ford van he drives contains, we suppose, his samples—though it contains other things on occasion, as naughty Tom Burt discovers. Mr Weston, accompanied by his assistant, Michael, comes late one afternoon to the small village of Folly Down, where he intends to call on a number of potential customers. Some of these people are expecting him, though not consciously; and indeed, the expectancy that something is going to happen lies over the whole village. We must remember that Mr Weston is God—he never makes any secret of it, although he never proclaims himself in so many words. To God all things are possible, and he begins by making time stand still in Folly Down: the clocks all stop at seven. He then moves from place to place, making his calls. He goes to the inn, where a wine salesman may reasonably look for a welcome; and to the church, where also wine is used. He goes to the vicarage, and to certain other houses; and most of his calls result in an order for the light wine, or the dark, though not all of the customers drink joyfully. Mr Weston himself is at first sight the conventional white-bearded old gentleman whom children think of as God the Father. He is good humoured, courteous, a little vague, even we feel naïve at times. He leans a good deal on his assistant, Michael, checking with him on the identities and addresses of the customers, and seeking his advice in business matters generally, although not always following it. Now and again he speaks with a stern authority, and we recognize that the mild manner is not everything, and there are forces beneath it which had better not be too often released. The winds will obey Mr Weston if he calls them, and the thunder.

The people of Folly Down display most of the characteristics of human beings everywhere, with the principal emphasis, as always in Theodore's stories, on the less attractive side of human nature: here are lust, and cruelty, and greed, and stupidity. Here innocence is mocked, love is despised or ineffective, hope falters. The one man whom the village might look to for counsel and guidance, the parson, does not believe in God.

Time stops in Folly Down, but life goes on, and at an accelerated pace. During Mr Weston's visit half a dozen dramas reach their climax and are concluded: all her life Tamar Grobe has waited to marry an Angel—and Mr Weston has brought one with him, for Michael is that same being who once 'quelled a mutiny' among Mr Weston's workers; Luke Bird for years has yearned to marry Jenny Bunce, and her father tells him he may when his garden well is filled with wine—and Mr Weston has come to the village with wine; the Rev. Nicholas Grobe has lost his belief in God, but Mr Weston's visit restores it, and with restored belief Mr Grobe finds his lost happiness again. But some of the evil in Folly Down is undone for ever, though perhaps not all. Certainly, Mr Weston's visit is fatal for Mrs Vosper,

the village procuress whose only joy lies in the destruction of innocence; and Martin Mumby, the worse of the two lecherous brothers, is
left an innocent of another kind, crouching in a corner, seeing something 'that don't please 'im'. He will never rape or seduce again. For
the unregenerate there is no mercy, but for some who deserve it a
second chance; and so John Mumby is allowed to marry Ann, and Mr
Grunter is restored to an honest reputation. Nobody is forgotten, and
everyone gets his deserts, before Mr Weston closes up his order book
and departs from Folly Down.

When Mr Weston visits Folly Down—or any other of the many
villages in which his old-established business has customers—he does
not neglect to carry with him samples of his wares; and we may follow
this precedent by offering a page of his book—or, rather, of the book
in which he is the principal character (for Mr Weston's own book is not
under consideration here) in the hope and expectation that the candid
reader of one page will wish to go on and read the three hundred
others. If Mr Weston does not appear in person in the following
passage—it is from Chapter 33—none the less his influence is upon it.

'. . . what were 'en John did take out 'is pick to do at this time o'
night?'

''E didn't tell I much,' replied Mrs. Grunter. 'Only there were
the boot he did once bury wi' Ada Kiddle, and he mid be going to
dig en' up again.'

'Folk do want their own,' observed Mrs. Meek.

'So they do,' replied her neighbour, 'and Grunter bain't the
man to allow any of 'is property to rest in peace as 'tis said on
stone, if so be 'is pick and spade will find 'en.'

''Tain't no madness that do want one's own,' remarked Mrs.
Meek.

'But 'tid madness', replied Mrs. Grunter, 'that do tell a plain
Christian woman that God Almighty be in Folly Down, and that
two bloody suns be shining in sky.'

'And what else did he say?' asked Mrs. Meek.

'Only this,' replied her neighbour, 'that I needn't hurry me
frying of they kippers, for 'tis everlasting life that be come, and
they fish mid cook for a thousand years before they be eaten.'

'He'll tell a different story when supper-time be near,'
remarked Mrs. Meek, 'but how came it that Mr. Grunter did
never mind 'is own boot before?'

'It do take years for 'e to mind anything but women,' answered Mrs. Grunter, 'though 'e did limp home thik day, swearing at the stones.'

Silence came, but again Mrs. Meek spoke. 'Time be slow and stubborn', she said, 'in a small village where there bain't much news to be told. Time be a slow-going wold cow wi' we, and Ford car by green do stay still as though 'twere fixed in road.'

'Little Tommy Barker did peep into van and did say there be something asleep in 'en that bain't no bottle,' remarked Mrs. Grunter.

''Tain't no ugly thing, I do hope,' said Mrs. Meek nervously.

'No, no,' replied the other. 'Tommy did say 'twern't nothing nasty, and maybe 'tis to be sold, for anything that folk will buy a tradesman will sell.'

Mrs. Meek grew thoughtful.

''Twas a sad silent evening,' she said, 'same as this be, when Ada Kiddle were found dead, and I do mind how me corns did hurt, and something be always going to happen when they do pain.'

'I do mind Ada's drowning too,' observed Mrs. Grunter, 'and only the day before she did it she did ask I what ways there were to put an end to a poor maid.'

'And what did thee tell she to do?' asked Mrs. Meek.

'I did tell Ada', replied Mrs. Grunter, 'that Dodderdown were the village for hanging, Madder the place to cut a wold throat, and that the folk of Folly Down do like drowning best.'

'Thee never mentioned Squire Mumby's pond, did 'ee?' replied Mrs. Meek.

'Oh, yes, I did,' answered Mrs. Grunter. 'I did say that there weren't no vipers in 'en, as folk do say, but only a few large toads.'

'Ada did look nice in a coffin,' said Mrs. Meek.

There is an engaging character sketch of T. F. Powys in these years as he appeared to a sympathetic observer, in *A Chatto & Windus Miscellany*, 1928, which also includes one of Theodore's best pieces of village humour, 'Archdeacon Truggin'. The sketch is by Sylvia Townsend Warner, and is an extract from a longer work which Miss Warner has not yet published. She has shown me the manuscript and generously says I may make what use I will of it, and the temptation to plunder her pages is strong, especially as they would add an unwonted

grace to mine. It seems to me, however, that her essay ought not to be
laid rudely under contribution, for it is something I would wish to see
published separate and entire, under her name and in a book of her
own. Instead, I borrow the first extract from the *Miscellany*, which
shows Theodore, his own work laid aside, assisting momentarily with
the details of domestic economy:

In December 1923 Theo's elder son left home for Africa, where
he was going to work on a stock farm belonging to his uncle. All
through the summer Violet had been busied in getting together
his outfit and preparing for the departure. For many years her
duties had not taken her further than to Weymouth or to Dorchester, but now her mind had to make a longer journey and
acknowledge a continent which imposed upon her shopping list
such items as a rifle, a sun-helmet, and a ticket costing £80.
However, though the purchases were new, there was nothing
new in the responsibility for making them, for Violet has always
conducted the family affairs, and has always conducted them with
the same unflurrying, unpretentious ability. Theo is disabled from
any practical dealings by two grave faults: an unappeasable
imagination and an insatiable carefulness. If he had taken a hand
in preparing Dicky's outfit his proceedings would have been
somewhat after this fashion. Whilst adventuring himself to
Dorchester in the carrier's van (equipped, I need hardly say, with
a shopping list that summed up the labours of days and the second
thoughts of nights, and mentally practised in every wary artifice
by which man might hope to outwit what an inscription in the
church of Steeple Ashton calls 'the uncontroulable Providence of
God') his fancy would conjure up some concatenation of chances
which would make it absolutely essential for Dicky in Africa to
have at hand a bottle of gum. Gum accordingly must be sought
for: not unadvisedly, lightly, or wantonly; no! but reverently,
discreetly, advisedly, soberly, and in the fear of God; duly considering the causes for which gum was ordained. A search conducted in this spirit cannot be the work of a moment. One must be
careful to buy the right kind of gum, in the right kind of bottle,
and to ascertain that it is rightly secured by a suitable God-fearing
cork. Moreover, one must be careful to buy it from the right kind
of shop-keeper: not one of those loose-living fellows at W. H.
Smith's, who dally in all manner of merchandise and would be as

likely as not to sell one green ink or an evening paper by inad-
vertence, nor yet a lean woman whose back parlour smells of rats;
and finally, one must be careful to pay the right price for it.
Weighed down with so many cares one cannot walk fast. Indeed,
under no circumstances does Theo approve of haste, and of all the
axioms of good living laid down by the philosopher Chilon, that
which pleases him best is: *Never let yourself be seen in a hurry.*
The gum being purchased, Theo, pulling out the watch which is
tethered to him by a finely-wrought old chain, would discover
that it was time to seek Mr. Balliboy's van in the market-place; for
one must be careful not to be left behind, and though there is yet
half an hour to spare, anything might happen: the van might run
away.

For a while Theo's mind might remain at rest. But there is an
aroma of disquiet in the neighbourhood of pessimistic thought,
and as the van passed Max Gate the shadow of Hardy's conifers
would sow a doubt. Suppose the bottle were to break? The elm-
trees at Owermoigne would only nurture the doubt with their
commiserating sighs, their heads shaken in grave disparagement.
Bottles do break; and glancing out of the window Theo might
even see a broken bottle lying at the roadside. *He that sees every
Church-yard swell with the waves and billows of graves, can think it
no extraordinary thing to dye*; and no experienced Christian can
doubt but in that First Curse there was made a provision for
bottles. The van would reach its last stopping-place, and Theo
would quit the other passengers with the sad civility of Charles
the First taking leave of his household. As he walked up the lane
he would wade through a dark flood of gum.

'Violet, my dear, I have bought a bottle of gum for Dicky. It
has a little brush tied on to it. But perhaps I have not acted very
wisely. The bottle might break. I do not like to think of poor
Dicky finding everything sticky, and he might cut himself on the
broken glass. I'm afraid that I have been foolish. I acted rather
impetuously.'

'Why, Theo, the bottle won't break if it's packed properly.'

'Perhaps not, my dear. Still I can't help thinking that I should
have done better to buy glue. And a little brazier to melt it over.
Though you always pack very well.'

During the evening Theo would revert once or twice to the
gum, and weigh the advisability of exchanging it for glue, and the

chances of doing so. Yet later in the evening Violet would hear a soft voice in the dark.

'Violet. Are you asleep? I don't want to disturb you if you are, but I have been thinking things over. There might not be room in Dicky's luggage for that brazier. It doesn't do to have too many parcels on board ship. So don't you think that the best plan would be to send the brazier to Africa by registered post?'

I do not know what Violet would say then. But I shall never forget the triumphant moment when she broke into one of Theo's bouts of dilly-dallying with the exclamation: 'Oh, get along with you, you old tea-pot!' [1]

[1] The sequel to this was a sad one. Theodore's elder son died tragically in Kenya in 1931. Soon afterwards Theodore and Violet adopted a little girl, Susan, and brought her up as their own.

——— 16 ———

D URING most of the decade of the twenties John Cowper Powys continued his lecturing in America. They were years in which of necessity he was much alone. Llewelyn was only briefly in the country after his departure for England in 1925, and Louis Wilkinson had given up American lecturing earlier than this, and returned to England. After publishing *Ducdame* in 1925 John remained silent, so far as books were concerned, until 1929, for the 'Little Blue Books' that appeared during these years were either short new essays or reprints of essays originally published elsewhere. He published essays, reviews and poems in various magazines, but these things were of slight account for a writer conditioned by temperament to a more extended utterance. Then, in 1929, he published *Wolf Solent*, the first of his books to attract wide recognition and large sales.

In 1929 John Cowper was a man of fifty-seven, and for almost thirty years he had lived a wandering, rootless life. The time had come to retire from full-time lecturing, and settle in one place. He chose a remote corner of upper New York State, the small community of Hillsdale, and moved in early in the new year. But the inquirer there for Mr Powys's house would find his journey not yet finished, for that is a scattered district and 'Phudd Bottom', the house in question, lies eight miles or so farther on, in the hills, a place remote enough even today, and surely in 1930 really at the end of the road. Close by is one small farm, and within sight a cluster of cottages, but to all intents and purposes it was as much off the map as Llewelyn's house on White Nose, or Willie's in Kenya. Phudd Bottom itself is a white frame house with the usual long American board porch where, no doubt, were set the usual American rocking chairs. It stands at the foot, and almost on the slope, of Phudd Hill, which rises sharply, its slopes thickly wooded. The whole area is wooded, except for the farmlands in the valleys, and

John could go out at night and enter the woods at the end of his garden and wander off into solitude. His neighbour, Mr Albert Krick, who still farms near by, recalls more than one occasion when he had to go looking for Mr Powys, who had gone off for a walk and forgotten to come back by one or two o'clock in the morning. At Hillsdale the neighbours were interested to see Mr Powys's 'manias' (as his own word calls them) quaintly in action. He would walk to the little triangle of grass where the roads forked, and post his letters in the iron mailbox set on a post in the middle; he would then lean over it, pressing his forehead against the cold metal, to pray to the mail-box to keep his letter safe and cause it to reach its ultimate destination. He had names, Mr Krick recalls, for various rocks and trees and hills. Once every six months or so he would journey to New York city to get his hair cut, and on these occasions Mr Krick would drive him to the station— itself a good many miles away. Once in mid winter when Mr Krick arrived to pick him up he found John waiting in the garden in the snow with no shoes on: he said he had not been able to find them, and indeed hadn't seen them for several months. They were at last unearthed, squashed flat and green with mildew, under an old sofa. There was no time to put them on if the train were to be caught, and John was last seen hurrying barefoot into the railroad depot with the shoes tucked tightly under his arm.

The solitude and remoteness of Hillsdale were of course entirely to John's taste, especially after crowded years in trains and noisy hotels; but he was not completely out of touch with congenial society when he felt the need for it. Not many miles away, at Austerlitz, lived Llewelyn's friends Eugen Boissevain and his wife Edna St Vincent Millay, and Llewelyn and Alyse were themselves at Austerlitz for the winter of 1930, while much nearer to Phudd Bottom, only a couple of miles away, lived John's old friend the poet Arthur Davison Ficke, whose grave may now be seen in the woods beyond his house. It is interesting to note that after John Cowper Powys's departure Phudd Bottom was inhabited by another sensitive spirit, the naturalist Alan Devoe, one of whose later books is an account of his life there, and of his observations of nature and wild life in the Hillsdale area—observations which must have been paralleled again and again by those of John Cowper, as he walked the hills with his black dog, 'The Old'.

Wolf Solent was the last book written before the move to Hillsdale, and it was written, as the author records, in trains and hotels up and down the country; and in his Introduction to the 1963 edition of *Weymouth Sands* Mr Eric Harvey notes that parts of the manuscript of *Wolf Solent* are on hotel notepaper. How many thousands and hundreds of thousands of words John wrote on hotel paper over thirty years or so would make a nice calculation; certainly, letters from him to a variety of correspondents scrawled in hotels at Utica, and Syracuse, and Saint Louis, and Oklahoma City, and Baltimore, and Detroit, and Sacramento and a host of other cities, will afford clues, when they can all be traced, to his criss-cross pilgrimages through all the States of America 'except two'. I once asked him, but I cannot recall that he told me, which were the two that escaped him; they were, in any case, States in which he never happened to lecture. I cannot believe that two States exist in which he never set foot [1]—that would be a strange fact, after so many years of such extensive wandering.

Wolf Solent is a completely satisfying book, without major fault, without any obvious shortcomings; it achieves exactly what its author intended. It is his first major novel, and one of the major English novels of the twentieth century. As a study in contrasting temperaments it can teach some of the professedly psychological novelists a great deal, and its faithful evocation of the Somerset and Dorset countryside is a triumph, especially (as Mr Harvey has pointed out) when it is remembered that this loving delineation of the lanes and fields around Yeovil and Sherborne was written four thousand miles or so from the scenes described, and by a man who had scarcely visited them, except fleetingly, for nearly a quarter of a century.

The character of Wolf Solent is the pivot upon which the story moves, but John Cowper possessed, and here displayed to perfection, the ability to make every character, even the lesser ones, round and solid, so that all the people in this novel are real, even when they are to appear only briefly, or rarely, in the development of the story. Thus we feel we know Roger Monk, and Mrs Otter, and Bob Weevil as we should know them after living two or three years with them in the same house; and, knowing them so well, we perceive how essentially different and individual they are. Surely no other English novelist of our time has so great a crowd of separate people. Even the shadowy Redfern, dead before the book opens, emerges as a personality, as the thoughts and reactions of others about him fit gradually into place.

---

[1] He was speaking before Hawaii and Alaska were admitted to statehood.

In his preface to the 1961 edition the author defines the 'purpose and essence and inmost being' of the book as 'the necessity of opposites'— 'Life and Death, Good and Evil, Matter and Spirit, Body and Soul, Reality and Appearance have to be joined together, have to be forced into one another, have to be proved dependent upon each other, while all solid entities have to dissolve, if they are to outlast their momentary appearance, into atmosphere'. He goes on to say that these principles apply equally to the individual, in whom there are differences and contradictions. Here indeed may lie the purpose and essence, but they are the disciplines behind a relatively simple story, the story of a man who loves two women, and who makes a wrong choice between them. This is no new story—and indeed what love story is?—but it is told with a freshness which makes the central catastrophe seem new, and to those involved it is of course scant comfort that this kind of thing has occurred plenty of times before; and, as commonly happens in John Cowper's novels, there are several side-plots and underlying themes supporting the main story, interrelated and conditioning it and each other; much indeed of the action is seen to arise from the influence of events with which the principal characters have nothing to do; the death of Redfern, the feckless behaviour of Wolf Solent's father, like Redfern dead before the story opens, and the incestuous relationship of the bookseller Malakite with his eldest daughter—these all exert pressures upon Wolf Solent which serve finally to sever him from Christie Malakite for ever, while forming a lasting impediment to any permanent reconciliation with Gerda. Indeed, in this book of opposites there is no tragedy more poignant than the fatal attraction of Wolf Solent and Gerda, so different from each other in every way, so utterly unsuited, joined in a marriage neither of bodies nor minds. The uncomplicated physical love that Gerda needs she finds readily enough elsewhere, but the restoration of the spiritual serenity which Wolf unwittingly has destroyed she cannot so easily accomplish, and her forlorn figure remains long in the reader's mind. Gerda is one of the finest of John Cowper's creations: she moves and breathes independently of the book: we expect to see her any time in the Yeovil streets—in some sort, she has the continuing life of Arnold's Scholar Gipsy, as real, as elusive, as unchanging as he.

Wolf Solent himself has been identified too closely with the author by readers looking upon the book as autobiographical. There is no autobiographical element in the plot, but it is true that Wolf comes closer to being a portrait of John Cowper than any of the other characters resembling him, in *Glastonbury*, or *Weymouth Sands*, or *Maiden Castle*, or elsewhere. Wolf's physical appearance is close to John's, and his habit of introspective analysis of his own motives and reactions, and of the actions of others, is closely akin to John's as displayed in the *Autobiography*. He behaves as John would behave, has the same tastes and habits and gestures—carries a great stick, loves walking, is all fingers and thumbs. But these similarities do not constitute 'autobiography', which must also be a record of events. The events in *Wolf Solent* are entirely unrelated to any events in the author's life, except in small particulars like Wolf's 'malice dance' at the school in London, which may remind readers of John's account of his own 'malice dance' at Sherborne. Another reason for the apparent autobiographical element in the novel is its setting against the background of Yeovil ('Blacksod') and Sherborne ('Ramsgard'). But here also it may be noted that the third place, 'King's Barton', is in no sense a portrait of Montacute, which it might have been expected to be. The only similarity here is in the presence of an ancient manor house—but there are other ancient manor houses in the actual vicinity of the twin towns. I think the author's remarks in the preface to the 1961 edition sufficiently indicate that he had Montacute House in mind for Mr Urquhart's residence, but his descriptions of the road to 'King's Barton' and of the village do not correspond with Montacute, nor does his specific observation that the manor was not a big house. His *idea* of a manor house may have been based on Montacute, but his execution was much less closely modelled. It is noteworthy that when he writes of particular places in their own name—as in particular of Weymouth, Dorchester and Glastonbury—John Cowper is a faithful recorder of the local scene; but when he uses fictitious names, though the true place intended is known, as, for example, 'Blacksod' equals Yeovil, then he no longer feels called upon to be topographically exact. But, real or imagined, his towns and villages of Somerset and Dorset, and the lanes and landscapes connecting them, bring the reader as close as he will get anywhere in books to the scene described. John Cowper Powys's west country is more real than Thomas Hardy's, because closer to our own day; and more real than Theodore Powys's because John's people and events are closer to everyday life.

How differently John wrote from either of these two, and how differently from the other great west country novelist, Phillpotts, the quotations already made will show. But into *Wolf Solent* he introduced new elements of descriptive writing—or, at least, gave these elements greater prominence. In *Wolf Solent* the weather, the effect of clouds, the movements of the air, the qualities of light, are frequently discussed, and some of the most beautiful short passages in a book the prose of which is always beautiful, concern these natural and often taken for granted matters. Let me give two short examples:

The fields of wheat and barley, pearl-like and opalescent in the swimming haze, sloped upwards to the high treeless ridge along which ran the main road from Ramsgard to Blacksod. On his left, lying dim and misty, yet in some strange way lustrous with an inner light of their own, as if all the earth had become one vast phosphorescent glow-worm, rolled away from beneath that narrow lane the dew-soaked pastures of the Blackmore Vale, rising again in the distance to the uplands of High Stoy.

It was one of those spring evenings which are neither golden from the direct rays of the sinking sun, nor opalescent from their indirect diffused reflection. A chilly wind had arisen, covering the western sky, into which they were driving, with a thick bank of clouds. The result of this complete extinction of the sunset was that the world became a world in which every green thing upon its surface received a fivefold addition to its greenness. It was as if an enormous green tidal wave, composed of a substance more translucent than water, had flowed over the whole earth; or rather as if some diaphanous essence of all the greenness created by long days of rain had evaporated during this one noon, only to fall down, with the approach of twilight, in a cold, dark, emerald-coloured dew.

How is one to define a classic?—no doubt in a dozen ways; it is certain, at all events, that no book can be a classic that is not worth reading more than once. *Wolf Solent*, I think, goes one better than this. It is better at a second reading, better again at a third; it is a book in which the reader may continually be finding new beauties, new subtleties and new insights. I have called it 'completely satisfying', and perhaps it was the first of John's books of which this might be said. It was not to be the last, and in the five years following the writing of *Wolf Solent* he performed the astonishing feat of writing three great books, his *Autobiography*, *A Glastonbury Romance* and

Weymouth Sands. That's why I felt so keen an excitement on a cold March day when Dr Robert Blackmore turned his car off the main highway from Boston to Albany and headed for the little white house of Phudd Bottom. There are plenty of places in which men have written books, but few which have given shelter in the writing of three such books as these.

─── 17 ───

LLEWELYN POWYS was in Palestine barely two months, and during that time he was ill with a return of his old complaint, and both he and Alyse were attacked and weakened by a local fever; so that he saw less of the country than he had hoped. 'I left the country with a sad heart,' he wrote to Marianne Moore, conscious of how much that interested him must be left behind. But he also experienced a great deal, and as might be expected got every ounce out of the things he was able to see. 'I also entered the inner cavern of the Holy Sepulchre with Alyse striking matches, and lay down in the grave of Joseph of Arimathea, which was shaped like an oven, and which I found fitted me well . . .' he wrote to H. Rivers Pollock; and to Naomi Mitchison: 'I saw a thousand things that diverted and entranced me.' Though so short, the visit produced three substantial books, the first of which he began at once when, leaving Palestine, he and Alyse settled for the winter in Anacapri. This was *The Cradle of God*, finished in February 1929. The next was *The Pathetic Fallacy* (published in the United States as *An Hour on Christianity*), and the third was *A Pagan's Pilgrimage*; both of these were finished by early spring of the following year, after his return to England. Of *A Pagan's Pilgrimage* there is not a great deal to be said. It is a travel book cut to the conventional pattern, with illustrations of places visited and scenes observed. A book rather of 'impressions' than of connected narrative, for, although it proceeds consecutively, it omits much. Certainly, *A Pagan's Pilgrimage* is entirely Llewelyn's book, and his voice can clearly be heard in the prose; it is like a long, in some sense a gossipy, letter. But it has not the weight of the two graver books, into which he put so much of the mature thought he had spent in meditating upon the Christian religion.

The Cradle of God is a *tour de force*, a long continuous essay without chapters (these divisions, present in the original draft, were wisely discarded for publication). The essay is a paraphrase of the Old

Testament, and of the story of Jesus, in so far as these interact upon one another; Llewelyn Powys shows how the Bible story prepares for the coming of Christ, and then what happened when he appeared. I call it a *tour de force* because it might well be argued that this story has already been told adequately in the Bible itself; but in fact the reader of *The Cradle of God* is kept continuously interested, even though he may know 'the story' perfectly already. The beauty of the writing holds him, and he is arrested time and again by the author's asides and comments. Here, as in all his writings about the Christian religion, and in particular when he writes about Jesus, Llewelyn Powys is as reverent as the truest believer—but he makes his dissent plain enough. He is quite certain in his own mind that Christianity is not true in essentials, whatever truth there may be in details. Perhaps Jesus lived and was crucified: why not? It is not this that is in dispute, but the claim that he was the son of God and saviour of the world. All the same, nowhere does Llewelyn write anything which a Christian may think in bad taste, or misleading, or unfair. Llewelyn's summing up of the whole business, when all the interest and poetry and pathos of the Bible story is allowed, is without compromise, and, like all his statements of his beliefs, eloquent, concise and moving. No matter with what persuasive charm he recounts the story of Jesus, it is dismissed as but a tale, in the light of such a passage as this, in which may be found—in two or three hundred words—the very essence of Llewelyn Powys as a writer, manner and matter perfectly married:

Even in the hour of death, upon the very threshold of the grave, I would not hesitate to speak out what is in my mind. I would have no boy or girl turn from the earth, with its ancient usages, its ancient messages, its ancient reassurance. When the hidden bell rings, when the chancel echoes at the time of high mass, let them be 'like the deaf adder that stoppeth her ear, which will not hearken to the voice of the charmer, charm he never so wisely'. Have care, O heathen youth! These matters remain unproven. Let not the free action of your minds, or the free action of your bodies, be impeded or checked by the resonant intoning of priests, as they walk in procession, dressed in lace. There remain raptures more real than any of these indrawn beatitudes. The wine of life is good, it is of the fruit of the grape-bearing earth. The bread of life is good, it is of the fruit of the corn-bearing earth. What though decay is inherent in all component things? We have our hour. All things flow away. All things tend to their end. 'What a cursed frenzy is this, to think that life is to be renewed by death!' Be generous, be free, be impassioned, be *understanding*, children of herbs and fruits and abstinences! Give no heed to these false teachers, but with emancipated hearts make your escape sure. Your heathen loyalties shall be deeper and truer than their loyalties. Leave these dingy temples with their unsnuffed candle-lights to the infirm and old. Even now your hour passes. With ineluctable glee dip your hands deep into the salt fresh sea of life. Lift up your eyes and behold the sun.

The Pathetic Fallacy makes a fitting successor to *The Cradle of God*, for it is a philosophical examination of Christianity as it strikes an unbeliever. Here again there can be no offence to those who do believe, but they had better take care that the book does not win them away from their obstinately held beliefs. There is in this book more of argument, more of polemic, than in the other. It is in some degree militant, the prose carries a deeper burden, for the author is no longer telling a story, but is presenting a set of convictions. Here as always in Llewelyn Powys the strength of the conviction lends strength to its expression.

In hours of deep emotion, in hours when danger threatens those we love, we chatter out uneasily the names of invented gods. We were wiser an we held our tongues. There is none to save, there is none who cares to save us. Time and chance happeneth to all men. From cradle to coffin is but a moment, though our span be eighty in number. Though we catch our tears never so diligently in bottles there is none to mark them. Darkness obliterates all. Our natural proneness to forget has its culmination in the oblivion of the grave. A few generations of human beings may be buried with their arms crooked upon their breasts, but the practice with its tender associations has had no significance outside our village boundaries. Generations will pass, centuries will pass, and Christianity will dissolve back into mist. Even though we are frightened, even though we are broken, even though our heads are bowed, it is prudent to disregard it. Christianity is impotent. Deliverance cannot come of it. A wise man can do no better than to turn from the churches and look up through the airy majesty of the wayside trees with exultation, with resignation, at the unconquerable unimplicated sun.

The writing of these two books so closely upon one another must have stimulated Llewelyn Powys to go on from the discussion of what he did not believe to the expression of what he did believe. Certainly, in these two books, in *A Pagan's Pilgrimage* incidentally, and indeed everywhere among his writings, he had freely stated his opinions and convictions on religion and on the terms of our life in earth. But the time had come for a positive, sustained statement of his beliefs. The stay in Anacapri had been marred by his continuing illness, and early in the new year of 1929 he and Alyse moved to Capri, where *The Cradle of God* was finished, and where he was again ill. In late spring they returned to England, to their coastguard cottage on White Nose. Here was an ideal place for a man wishing to meditate upon life and death and eternity.

The great headland, last or first bastion of the chalk, for west of it lie the sandy cliffs of Ringstead and the coloured slopes of Jordan Hill, is remote and aloof. Those coastguard cottages lying just back from the summit, with its treacherous slide and sheer falls to the sea six hundred feet below, make an observatory from which to scan the heavens or the workings of the human mind. Llewelyn Powys was deeply moved by this environment, as many references in his writing show—'it is not possible for a man to stand on its wind-swept forehead and remain dead in spirit'. Here could be seen nature in all aspects—the flowers, the birds, the animals of the headland; the sea, never still, never the same; the distant landscapes of Dorset, stretching away; the sun, the clouds and a sky full of stars. Here he gathered all his mature reflections and began to write *Impassioned Clay*, conscious that it was to be his most important essay—a 'positive "constructive" trumpet call to youth', he called it in writing to John Cowper before ever the work began. 'Something of a Devil's Handbook,' he went on, 'such as we used to plan, only setting forth clearly from a dug-in Dorset "viewpoint" the human situation touching upon astronomy, biology, geology, anthropology, and gradually closing in upon a system of practical ethics as explained by Epicurus, only ending with a chapter upon death.'

He kept pretty closely to this definition, but as always he is personal in his approach: here is no 'abstracted meditation', and from the first words we are in the presence of a man talking familiarly, though the matters spoken of are grave. Llewelyn Powys never divorces philosophy from the everyday. He tells—in the essay's very first sentence—of stepping into the silence of the night outside his cottage and looking up to the heavens. He falls under the spell of those remote distances,

that unimaginable vastness and silence. But, 'in my room upstairs a
peat fire was glowing. All was snug and secure and actual there'. It is
this very security and actuality that point the moral and underline the
fatality, and again and again the 'remote inquiries' are brought back to
earth, 'back, back to humanity', by such touches.

Impassioned Clay is not a long book. Printed straight on, without
chapter divisions, it makes 120 pages; but every page, every paragraph,
is filled with matter—there is no superficial word, no inconclusive
thought. The essay reviews the place of our world in the universe—a
speck of matter inconceivably small—and goes on to consider the first
coming of life to the planet, the ages of prehistory, the appearance of
man. It discusses man's gradual increase in wisdom and understanding,
from the brute, subhuman, to the poets, teachers, conquerors, saints,
of a later day. It shows how men have made religions to guide, comfort
and restrain the generations; and how, in the author's opinion, all are
vain. He then goes on to state his positive beliefs, springing from the
teaching of Epicurus and Lucretius and specifically rejecting Christianity, with its laying up of treasures in an imaginary heaven.

We have our hour. *We are alive now.* Those not yet born know
not life any better than the dead. It is ours, ours this unmatched
experience: ours to wait upon the winters, ours to smell the snow,
ours to watch it falling, falling, each flake with exquisite uncertainty, now up, now down, fluttering to its appointed place on
stone or bench or on tiled roof; ours to tremble at the approach of
spring; ours to kneel down to the first crocus smelling of the
colour of yellow; ours to hear the cry of the blackbird disturbed
in its nest in the fork of the elder-tree; ours to spend with careless
aplomb the opulence of summer days, lying with the one we love
between the yellow acres of corn.

He does not preach this as a selfish philosophy. He is fully conscious
of obligations, and observed them as punctiliously as any follower of
the most demanding of religious systems.

We must temper our liberty. Merely to possess senses is to
possess rights, and these undemanding and pitiful rights are
never disregarded by the magnanimous spirits that we love.
Epicurus said that it was not only nobler but a more blessed thing
to do good than to receive it. Out of the natural largesse of our
joy we must give wide scope to our compassion.

My quotations are short: I would prefer to quote the entire book. There is something wise, arresting, certain, on every page, be it a sustained passage like that on page 95 beginning 'I appeal to youth', or any one of a hundred detached sentences of which here is a single example: 'In every strong and healthy human being there is an inner knowledge of what it is good to do and what it is not good to do.' Let no one suppose, as some of his detractors have supposed, that by liberty Llewelyn Powys means licence. He is strictly a moralist, and anyone who lived fairly by his teaching would be as deserving of esteem and respect—and would be on a nearly parallel course—as a follower of the teachings of Jesus. 'Love one another' is not exclusively a Christian precept.

As Llewelyn found he could not say everything in his first examination of the Christian religion, so he found he needed to make supplementary statements in setting down his own. *Impassioned Clay* has two such footnotes, *Now that the Gods are Dead* and *Glory of Life*, published respectively in 1932 and 1934, both in finely produced limited editions, the first in America only, and the second in England only. Lynd Ward's striking illustrations to *Now That the Gods are Dead*, and Robert Gibbings's intuitive engravings for *Glory of Life*, are rare examples of text and illustrations happily marrying, and it is to be regretted that later reissues of these essays have had to be made without their illustrations. On the other hand, the limited edition, so characteristic of the publishing tradition of the thirties, has its disadvantages for such a writer as Llewelyn Powys, whose maturest work ought to be in the hands of as many readers as possible, for its message is designed for all. Ideally, one would wish to see these three essays united in a single volume, an affirmation of the happy, constructive and positive faith which he held all his adult life long, and proclaimed so consistently in all that he wrote.

Although the beginning of *Impassioned Clay* speaks of the author stepping out from his cottage on White Nose, at the end it carries the colophon 'Steepletop, Austerlitz, N.Y.' and the dedication is to Eugen Boissevain, 'under whose roof' the book was finished. The book was begun, Llewelyn tells us, on June first; and in August he and Alyse decided to take a trip to America. They spent some time with John at Phudd Bottom, and some time in New York, and then retired to Austerlitz to spend the winter in a cottage on Edna St Vincent Millay's estate.

Steepletop is a complex of buildings and barns, part farm, part private house, some seven hundred acres of wild hill and woodland; the 'cottage' Llewelyn and Alyse occupied is a substantial wood-frame house lying a little downhill from the main residence, with superb views across the hills opposite, where deer and other wild animals can often be seen. Steepletop, incidentally, has nothing to do with steeples. The place is named from a weed common in the area, *Spiraea tomentosa*,[1] which has pink spire-like flowers. Llewelyn and Alyse had known Edna Millay and her husband Eugen Boissevain for some years, and Miss Millay was later to visit them at East Chaldon. At Steepletop they could be quiet and undisturbed, but when they felt the need for stimulating society the Boissevains were no more than a hundred yards away, and at their house from time to time other interesting folk would gather. John Cowper was only a few miles away, at Phudd Bottom, and another neighbour whom Llewelyn and John loved well was Arthur Davison Ficke, the poet who addressed verses to both of them. If, for Llewelyn, the great attraction of Steeple-top was the famous poet who lived there, that was understandable, for Edna St Vincent Millay's beauty and vivid personality made an indelible impact upon a wide circle of artists and writers, many of whom have paid tribute to her. Her practical generosity was demon-strated a few years later, when Llewelyn lost his libel action, for she sent him a cheque towards his expenses, which stood finally at over £600 at a time when he was not making a great deal of money. How warmly Miss Millay and her husband felt for Llewelyn and Alyse appears in her published letters.

The winter at Austerlitz was interrupted by a trip to the West Indies, which Llewelyn wrote about in the long essay afterwards pub-lished by Mr Malcolm Elwin in his miscellany *The Pleasure Ground*. In this essay he mentions in passing his winter at Austerlitz, and its pleasures—the sledge rides, the cheerful company, the fireside reading of Malory, the buckwheat honey and brown bread . . .

As I look back now upon the months I spent in the mountains above the small village of Austerlitz I know that I was given many chances of touching in time the flying wings of eternity. In the dead of winter on moonlit nights I used often to visit a ruined farmhouse. I would feel my way up the creaking narrow stairs,

---

[1] Another name for the plant, 'Hardhack', was used as the name for Arthur Davison Ficke's house, a few miles to the west.

cross the floor of the upper room, avoiding as best I might the holes in the sagging boarding, and, kneeling down at the frameless window, send my spirit out into the night, out over the white valleys where foxes with bellies as empty as purses were treading and sniffing, out over the mountain tops where ridges of trees were visible, fretsawed against the naked air. Alone in this forlorn, unvisited chamber where draught-driven snow lay in precise heaps, my identity could often win to a liberation beyond the yearning outcries of the blood and bones of my fleshly body.[1]

Here, as always, we see him putting his own precept into practice: 'By day and by night no sight that we see, no sound that we hear, but has its own poetical burden.'

[1] From 'A Voyage to the West Indies', *The Pleasure Ground* (Macdonald, 1947).

18

The year 1930 is of some significance for the collector of books by the Powys brothers and their circle, for it affords no less than eighteen items separately published, though not all of them are substantial, and not all call for extended comment here. The reader of *At The Harlot's Burial*, a small gathering of poems by 'Laurence' Powys (that is, Mr Francis Powys, Theodore's second son), may note a cast of mind akin to Theodore's, especially in the title poem. The reader may note that Louis Marlow's *The Lion Took Fright* is dedicated to Theodore, and may recall the characteristic letter of thanks from Theodore, printed in *Welsh Ambassadors*. He may mark such items of general Powys interest as a new novel by Louis Marlow's wife Ann Reid, the appearance of A. R. Powys's useful handbook on *The English Parish Church*, and two books by Philippa Powys, her only publications.

Philippa Powys, called in the family 'Katie', from her first name Catharine, had, like her brothers Theodore and William, been early attracted to the land, and had for a time run a small farm at Montacute. Like all the Powys children, she was able with care to live without paid employment, and most of her life was passed in country pursuits. She lived for a time at Sidmouth, where she was friendly with the novelist Stephen Reynolds, and then for many years at Chaldon Herring. She died in 1962 at Buckland Newton. In his paper on the family Littleton Powys says he had read other works of hers besides the one published novel, and that 'if only the gods had given her as great a mastery of language as she has of imagination, the world would have welcomed more of her novels'. 'The only poet in our family', Llewelyn once called her, though he cannot have meant this literally, for he was a fierce champion of John's poetry too.

The Blackthorn Winter was dedicated to Alyse Gregory, and published by Constable, who at this time were publishing Ann Reid and Alyse Gregory also. I am not clear about Littleton's exact meaning when he suggests that Philippa lacked a mastery of language; certainly, her book has a certain air of the amateur, rather engagingly so, and the language is simple and direct rather than eloquent or stylish; but her brother can hardly have intended a criticism of this. Philippa's style indeed very well suits her story, which also is simple and direct. It concerns a small village in Somerset, having features in common with Montacute, and the love of an itinerant gipsy lad for one of the village girls, engaged to the young blacksmith. The girl at first will have none of the gipsy, but he persists and finally seduces her, and then she falls entirely under his spell and at last elopes with him. Her life with the gipsies, her child, the gipsy's desertion of her, the blacksmith's despair at losing her, are all in a naïve tradition, perhaps, and it might be argued that unnumbered girls have read such tales in scores of novelettes; but there is more in Philippa Powys's story than that. Under the melodrama these characters feel deeply, and the author shares their passions. The poems in *Driftwood* are about the Dorset coast, the wind, the sea, the birds, the weeds. They are undisciplined and halting, rather 'notes for poems' than poems. They have some similarity with the short unrhymed poems of D. H. Lawrence. Among them there is a poem on the death of Walter Franzen, which makes a footnote to Llewelyn's essay 'A Grave in Dorset', and might one day be printed with it.

Llewelyn's publications in 1930 have been noticed—*Apples be Ripe* and *The Pathetic Fallacy*. Readers who have both novels may observe points of similarity between *Apples be Ripe* and *The Blackthorn Winter*, but there is no question of the one influencing the other. This is a similarity born of similarities of temperament and outlook. There is a closeness to nature in both novels, almost as though nature were operating as a character; Philippa's heroine Nancy and Llewelyn's hero Christopher might both have lived happier lives if they could have met. A great part of the action in both novels takes place out of doors, in hedgerows and fields, in all weathers. If some allowance be made for the brother's defter practice, it might be argued that the following passages might be from either of the books; but it could never be supposed that either was by Theodore or John.

But very soon Mike turned with Nancy into the shadow of a lane deeply imbedded with brambles and long uncut thorns. A few stars vaguely appeared above it. Here they met their horses grazing, some feeding, some with hobble-bands around their fetlocks, others lying stretched as if dead, their long necks resting upon the earthen track. They passed them by without a word or sign until they reached, by a broken gap, the shelter of a rick.

There where an open cut brought ease to their limbs he made her lie. Out of the blaze of moonlight, hidden by the dark obstruction of the hedge, he followed the way of his love. Every nerve in Nancy's body caught his desire. They were wrapped in the wealth of its abundance. Much was forgotten; the regret of Walter, and her own mistaken elopement. The pain of her shoulder was lessened, and the moonbeams became bleared beyond the jagged fringe of hedge. The love of her gipsy sufficed her. By the wild weed of passion she was entangled.

The sun had gone down and the dew was falling. Away over the roofs of the village a full moon was visible. 'Let us go into the wood,' he said. They scrambled through a gap. A long trailing bramble hooked itself into the girl's dress, and Chris with trembling fingers disentangled it. Nelly stood motionless, watching for the moment of her deliverance, her head half turned. 'She is beautiful,' he thought when, freeing her at last, he looked up at her concerned face. They walked down a small footpath. Foxgloves in all their pixy glamour stood in conspiracy on both sides of the way. He took her hand. She made no protest, and thus they went forward to the farther side of the spinney where the oak trees and beech trees gave place to a grove of hazels, the brown wands of which had been cut close to the ground in the early part of the year. The woodmen had stacked their faggots in heaps in readiness for the winter hauling, and between these heaps the bracken had grown up with great luxuriance, completely concealing the bluebells with their fading seeds.

'Let us rest,' he said. His companion made no demur. He took off his rough labourer's coat, the same that he had bought on his way through Southampton, and spread it on the springing ferns. She sat down in silence. Without a word spoken he drew her to him and kissed her.

In this year John Cowper published one substantial book, and it proved to be among the most successful of all his works—*In Defence of Sensuality*. The English edition passed through six impressions in three months, and the book continued to sell well in later, cheaper editions. It was widely read in the United States also. Perhaps initially the striking title may have helped the book to be noticed, but its continuing success lay in deeper causes. It was the first of John Cowper's essays in didactic philosophy to appeal to a large audience; its success may have helped to obtain currency for those which followed, so far as his English audience was concerned. It may be noted that in the United States he had already met with a large success with *The Meaning of Culture*, published in 1929, of which I have a copy dated the same year and marked on the jacket 'Eleventh large printing'. The book was published in England in 1930, and passed through half a dozen editions, but more slowly.

Undoubtedly, John Cowper Powys's greatest strength lies in his novels; it is they that set him among the greatest writers of his time. They overshadow and they will always overshadow his other books; but they need not conceal them. Thousands of readers have been strengthened, and comforted, and encouraged, by his essays in compromise, his hints on how to confront a hostile and puzzling world. These essays speak to everyone, and they were published in a time when the ordinary man everywhere was in need of advice and reassurance. Those were years of depression, of strikes, of the threat of war, of uncertainty and stress. People everywhere were living unadjusted, frustrated, incomplete lives—as indeed many are today. As Llewelyn had noted, the churches were losing their hold; but nothing had replaced them, and few people in any generation have the resolution to take up an attitude like Llewelyn's own, accepting man's essential loneliness 'from the cradle to the grave'. Almost everyone needs something to lean on, and John's philosophies show how support may be found from within.

He does not lay down a set of rules, but rather offers intimations, hints, suggestions, by which the reader may work out a personal philosophy for himself, designed for the particular circumstances in which he is placed. There are a number of these volumes of what may loosely be termed 'philosophy', and undoubtedly a 'system' could be built up from them; but their value will always lie in the detached passages which the individual reader will pick for himself as most applicable to his own need. The titles are in general self-explanatory: to those mentioned already may be added *A Philosophy of Solitude* (1933); *The Art of Happiness* (1935); *The Art of Growing Old* (1944);

and *In Spite of* (1953); the essay on war called *Mortal Strife* (1942) is also more nearly related to philosophy than to anything else.

These philosophies, or aspects of the same philosophy, are of course paralleled in the novels, where time and again the major characters either express related philosophic views, or are shown to live by them. John Cowper's philosophy is not rooted in religion, any more than Llewelyn's is, but it takes from religion—whether Christianity or the religions of the East—what it can use; and the reader who is unwilling to give up his own religion, be it Christianity or another, can in his turn take from John Cowper. Such a reader may be unwilling to go all the way with the author, and yet find striking and thought-provoking passages on almost every page.

'Our rulers at the present day, with their machines and their preachers, are all occupied in putting into our heads the preposterous notion that activity rather than contemplation is the object of life.' That is picked truly at random from *In Defence of Sensuality*. The passage is footnoted by this, from *A Philosophy of Solitude*: 'An original mind has no more respect for modern ideas than it has for any other ideas. All ideas are human. All are stamped with the sign-manuals of our race: short-sightedness, maliciousness, prejudice, unimaginative literalness, complacent dogmatism, parrot-like pedantry.' 'Driven as we are', so the story is taken up in *The Art of Happiness*, 'by the urge of economic necessity, hemmed in as we are by the fatality of our material environment, there is a margin in all our lives when, whether we like it or not, our thoughts and emotions wander from the matter in hand, and our imagination finds itself confronted by mysteries beyond the improvement of any human society.'

Writing in 'The Modern Thinker', at the time of publication of *A Philosophy of Solitude*, John Cowper explained what he was attempting. He was trying to show the individual ego how to confront the vast hostile and mysterious universe in which it found itself, a lonely, sentient speck, in such a way as to be happy *in spite of everything*; and to show that this happiness could be attained no matter what the material circumstances.

In conclusion [he wrote] I seek to show how by simplifying life to an extreme point, and by rejecting all the 'pleasures' and 'entertainments' of the crowd, it is possible to share not only the exultation and the non-human aloofness of the elements, but that tragic and patient expectancy with which these tremendous presences await the final dissolution of our 'insubstantial pageant', and the possible substitution for it of some totally different dimension of the ultimate mystery.

John Cowper Powys also published in 1930 his curious and little-known story, *The Owl, The Duck, and—Miss Rowe! Miss Rowe!*, in an edition limited to 250 copies, printed at the Black Archer Press, Chicago. It is a sad little story, on a superficial level, of two old people living in poverty on the small top floor at 4 Patchin Place, Greenwich Village—the New York house in which at that time John was living, which had formerly been the home of Alyse Gregory and Llewelyn Powys, and was afterwards the home of e. e. cummings. But like any story of J. C. Powys, the superficial level is not everything; and the final effect of the story is not really sad, even though the old man and the old woman are gassed at the end by the tap of the stove becoming unaccountably turned on, on the very eve of their removal to a 'Home'—which for them would be a fate worse than death. For a tale of sixty small pages *The Owl, The Duck* is uncommonly full of characters, for the old man and the old woman only appear to live alone. There are other entities present too: a stuffed owl, a china duck, a doll, a wooden horse, a glass fish, a ghost, two shadowy beings who were characters in an unfinished novel, a headless figure of Lao-tze, and a tiny image of Kwang-tze. It is a moving little story, absurd and charming and odd, interesting of itself, and interesting also as an early intimation of John Cowper's later use of inanimate articles as characters which reaches its culmination in the remarkable first chapter of *Atlantis*.

This publishing of a single short story in a limited edition was an isolated occasion with John Cowper, but Theodore did it on a number of occasions, beginning with *A Stubborn Tree* in 1926, and ending with *Goat Green* in 1937—although this was not a limited edition in the strict sense of the term; it was, however, a single short story in a finely produced edition. The year 1930, which is under review in this chapter, offers no less than four of these single stories from Theodore: *The Key of the Field, Christ in the Cupboard, Uriah on the Hill* and *Uncle Dottery*, and it is symptomatic of Theodore's widening reputation that these stories were offered by four different publishers up and down the country; the publishers of fine and limited editions considered Theodore a suitable author for their lists, at a time when the market in first and limited editions was foundering in the aftermath of the great slump of 1929, and the collectors who survived it were becoming more cautious and more discriminating. Very many authors who had been introduced injudiciously into this specialized publishing field now disappeared from it—it would be unkind, perhaps indiscreet, to mention names. Theodore survived, and his limited editions range from the splendour of the Golden Cockerel Press to the less ambitious paper and wrappers of the Blue Moon. It is also interesting to note that he appealed to the younger generation of publishers; *Uriah on the Hill* was one of the earliest publications of Mr Gordon Fraser, and *Uncle Dottery* was an early venture of Mr Douglas Cleverdon. Also in 1930 Theodore published a full collection of short stories, twenty-six all told, in *The White Paternoster*; the emphasis in this gathering is on the humorous stories, Mr Truggin, Mr Dottery, and others of their kind figuring largely, but there are examples of Theodore's tragic manner, as in 'What Lack I Yet?' and 'The Hunted Beast'—a story of haunting horror.

But the emphasis was on humour, and nowhere more so than in Theodore's other 1930 book, *Kindness in a Corner*, his one predominantly humorous novel, and so much a masterpiece of its kind that it must be always a matter for regret that he never wrote another. The distinction of his humour has not been sufficiently recognized, and indeed has sometimes been dismissed in a passing reference by critics concerned with his admittedly major work, which lies elsewhere. Humour seldom gets much serious critical attention, but our literature would be much impoverished without it; among the humorists of the twentieth century Theodore Powys takes a high place, and a place no other could occupy, for his is a very personal and individual humour, immediately recognizable and inimitable.

The 'corner' of this novel is the village of Tadnol, which is singularly free of the unpleasant characters who inhabit so many of the Powys villages. There is an occasional sly sadism here, but nothing comparable with what goes on as a matter of course in Dodderdown, Shelton, Madder and Mockery Gap. Tadnol people are simple, honest and friendly, take them for all in all. The 'kindness' in this corner is provided by the Rev. Silas Dottery, its rector. But there are other kindnesses: the reciprocal kindness of the villagers (when the rector is out of sorts they offer him their daughters), and the kindness of the grave, which Sexton Truggin is always extolling, and over all the kindness of God, which passeth all understanding. Tadnol is something of an earthly paradise. But this title is a punning title (perhaps the

only pun in all the Powys canon, for these brothers were not given to
jests of that sort). Mr Dottery is in a corner right from the moment he
forgets there is to be a Confirmation service, and remembers only when
the Bishop is already waiting to lay on hands—and no heads have been
prepared to receive them. This misfortune he surmounts, but it leads
to worse, for he has enemies in the Church, and these now accuse him
of keeping a mistress in his study cupboard. Perhaps only in a T. F.
Powys story would a Canon of the Established Church really believe
that a wanton girl would live in a cupboard—and as we have already
noted in passing, in another story the figure in the cupboard was Christ
himself—but in Theodore it seems perfectly natural, just as it is
natural for the unworldly Mr Dottery to think his own servant girl,
dressed in his own white surplice (and very little else) is a martyred
saint sent by God to give him counsel.

The humour of this novel is threefold. First, it has a humorous plot,
original, plausible (within the author's standards of convention) and
complete—that is, logically unfolded and logically rounded off. Next,
the individual characters are humorous—Mr Dottery and Mr Truggin
richly so: triumphs of character creation. Lastly, the narrative is
humorous, the style exactly suits the matter. But this is not all; like all
great humour, this has its pathos, its serious undertones. Mr Dottery
is not a figure of fun, but a gentleman and a man of God whom we
respect and honour. Truggin is a sterling character, shrewd and earthy,
no fool, but on the contrary the possessor of a good working philosophy which he will share with all. His eloquent defence of death is
central to the book, in which death, or the implications of death, are
often under discussion. Theodore has the power of invoking compassion for the most arid of his people. The Bishop's wife, whom as
Miss Pettifer we have met and disliked in *Innocent Birds* and elsewhere,
we now begin to feel sorry for; only a mind diseased could work so
eagerly to bring a good man down.

It may be argued that in this book Theodore—despite the book's
merit—was not entirely sure where he was going. There is some
parallel in this with *Pickwick*, where the beginning is much more
superficial than the end. Both books commence almost in the realm of
farce, and take on their warm humanity as they proceed. There are
chapters towards the close of *Kindness in a Corner* which are not
humorous at all, nor are they meant to be. 'Mr Dottery sees new
Company' is one, 'The Dirt of God' another. There is also some loss
of effect in the absurd efforts of Canon Dibben to make a live sacrifice

with two stolen doves. Perhaps the story is rounded off a little hastily. But, if these be defects, it is still true to call this novel a masterpiece, for the sustained comedy of the first thirty chapters. Moreover, although here on an admittedly lesser plane, the writing shares a quality notable in Theodore's more serious works : it does not yield everything up at a first reading. There are subtleties of humour, and insights into character, which appear on a second reading and were overlooked at a first.

19

In April 1930 John Cowper Powys settled at Phudd Bottom and commenced his longest and greatest novel, *A Glastonbury Romance*. The book contains rather under half a million words, and it was written in a year and nine months. Here indeed is a contrast between the brothers: such a book would not be written in so short a time by Theodore's method of completing two or three hundred words a day. and two or three hundred words would sometimes barely suffice John for a single sentence. Like the boy in Prior's poem, John must 'down with all he thinks', whereas Theodore would carefully select and consider what he wished to say before ever setting it down. We do not need to prefer one method, or the other, while we can rejoice that two such writers await our pleasure. Each wrote in the manner suited to his genius.

Naturally enough, John Cowper's energies were all reserved for this big book during the time it was being written, and his name disappears from the bibliographies for a couple of years, except for the curious little report of his debate with Bertrand Russell on 'Is Modern Marriage a Failure?' in which John said it was not and Russell said it was—and 1,010 people in the audience agreed with Russell, and 990 with John. I was once told by a member of that audience that there was an odd contrast between the speakers. Russell made his point and sat down, but when it was John's turn 'you had time to go out for a drink and know he would still be at it when you got back!'

One other small item came from John during the writing of *Glastonbury*. This was his essay on Dorothy M. Richardson, a writer whose genius he considered to have been consistently underrated. In 1931 her long sequence of novels under the overall title *Pilgrimage* was nearing completion. This work is, of course, a cornerstone in developing the 'stream of consciousness' technique of the novel, and indeed the term 'stream of consciousness' was apparently first used (by May Sinclair, in 1918) in discussing Dorothy Richardson's novels. John Cowper's essay, published as a small book by Joiner and Steele in 1931, was perhaps designed to send Dorothy Richardson new readers; and perhaps it did. But it is not one of his major critical essays; there seems to be in it an element of special pleading, as though he were concerned not only to convince his readers, but to convince himself. It lacks the sustained excitement and enthusiasm of his essays on the masters: unless indeed this is the reaction of a reader not carried along by it. John says that there are readers who will find the story of Miriam 'dull', and this certainly is the danger the vast novel must face; *Pilgrimage* is easy to begin upon, not so easy to follow to the end. In this it is at a disadvantage compared with long novels written in the traditional narrative style, such as (say) Henry Williamson's *A Chronicle of Ancient Sunlight*, which is as fresh at the twelfth volume as at the first. It is of interest, however, to note that John Cowper was writing an essay on Miss Richardson *at this time*; because *A Glastonbury Romance* exhibits the stream of consciousness in a new way; the stream of consciousness here is not of a person, but of a place. The town of Glastonbury is essentially a character (and a major character) in the book, its history, its legends, its *mystique* being almost consciously and physically present, brooding over the human events, influencing, conditioning, modifying them. 'There is all the way through the book', the author wrote, 'a constant undercurrent of secret reference to the Grail Legends, various incidents and characters playing roles parallel to those in the old romances of the Grail, not without various furtive dips into that world of weird ritual and mythology made so much of in T. S. Eliot's "Wasteland". It does not go to work with the pedantry of Joyce using the *Odyssey* in "Ulysses"—but there is a vague sort of parallel to all that!' More formally, in the Preface to the 1955 edition, he speaks of seeking to describe 'the effect of a particular legend, a special myth, a unique tradition, from the remotest past in human history, upon a particular spot on the surface of this planet together with its crowd of inhabitants of every age and every type of character'. But this is not all: for as we read, not only are we aware of the Grail legend, and the old Glastonbury legends exerting an influence on the characters, but we become aware that this influence is *consciously exerted*. The Grail, King Arthur's sword, the tormented entity at Mark's Court, are all 'taking a hand' and working definite changes in men's thinking and behaviour, just as the sad wraith of Miss Rowe does in *The Owl, The Duck, and—Miss Rowe! Miss Rowe!*

Glastonbury is not only as long as five or six ordinary novels. Each of those five or six might be expanded into another; for there is an astonishing wealth of plot and characterization, and the book is much more than in the usual use of the phrase, 'a slice of life'. It is, again in a trite phrase, 'taking the lid off' the town of Glastonbury. Love, politics, religion, commerce, affairs, are all exposed and examined. The reader is in like position with the observing Immortals in Hardy's *Dynasts,* looking down.

There are, for example, half a dozen love stories, and these are each concerned with a different aspect of love. There is the frustrated love of the elder Dekker for his son's mistress, Nell. There is Sam Dekker's love, at first innocent and natural, and later tainted by religion into something abnormal and unrewarding. There is Philip Crow's illicit love for Persephone Spear, and the love of her husband Dave, undemanding of her, unsatisfying for her. John Crow's love for his cousin Mary the author speaks of as 'vicious', as he does of Wolf Solent's love-making with Gerda; just what is here implied we are not told, but it would seem to be in some degree a perverted love in which there is no physical consummation. More conventionally 'earthy' is Will Zoyland's love for Nell, and Tom Barter's for Tossie Stickles. These are not all, for I have not mentioned the strange, sad love of Owen Evans for Cordelia Geard, the love of Crummie Geard for Sam Dekker, or Rachel Zoyland's for the young poet Athling; but all these are separate stories, separately worked out, some, it is true, at greater length or in greater detail, but all sufficiently for the reader to know 'what happened'. They cover almost every aspect of love, its ecstasies, its disappointments, its sacrifices, its fulfilments. The love of young people for one another, the love of young for old and old for young, the loves of ordinary folk and the loves of madmen, misfits, saints and sinners! Here too are love of God, love of one's neighbour, love of power, love of self, love of money; selfish or generous or hopeless or triumphant love, they are all here.

I have said that the town of Glastonbury is a major character. The crisis of the whole book lies here. What is to be Glastonbury's future, the future of a town saturated in history and legend? Is it to be fixed and unalterable, like a fossil; or to go forward to new ways? This is a question that may well be asked in many towns, and it is an urgent one. One thing or the other: crumbling walls and ruins, or springing factories and prosperity, these seem to be the alternative prospects, until Mr Geard comes along with his plans for a religious pageant and a religious revival. These would revitalize Glastonbury, bring needed money into the town, but capitalize on assets already apparent, the abbey, the Grail legend, the ancient association with Joseph of Arimathaea. The commercial interest is represented by Philip Crow, owner of a large local dye works, who is exploiting the tin deposits in and around Wookey Hole Cave. Mr Geard represents the faction (is indeed himself almost its only member) which seeks to develop a religious centre at Glastonbury. A third interest lies with the workers —Philip Crow is the town's largest employer of labour—and these are Communist dominated. These three incompatible elements do battle for the soul of the town.

In his *Autobiography* John Cowper Powys says he was always at home with Catholics, Jews and Communists. He seems hardly so when he writes about them, which is curious. Catholics figure hardly at all in his novels, and Jews make no separate impact. His Communists are caricatures and this is especially so in the case of Red Robinson in *A Glastonbury Romance*. Robinson, with his exaggerated Cockneyisms and his violent speeches, is altogether unsuited to run an important political machine, and would not have been given the opportunity in real life. He is out of scale, too much of a good thing. Dave Spear, on the other hand, is wishy-washy and ineffective. I don't think the Communist Party would have had much use for either of them. There is in *Weymouth Sands* a character who would have been perfect in Robinson's job—the young 'town official', Sippy Ballard. In that novel he is not a Communist, but by general temperament and character he would have made an excellent organizer for the Glastonbury experiment.

It is an oversimplification, in looking at so vast a novel, to make any one or two events central and decisive, and to say, here is the main theme, or this is the climax, the crisis. The pageant is central, certainly, but simultaneously with its preparation many other events are going forward, and their omission would impoverish the tale. The flood is also a key to the whole, but not the only key. Of great significance is the story of Mr Evans, slowly unfolded, submerged often but never far under the surface, a great lost unhappy character such as few contemporary novelists could have created. Another entirely convincing and pathetic character is Tom Barter—and readers of John's *Autobiography* will be reminded in him of Tom Jones—a man savagely frustrated, a failure, looking for what consolation he can find with tea-shop waitresses and barmaids, but capable of a loyalty, a generosity and an integrity even the 'saint' Sam Dekker might envy. There are rich lesser characters, a score of them, Young Tewsy, the brothel door-keeper, and old Weatherwax with his bawdy songs, and the dying Tittie Petherton. The great creation of course is Bloody Johnny Geard, complete, rounded, alive. Bloody Johnny is surely one of the most *convincing* characters in all of English fiction. He behaves as we expect him to even though until we open the pages of this book we have never heard of him. What he says and does (we feel) is what Bloody Johnny *would* say and do. There is great skill in the build-up of this character, and by a hundred small touches he is brought vividly alive, from his first appearance, when he announces his grand design through a mouth filled with sponge-cake, to the moment when he deliberately allows himself to drown: and never more alive and aware than at the end. Geard is preposterous on a grand scale, and that is why he is convincing; Robinson is preposterous on a normal scale, and that is why he does not convince.

In *A Glastonbury Romance* we find John Cowper's first large-scale employment of the supernatural as an integral element of the story. There are forces invisibly working, and not in support of the human characters, from the very first page; we see very little of them, but we are always aware of them. Glastonbury is the shrine not of the Holy Grail only, but of unnamed, unnameable pagan mysteries rooted in pre-history; it is impossible to say what forces the madness of an Owen Evans, the faith of a Johnny Geard, might not unleash. We cannot be sure exactly what happened when Geard slept in the haunted chamber at Mark's Court, or of the overall significance to the story of John Crow's vision at Pomparles Bridge. The 'saint', Sam Dekker, has his vision, too, and John Cowper's sure insight is apparent in a characteristic touch here, for amid the ecstasy of seeing the veritable Grail itself in glory Sam wonders what kind of a fish it is shining within: 'Is it a tench?' More, at that moment of supreme revelation Sam cries out to Christ himself, 'Is it a tench?'

This novel is an inexhaustible quarry for the commentator. It has scores of magnificent passages, scores of crowded unforgettable scenes. The bawdy party at Mother Legge's, with the moaning figure of Tittie Petherton propped up by the fire. The vigil in the haunted room at Mark's Court. The triumphant fiasco of Geard's grand opening of his Saxon Arch, when he arrives drunk and stupid, and raises a child from the dead. The conspiracy to murder John Crow, initiated by mad Bet Chinnock because she loves him. Geard's night in the bed of the

dying Tittie. The crowded canvas of the pageant. The tender hours
of Nell and Sam together at Whitelake Cottage. The reviewer [1] who
quoted from Dryden, 'Here is God's plenty!' used the right phrase. It
would be absurd to try to represent the book by a quotation. The
writing always has beauty, sometimes rises to sublimity. It has humour,
richly and generously. It has compassion, humanity, understanding. It
is bawdy and religious, gross and tender. I see no cause to dissent from
J. D. Beresford's judgment that *A Glastonbury Romance* is one of the
greatest novels in the world.

[1] Canon Norman A. Matthews, speaking in the B.B.C. Welsh Home Service,
4 August 1955. Professor G. Wilson Knight uses the same phrase of *Owen
Glendower* in *A Review of English Literature*, January 1963. Dryden—a master
of the apt phrase—used it of Chaucer.

─── 20 ───

WHEN T. F. Powys published *Mr. Weston's Good Wine* he published a new work, recently completed, not something taken from the pile accumulating 'in the cupboard'. From this time on the successive publications represented new work, with only trivial exceptions, and, again with trivial exceptions—a few of the short stories—they are works conceived and written in full maturity. Where there are weaknesses (and what writer is without these?) they are inherent, and do not arise from the inexperience or uncertainty of a prentice hand. The next major publication after *Mr. Weston*—a collection of stories intervened—was *Fables* (1929), and this some critics would set beside *Mr. Weston* as the author's crowning achievement. Of the short stories in *The House with the Echo* something has been said already; a few of the stories are early, all are short, and the general balance of the collection is uneven. It does not carry the weight of *The White Paternoster*, which followed in 1930, or of the two later collections, and none of them individually has the authority of Charles Prentice's nearly faultless selection in *God's Eyes A-Twinkle*, published in 1947 after Theodore himself had 'gone out of business'.

The fables—nineteen of them—are of course short stories, but from their special nature as fables the book has a unity and cohesion no random gathering of separate tales could have, and it gains by being read straight through (though not quickly) as a novel would be read. Here if anywhere in a single book of his may be found Theodore's major ideas and his particular philosophy—though this is never to be understood directly from what he says, for no writer more certainly needs to be thought upon and pondered over than he, if the marrow is to be reached.

Traditionally, the fable is didactic; it points a moral, and typically only one; we learn from 'The Tortoise and the Hare' that the race is not always to the swift, and by implication we learn the values of modesty, humility and perseverance. But Theodore extends the scope of the form, so that any one of his fables may teach the attentive reader several lessons; if he had written 'The Tortoise and the Hare' he would probably have shown that the race *is* to the swift, but that it is better not to win. Moreover, his intention is not primarily didactic; there may indeed be a lesson stated, and a possible answer given, but he is not telling the reader to attend, rather he is inviting him to think.

The idea of taking sticks and stones for characters was given to Theodore by Llewelyn, who said, 'Write about anything; write about that log of wood and that old boot', and perhaps the hint was enough to start him off, just as a similar hint set Cowper to *The Task*, and many another writer to his work through the ages. But, from the moment of beginning to write, a writer is on his own; when Charles II suggested the plan of *The Medal* to John Dryden (if he really did) he cannot have had any notion how the poem would turn out. There is nothing of Llewelyn in the *Fables*, but there is everything of Theodore.

These fables have originality of situation, plot and climax, and it is a 'Theodorian' originality; it is not only that nobody else has thought of that touch, or this, but also that nobody else would or could have thought of it: for example, a uniquely Theodorian character is Mr Pim, the church clerk at Madder, who not only had never taken holy communion, but was quite ignorant of what the affair implied, until the vicar got him in a corner one Christmas morning and explained it all; at which Mr Pim feels impelled to instruct all the congregation:

'Mr. Tucker do tell I', said Pim, addressing himself to Miss Jarrett, 'that the Lord God, the Creator of the world, who be named Christ by drunken folk when pub do close, do change 'Isself into they scrimpy bites of Mr. Johnson's bread that thee do take and eat up at church railings.'

Finding no sympathetic response in the living, Pim goes on to tell this piece of news to his friend John Toole, who is buried in the church-yard, and Mr Toole replies with another typically Theodorian reaction.

'If 'ee do happen', said the muffled voice, 'to get a word with thik crumb of bread that be the Lord on High, ask 'E to be kind enough to look over Johnnie Toole at the last day, for I be well content to bide where I be now. There baint no work to do here and all be ease and comfort, and many a merry story do we bones tell together.'

This might almost be Theodore speaking for himself. 'Powys likes monotony.' When in his later years he would tell visitors if they did not find him when next they visited the house to 'look for me there', with a gesture towards Mappowder churchyard adjoining, the gesture implied no regret and something more than resignation. He would sit in the church, not from a belief in the religion practised there, but because it was quiet.

Mr Pim goes along after he has finished ringing the bell to share in the rite of communion for the first time in his life; and, being unpractised, he drops a bit of the wafer. After the service he lingers in the church, thinking upon this new experience and speculating about the nature of God.

After he had eaten God, Pim wondered what God was like. He supposed that God would very much resemble the landlord at the village inn. Mr. Hookes, the landlord, looked like a judge, and indeed he might well have been the creator of all men.

''E did draw I out of 'Is great barrel into a little cup,' said Pim aloud, 'and when I die 'E do but empty I again into the dirt from whence I came. They be 'Is notions. But if I do eat 'E, between meals, and become as lordly as 'Isself, all me happiness be gone.

'And 'tis likely', continued Pim, eyeing in a cautious manner the crumb upon the floor, ''E won't be best pleased wi' Pim for dropping 'E upon church carpet so carelessly. 'Taint proper for a Holy Crumb to be so fallen. And what be I? Only a small worm of the earth, while 'E it were who did make the round world, the seas, and wold Madder Hill. 'Twouldn't do for Pim to go to heaven no more than for Johnnie Toole. Maybe 'E'll let we bide a merry family. Some do fall of a sudden, some bent and tottering like wold Barker do tarry long, but all do go to dust.

'I be sorry', said Pim, addressing himself to the crumb, 'that I did swallow t'other half of 'E.'

At this point the crumb joins in the talk and points out the delights of Heaven, but Pim persists in requesting that he and Johnnie Toole may be allowed to 'bide in ground at last day'. Although the crumb is God, Mr Pim leaves Him with a poorer conceit of himself—'Shepherd do shout Thee's name to 'is dog, Carter Beer do damn old Boxer wi' Thee . . .'—until the crumb remarks 'in a low voice', 'I almost wish I had entered into a mouse instead of a man'.

Mr Pim has the last word, '. . . Thee may do thik now . . .' and the church mouse creeps out and devours the Holy Crumb. Although it is one of the shorter fables, 'Mr. Pim and the Holy Crumb' is not to be digested all at a single reading. Moreover, the lesson when learned is not always just what one might expect it to be. A persuasive case is made that Madder churchyard be a better place to bide than the shining courts of heaven. Again, in 'The Hassock and the Psalter' we perceive from the moment when the psalter first speaks that it is vain, arrogant, disobedient and selfish; and the hassock is dutiful, humble, loyal, etc. etc.—exactly the hassock to be given a new cover as a reward for its virtues. But when Mr Spurdle the new churchwarden comes—and it is Mr Spurdle for whom the hassock has been praying, and for whose welfare the psalter hasn't given a damn—it is the psalter with its fine golden clasp which Mr Spurdle takes up with pleasure, and the old, worn, faded and virtuous hassock which he casts into the fire. Consider also that when God himself drops in one Sunday morning at the church he is apparently put into an excellent humour by the prayer of Farmer Shore: 'Farmer Shore was praying that all the corn in the country, except his own, should be eaten by rats, worms and birds, spoilt by rain, or left to rot in the fields.'

The hassock's loyalty is its own reward, if there be a reward, but in 'The Corpse and the Flea' the Flea meets with a generous appreciation of its loyalty when it elects to remain in the coffin and be buried alive. The dead Mr Johnson is deserted by all—by friends, relations, neighbours—and the life that remains in the house, mice, beetles, spiders, is much preoccupied with its own narrow viewpoint—the spider, for example, is enraged because the old woman who laid out the corpse tore down its web. Only the Flea cares that Mr Johnson is alone in his death, and determines to share his end. 'I will be with you always,' it affirms, and the shadow of a figure passes over the coffin, with arms outstretched.

Here, and often in the fables, the symbolism is clear enough. We remember the words of Jesus, 'Lo, I am with you always', and we can think that He is the Flea, or that the Flea is quoting scripture; and we know what the shadow is that passes overhead. The symbolism is not so integral here as in *Mr. Weston*; it is an added extra, in no way essential to the principal themes, and perhaps even an embarrassment to them.

Every reader of these fables will choose his own among them as the most moving or the most impressive. Each is a sermon, apt to its occasion. They display all the virtues—and not seldom show them going unrewarded, unless the reward be something not at once apparent; and they exhibit all the vices, neither approving nor disapproving, merely recording and leaving the reader to choose.

In general the characters reason, speak and behave like humans, (although, admittedly, like Theodorian humans, always a little odd). In this they follow the main stream of the tradition, from Aesop on, and in this they differ from John Cowper's articulate inanimates whose language is close enough to common speech, but whose impulses, reactions and motives are sub- or super-human—and even this is only a part of it. The club in Chapter One of *Atlantis* is aware of being a club, thinks club-like thoughts, has a club-like point of view, and is at once reconciled to being a club and glad about it. But the dish clout and the old pan in Theodore's first fable are characterized on the very first page as 'trusty old household servants' and there would be no essential shifting in emphasis if they were spoken of throughout as a cook and a butler; the terms 'clout' and 'pan' are used within the literary convention of the fable form; clout, pan, lantern, slate, stone, tree—they are used to underwrite human paradoxes and human preoccupations. In John Cowper the introduction as characters of such things as a club or a worm *extends* the human experience and supplements it; the fable has a narrower scope, whether by Theodore Powys or Aesop, or any of the writers in between; it does not extend the human experience by its use of inanimates, but it does underline it. The purpose is to arrest, surprise and startle the reader, to make him think, to make him pay attention. Such a use is abundantly justified when— as here—it forces the reader to linger over the implications, disturbing, comforting, or enlightening, which may be found in 'Darkness and Nathaniel' and 'John Pardy and the Waves'.

The *Fables* were followed in 1930 by *Kindness in a Corner*, after which there remained only one major work to come, although Theodore was to live more than twenty years after its publication. This was *Unclay* (1931), the last of the novels.

I confess I find the title itself a rather absurd one; the word means the act in which Death takes away life; Death's warrant to kill, without which he cannot proceed, carries the command 'Unclay', with the name or names of those to whom Death must come. For Theodore it undoubtedly had a special metaphysical significance related to the mortal clay to be 'undone'; but I find the word does not look right, does not feel or sound right; I think it is a failure.

Perhaps this is true also of the book, which certainly lacks the easy untroubled authority which impresses itself upon every page of *Mr. Weston*, a novel in which we feel the author's powers are never fully extended, in which there is never any suggestion that he has undertaken more than he can perform. Such a doubt does offer itself, once and again, in *Unclay*. But all the same for that it is a unique and extraordinary book, full of excellence and originality; a book entirely its author's.

With *Unclay* we find ourselves back in Dodder, a village we have visited before. Canon Dibben—whom also we know—has been given preferment from Dodder to the larger parish of Stonebridge, and Mr Hayhoe, a mild and somewhat melancholy man, is to replace him—if and when Lord Bullman decides to confirm his appointment. The usual village events and intrigues are in progress when the story opens, one seeking to marry, another to rape, a third to swindle, and these several ambitions are furthered or hindered by the arrival of a stranger, John Death. The argument so far is the same as in *Mr. Weston*; Weston comes to Folly Down, Death to Dodder, and for a while everything is conditioned by their presence. But whereas Mr Weston is able to conduct his business satisfactorily, Death is inhibited by two factors: first, that he has lost the written orders under which alone he can operate, and second that Mr Jar the tinker, who is in some sort his employer, is also in the neighbourhood keeping an eye on what goes forward.

In no writer is a willing suspension of disbelief more necessary to the reader than in T. F. Powys; pause for a moment to consider the implications of his plots, and all is lost. In *Unclay*, for example, we are told that Death carries a bit of paper, signed by God, upon which is written the name or names of those he is to kill or 'unclay'; and without this paper he cannot operate. On his coming to Dodder Death loses his piece of paper, and one of those named in it finds it and retains it. Death spends some time in Dodder looking for his paper and also 'taking a holiday', and during all that period, if the implications are followed, nobody can have died in all the world: a big absurdity to swallow. For Theodore it can hardly have seemed so, for it has been suggested that for him East Chaldon, which equals Dodder, or Madder or Tadnol and the rest, for him this *was* the whole world. So Death might restrain his hand for a couple of weeks. He employs himself in sharpening his scythe, looking in a desultory manner for the missing warrant, and making love to the girls of the village. He mixes with all, of course, as a mortal, and only occasionally by a hint or a gesture gives an intimation of his true nature. Tinker Jar, on the other hand, keeps mysteriously aloof (although now and again he mends a kettle). His appearances and disappearances stamp him an immortal, he moves in a supernatural haze. He loves to walk on Madder Hill, which overlooks the village; on this hill there is a bush which is sometimes seen to be burning, but is never consumed.

It is something of an oversimplification to say that the story hinges on the fact that Death falls in love with the girl he is in Dodder to 'unclay', and that the action lies in whether he or the man she already loves shall win her; for there are a number of lesser but important other threads to the story, and indeed *Unclay* contains more, in this sense, than any other of Theodore's novels. There is the sad story of Mr and Mrs Hayhoe and their love for their young dead son. The story of pretty Susie Dawe, loving Joe Bridle, loved by Death, married to the brutal Farmer Mere. The story of Winnie Huddy and Mr Solly, who fears all women and can only live with his sister because she thinks herself to be a camel. And the related threads of cruelty, avarice and malice, which are present always in Theodore's stories. This novel has memorable characters among its supporting cast: the unpleasant Mr Dady, who loves to kill, his thumb eternally poised to press down upon a trapped fly; Mr Titball, the obsequious retired old retainer, with his uncritical reverence for Lord Bullman; Mere, the evil farmer; Sarah Bridle, the camel lady, and Solly, who thinks of girls as turnips.

Unclay is full of the detached, detachable aphorisms which are Theodore's alone; if anyone put together, in the manner of the nineteenth century, a 'T. F. Powys Birthday Book' ('compiled by a Lady') it would be a remarkable affair, and it would lean heavily upon *Unclay*. Like *Mr. Weston*, but in a different manner, this book is about Death and Love, the two inescapable facts of life.

Sometimes the passages a reader will mark with his pencil in the margin as he goes along have the polish of La Rochefoucauld—'As one begets a child, so one begets an enemy—unknowingly.' Others carry the simplicity of George Herbert: 'Love is heavy to carry. Though at first it settles upon its victim like a butterfly, it quickly changes into lead.' 'In all the wide world there is no flattery like the flattery of an old servant.' 'One would like to know what the ground thinks when a girl steps upon it'—but this last, surely, could be none but Theodore's.

21

IT is easy to keep track of Theodore biographically, for he stayed in one place, and even his day-to-day, almost his hour-to-hour, movements may be plotted and predicted; but he is for this reason an impossible subject for biography proper, which must be concerned with diverse events if it is to continue interesting to read. It is less easy to follow John Cowper's movements up and down America, and probably this random itinerary can never be plotted; but we saw him last settled with apparent permanence in Hillsdale. We now turn again to Llewelyn. In spring 1931 he and Alyse returned to England, and in the autumn they settled at the cottage called Chydyok in the downs above East Chaldon; here they remained, one or two short excursions apart, until the time came for Llewelyn's removal to Switzerland in the winter of 1936. The five years at Chydyok did not see the production of any long major book, although in this period *Love and Death* was begun; but they saw the publication of many of his finest short essays. It was probably *Earth Memories* and *Dorset Essays* which first made the English reader fully aware of Llewelyn, and these collections would be supported by the frequent appearance of his essays in periodicals of wide circulation—for example, a series in the mass circulation newspaper, the *Daily Herald*. Through such a medium Llewelyn would be reaching a general reading public John came before much more rarely, and Theodore never at all. Llewelyn was also at this time consolidating his reputation in free-thinking circles by such work as the essays in *Damnable Opinions* and *Rats in the Sacristy*, many of which appeared serially in such journals as *The Rationalist Annual*, the *Aryan Path*, and the *New English Weekly*. The years at Chydyok were years of journalism rather than of writing books, and this is a point worth making, because the writing of journalism imposes a different discipline upon the writer; there are press days and deadlines to be met, and the subject written upon dictates to the writer its own necessities of scale, treatment and length, which must be reconciled with the needs of the periodical in whose columns it is to appear. Alone of the three brothers, Llewelyn was a journalist in the way Fleet Street knows the term, and in this sense he alone of them was a professional. Theodore indeed is not in competition: he never 'wrote for the papers'. John's journalism was occasional and erratic.

During the years at Chydyok Llewelyn published seven books: *The Life and Times of Anthony à Wood* (1932); *Now that the Gods are Dead* (1932); *Glory of Life* (1934); *Earth Memories* (1934); *Damnable Opinions* (1935); *Dorset Essays* (1935) and *The Twelve Months* (1936). Two others published in 1937 were written at Chydyok, *Somerset Essays* and *Rats in the Sacristy*. Many essays published in periodicals at the same time are uncollected, and some essays of the period are unpublished. It is an impressive output of work for a man in Llewelyn's state of health, and he was seriously ill, apart from his usual need for care, on three occasions—in 1932, in 1933 and in 1934. In 1936 he had pleurisy. He must often have worked under great stress and difficulty, but if so this does not appear in his work; the polemical essays are vigorous and uncompromising, the others enshrine his sunniest affirmations of the bounty of life, the beauty of nature, and the delight of living.

His controversial beliefs and ideas he gathered mainly into *Damnable Opinions*, where the essays often enough reiterate his lengthier and more formal utterances in *Impassioned Clay* and the other two long philosophical essays. The biographical essays are mostly gathered into *Rats in the Sacristy*, although several were more appropriate to *Dorset* or *Somerset Essays*, and appear there. Because the subjects chosen for biographical commentary are so often originals, eccentrics and enemies of the Church, there is scope in these essays for the expression of Llewelyn's own opinions, and they may well be read alongside *Damnable Opinions*. No reader having in his recollection the quotations I have made above from *Impassioned Clay* and *The Pathetic Fallacy* could fail to recognize the same mind, and the same pen, in *Damnable Opinions*:

For two thousand years the Christian Churches have had at their service the best minds of each age, and yet even so it is not easy to give credence to their anthropocentric explanation of life. The riot of the universe, with its star streams and star clouds, with its unpredictable electrons and quivering wave-groups capable of aggregating into forms of vegetable life, animal life, bird life, fish life, microbe life, as conspicuous for ferocity as for brevity: life living upon life, the cow destroyed by the lion, the grass by the cow—and this tumultuous torrent of sap and blood under the spell of hate and desire existing apparently at hazard, disorder rising out of order, discipline out of rebellion; heartlessness here, compassion there, intermixed at random, all at odds, all rushing forward into an unknown future pell-mell, does not suggest that a cosmogony too closely identified with man's wishes is likely to approximate to the real metaphysical solution.

('Cardinal Newman'.)

Such a passage moves with a breathless conviction, the long sentence piling up its effects as it proceeds, and ending with the irony of a man master of his argument. Sometimes Llewelyn's style is a little self-conscious, but only when he is writing of less weighty matters. When he writes directly from the heart, on some theme which is in his blood and marrow, he has no need to hesitate over words to choose the very one.

I have said that Llewelyn was a journalist, and this book supports my point. These brief essays on 'The Oxford Group', 'Morality', 'The Poetic Faith' and similar themes are never 'last words' on their subject, nor are they complete statements of a point of view. They offer starting points, points for discussion, sometimes a superficial view—superficial in the sense of not striking deep, rather than in the sense of trivial or mean. They are often enough parentheses and foot-notes; no one would suppose morality to be a subject fully covered in five pages. But because they are journalism they are not negligible. Works of enduring literature have begun as journalism, and these papers have a distinction of thought and style which will carry them far and long from the columns in which they were first printed.

Naturally, Llewelyn thought highly of the essays in which he gave the most persuasive and eloquent expression to his religious beliefs; but it was not by these that his influence as a writer during his lifetime must be measured. From the days of 'Are you the Llewelyn Powys who writes on Africa?' it was his familiar essays that brought him the widest recognition. And how good they are! He was fortunate that he wrote at a time when the essay was an acceptable form, widely published in newspapers and magazines, and at a time when publishers were prepared as a matter of ordinary publishing practice to issue collections of essays in volume form. Neither of these factors has operated so favourably for the writer in the past twenty-five years. Scores of journals and magazines have disappeared since the war, including most of those to which Llewelyn regularly contributed; and few have taken their place. The book of essays is probably less easy to place with a publisher even than the book of poems, and we find ourselves today in a situation where a literature rich in great poets and great essayists has almost ceased to function in either of these two directions. Poetry, it is true, is healthier now than at any time since the internal renaissance always briefly produced by a war; but the essay remains an outcast, so far as the book publisher is concerned. Gone are the professional essayists of the twenties and thirties—Hilaire Belloc, G. K. Chesterton, E. V. Lucas, Robert Lynd—and we cannot foresee the return of conditions in which their kind might flourish. That Llewelyn Powys was able to write essays is a matter for satisfaction, because economic necessity always dictated his course, and if he had not enjoyed a market he would of necessity have abandoned the essay form for some other. He would have persisted, perhaps, in the writing of novels.[1] He might have tried again with biography. He would have written well, whatever happened. But the essay is so exactly suited to his genius, and makes so large an element in his work—both in quantity and quality—that without it he must have been another, and I think a lesser, writer.

There are a total of ninety-one essays in the three principal collections now under notice, and *A Baker's Dozen* (1939) and *Swiss Essays* (1947) added forty others. These, with a handful that may be taken from other volumes, and with a somewhat larger handful omitted as nearer akin to biographical and critical studies, represent the body of familiar essays by which alone, if his other writings were lost, he would inevitably hold a high place in modern English letters. I will single out one or two from each volume, for it would be impossible here to discuss all those I have specially marked for comment.

Earth Memories includes the two obituary essays already mentioned, on the deaths of Ann Reid and Walter Franzen, and the account of his father's birthplace, Stalbridge, in one of the most evocative of all his essays, 'Out of the Past'. Here also are examples of his close, sympathetic, but realistic observation of nature, notably in 'The Partridge' and 'An Owl and a Swallow'. Llewelyn is never sentimental about

[1] Among his projects was a smuggling book for boys on similar lines to *Treasure Island*, but against a background of the Dorset coast.

wild life, but his account of the death of the hen partridge, leaving her unhatched eggs to perish, is the more moving for being quietly matter of fact. The essays in this collection are somewhat wider in range of subject than those in the Somerset and Dorset series, but they are stamped with the landscapes he loved as deeply as any that followed; and as always, he is prompted to reflection as he walks on the hills by the sea's edge:

> Every religion is as brittle as an empty snail shell in dry weather, as quick to disappear as cuckoo-spit in a summer hedge that conceals at its centre no green fly. The secret to be remembered is that nothing matters, nothing but the momentary consciousness of each individual as he opens his eyes upon a spectacle that knows naught of ethics. Let us, as best we may, reconcile our minds to the fact that all our self-imposed tasks, our political engineering, our brave talk have actually, under the shadow of Eternity, no consequence. Our idealism is treacherous. It is a moonshine path over a deep sea. We are cursed souls each one of us and resemble nothing so much as jackdaws flying about the radiant cliffs of God pretending to be sea-gulls.
>
> And yet there is no cause to despair. Merely to have come to consciousness at all constitutes an inestimable privilege. The past is nothing, the future is nothing, the *eternal now* alone is of moment. This is understood well enough by every living creature but man.
>
> ('A Butterfly Secret'.)

The two series of country essays, Dorset and Somerset, differ from most writing about the rural scene. They are less descriptive than interpretative. They are landscapes with people, for even on the empty downs above his house Llewelyn observed a constant movement, if not of shepherd and crofter, then of fox and cormorant, and if not of these, then of the ghosts of the ancient peoples whose villages lie under the turf. Often enough, he is conscious of all these elements, as these closing paragraphs show:

> At the top of this open hedgeless track-way there may be seen a most awe-inspiring acre, an acre used at one time by the ancients as a burying place for their kings. To come up this ordinary Dorset cart-track between fields of grass-green corn, and to find oneself amongst these silent tumuli, is a signal experience. It becomes suddenly apparent that this homely work-a-day lane

leads to the august necropolis of a people contemporaneous with the later dynasties of Egypt. I know of few hillsides that offer a more harmonious resting place than does this down above Sutton Poyntz. The short turf here is fragrant with thyme; and the Bay of Weymouth, with its wonderful classical curve, lies full in view. Presently the Lulworth pleasure steamer comes churning across the calm waters of the bay, its old-fashioned paddles on larboard and starboard, working as steadily as mill wheels to bring holiday passengers safe into port. It is evening and in the field at the foot of the downs a chestnut mare is peacefully grazing. Her foal, with starts of simulated panic, from time to time comes galloping up to her on unsteady spindle legs, its young shapely head held high after the mettled manner of its kind. A herring gull crosses the valley in the direction of Redcliff Bay. The bird flies with the leisurely flight of a wild fowl whose creature wants have been satisfied without stint.

A boy and a girl have even yet the most beautiful of all their hours to spend together, the twilight hour of a summer's evening. Tangible, audible, visible, it is the poetry of life to those lovers, their awakened insights apprehending deep mysteries.

> *Tho' thou art worshipp'd by the names divine*
> *Of Jesus and Jehovah, thou art still*
> *The son of Morn in weary Night's decline*
> *The lost traveller's dream under the hill.*

('The White Horse.')

But he knows also that the most peaceful of evenings is less than wholly idyllic, and this is no pretty week-end view of the country scene. Time and again he reminds us of the pitiless, relentless cruel struggle for life of every creature that is born, from man to maggot. The rat kills the partridge, the dog kills the rat, and the maggot kills the man.

It was once said of John Cowper that 'he makes you feel important'. His enthusiasm took no account of appearance, but he looked beneath it and saw that the beginning poet might yet become a Milton. Llewelyn Powys exercised this same sympathy in writing of his west country heroes and worthies. He approaches the Montacute poet Thomas Shoel with the same respect that he would accord to Shelley, and this quality of disinterested inquiry is all too rare among literary critics. It is a pity he did not write more essays on these minor but not negligible figures; another, on the Rev. Henry Hardin, contains the justification: '... how rewarding it is to read of the simple life of so dutiful a servant "of the God of the burning bush"'; by such a study the bluebells beneath the beech trees in Park Covert, the Abbey pond by the great sycamore, the quarry-men with their yellow trousers come to lose something of the inconsequent mirage quality they often possess for my mind; lose it to become, below the mocking mackerel skies of my childhood memories, part of a solid reality as firm, tangible, and stubborn as the Ham stone in Washlane'. For simple goodness Llewelyn has an immediate sympathy, whatever his reservations about the Christian faith; and some of his finest essays speak eloquently and persuasively of the clergymen in country places, Henry Hardin the Baptist, Sidney Osborne the Anglican of Durweston, William Langdon and his own father, of Montacute, and others. He did not associate these harmless and helpful lives with the great untruths, as he saw them, of the organized Churches. He has another gallery of country folk, Nancy Cooper the beggar-woman of Montacute, whose life possessed a 'ballad quality', and the stoical, honourable, unostentatious Herbert Parker of Osmington. Like John, Llewelyn felt a high appreciation of the qualities of such unlettered folk—he dedicates *The Twelve Months* to his farmer-neighbour James Cobb—and everywhere in his writings he shows a special appreciation of those who work with their hands. I remember his quick approval when I told him my father had been a shoe-mender,[1] and his praise of the honest calling of an ironmonger, when I told him I followed it.

There is a certain territorial unity in *Dorset Essays* which is lacking in its successor. The author strays outside his native county only in a page here and there; but *Somerset Essays* contains many complete essays which lie entirely within Dorset, and others ranging into Devonshire, Capri, the Rocky Mountains, though back they come firmly to the fields and streams of his home. In a prefatory note to *Somerset Essays* he tells the purpose that guides him. It was not 'to produce formal handbooks', but 'rather it has been my endeavour, through meditations upon the past, and through memories of my own life-experience, to catch at moods common to all reflective country-bred people who feel themselves emotionally attached to cities, villages, lanes, and fields familiar to them since childhood'. Undoubtedly, the individually felt and recorded vision in these essays is what gives them

[1] 'A shoemaker's son is a prince born'—Llewelyn quotes this saying in *Swiss Essays*.

their unique value; not the fact that here is an account of Cadbury Camp, and there a notice of Sir John Harington, but the fact that they are Cadbury and Harington as seen by Llewelyn Powys and none other. He is the most involved personally of all the great essayists, whatever his subject; time and again the very starting point is a personal moment in time, be the subject entirely alien from that moment. His account of Nancy Cooper begins in the city of San Francisco, of which likely enough the old woman had never heard. He begins an essay on the Duke of Monmouth by recalling the gift of a bicycle when he was a lad at Montacute. An essay on the partridge of Switzerland is suggested by memories of the African Rift Valley.

'Princely journalism', so Ruskin once described the essays of Alice Meynell; and princely journalism were the essays of the twelve months which Llewelyn wrote for the *Daily Herald*, and which make so attractive a book under the design and with the wood engravings of Robert Gibbings. For information Llewelyn leans heavily on *The Book of Days* (as he acknowledges) but he writes of the seasons with a grace altogether beyond the excellent brothers Chambers. And here again the historical and legendary information is supplemented by facts and observations within his own experience, memories of Montacute, tags of country-lore from Chaldon, in among the high matters of Roman emperors naming months, and the natural lapse of the seasons running through them. Here as always he quotes felicitously, and indeed few contemporary writers are happier in quotation and allusion: his gift for it is perhaps best displayed in *Love and Death*.

But if he quotes happily from Lamb and Marvell and Spenser and the Bible and the old ballads we are not deceived into thinking all quotation ends here; and generations of later writers will find Llewelyn Powys a rich quarry to quote from. For classical quotation, says Johnson, is the literary man's parole; and Llewelyn Powys will be a classic.

22

THE extraordinary and concentrated effort required to write such a book as *A Glastonbury Romance* in less than two years would have left most writers exhausted. If not physically exhausted (but that too) certainly exhausted of invention. This was not so with John Cowper. Beside *Glastonbury*, *Weymouth Sands* is dwarfed, so far as bulk is concerned—it has less than six hundred pages. But it is dwarfed in no other respect. The invention is as rich, the characters as varied, the situations as engaging; and they are quite different from those in *Glastonbury*. That was a struggle between opposing powers, operating through people. The struggle in *Weymouth Sands* is all personal and human. There is nothing political involved, nothing religious, nothing ideological, apart from the tenuous thread of anti-vivisection feeling, which was to reappear so much more forcefully a year or two later in *Morwyn*. John Cowper would seem to have begun upon *Weymouth Sands* as soon as the last pages of *Glastonbury* went to the typist. The third great achievement of the years at Phudd Bottom was the *Autobiography*, and both these last works were published in the same year, 1934. It will be convenient to examine *Weymouth Sands* later, with the companion Dorset novel, *Maiden Castle*.

John Cowper Powys has written three or four works which must long endure and one cannot predict which will endure the longest; but perhaps it will be the *Autobiography*. As L. A. G. Strong has said, 'This book would have held and astonished me even if I had never heard Mr. Powys's name before'. Exactly: this book does not depend on the author's reputation, and indeed when opened it will not be found to be the life of an author or of a public figure. John Cowper rarely mentions any of his books, and although it is true there are many passing references to famous contemporaries, the book is not rich in anecdote and memoir. It goes far deeper; it is not a portrait of a man seen from the outside, but *seen from the inside*. Such a portrait will not be pretty, but it will be about as near to truth as human vision can get. That it is the greatest autobiography in the English language I have not the smallest doubt. I am aware that it may be asked, have I read them all?—and I am prepared to allow that until I have read the autobiographies of some hundreds or thousands of nonentities I must be prepared for this question. But I do not say I am certain of it, only that I do not doubt it.

How is the commentator to approach this great book? No amount of talking about it will be any sort of substitute for reading it. One may misquote Johnson and say, 'I would rather read it than praise it'. But some reflections and observations may be attempted.

This is not a formal autobiography with exact details and dates, and in a number of particulars it is admittedly incomplete. As I have said, John Cowper briefly mentions a few of his books, but most he doesn't refer to at all. He does give, it is true, a number of passages which add up to a sort of manifesto of his aims as a novelist; and throughout the *Autobiography* affords parallels and correspondences with the philosophical books. But for anything like a history of his life as a writer it is necessary to turn to the *Letters to Louis Wilkinson*, and these of course do not begin (in the published volume) until after the autobiography breaks off.

The other marked omission lies in his discussions about women. The book is dedicated to his dead mother, and the dedication in the American edition carries additional wording: 'Dedicated to Mary Cowper Powys, whose spirit I have followed in the only reticence in this book.' Just how this 'reticence' is allied to his mother's spirit I am not clear, but throughout the autobiography women appear but superficially. He never speaks of his wife, beyond an occasional brief mention. He says almost nothing of his mother or sisters. Of his loves and friendships with women he says, again, almost nothing. That he can write with unique insight of women any of his novels sufficiently shows, and in his philosophical writings there is a great deal about the relations between the sexes. He tells us a great deal also, by inference, about his personal sex impulses, both here and elsewhere; nor is this any sort of reticence based on shame or shyness (save the mark!). It goes deeper than I can follow.

It is not a formal autobiography in part because it does not proceed logically and chronologically, and in part because it does not take account of dates and similar exact data. It is true the book begins with the author's birth, and it ends when the narrative reaches the point his life has reached in the telling. It is also true that, very broadly, the external events follow one another in the right order. But this autobiography is most properly 'the growth of a poet's mind'. The external events are relevant only so far as they contribute to that growth—or hinder it, or modify or nourish it. It is the same with people, it is the same with places: never was the record of them more subjective. As for dates, the author says frankly he can never remember them, and he never tries to; this makes occasional difficulties for the biographer, because the *Autobiography* is the authority for a good many passages in John Cowper's life not comprehensively written of elsewhere. But as more and more letters and other material are published, this difficulty will in some degree disappear. The superficial appearance of a chronological progression suggested by the chapter heads—'Prep School', 'Cambridge', 'Europe', 'America', 'The War', is not supported by the text because within this framework he ranges freely over his life, and this is especially so in the central and later chapters. Again, the difficulty is created for the biographer, the student, the commentator. The general reader may be content to let it go—may indeed never notice this purely biographical inconsistency, in the fascination of seeing a mind and spirit grow.

The central portrait of John Cowper is surrounded by a memorable gallery of others. There is a great deal here about Llewelyn, and a notable character-sketch of their father; rather less about the other brothers, and this is particularly disappointing in the case of Theodore, for whom biographical material is so scanty elsewhere. But the short passages are rewarding, and they will always aid Theodore's readers and admirers in their attempts to reach an insight into that withdrawn and enigmatic character. John's generous appreciation of his brother Littleton has always interested me, for these were the two greatest opposites in all that diverse family, the nearest in birth, in all else poles apart. They would seem to meet only in a shared love of nature, and even here the approach was on the one hand a schoolmaster's and on the other a poet's.

But the great studies in character are not of his family, but of a group of his friends—a group scattered through his life. The fantastic and pathetic figure of Alfred de Kantzow comes first to mind, the old aristocrat with his pantheistic poems, praying late at night to a nameless 'first cause' for support and furtherance of his career—the career of a man in his seventies which had not yet even begun. Old de Kantzow, striding the hills behind Brighton, declaiming in pubs, composing stoical addresses to the Inanimate, making his wry comments on life: 'What an engaging situation, Powys!'

Another is Tom Jones, alone in Liverpool with his game leg, his soul-destroying job, his girls and his cigarettes, courageous and hopeless. 'Tom's a-cold now until the end of the world,' but he can no more be forgotten by a reader of this autobiography than the lad in the old Margate Hoy by the reader of Lamb. So, in a page or two, can a thing be placed and secured for ever. Longer, more spread over, are the portraits by inference of Louis Wilkinson and Arnold Shaw, the 'circus-manager'. Briefer, less rounded, those of some of his literary contemporaries: but these have their value, too, and there are good, satisfying glimpses (not always satisfyingly long) of Arthur Davison Ficke, Theodore Dreiser, Edgar Lee Masters and other formidable figures in modern letters. Moreover, the incidental *dicta* on contemporaries like D. H. Lawrence, James Joyce, Henry James and Thomas Hardy frequently have a value quite out of proportion to their brevity. The range of his reading in contemporary literature—and in much that has no pretentions to literature—was very great, far greater than Theodore's or Llewelyn's. No doubt this was due in part to the necessities of his lecturing, for not all his courses were on classic literature. But he quotes, or refers to from an obviously informed memory, such diverse writers as Dorothy Richardson and Charles Fort; Vachel Lindsay and Romain Rolland; Gertrude Stein and William James; he refers again and again to contemporary German and French and Russian novelists and thinkers as well as to a host of lesser figures whom also he has obviously read with attention. Readers of the *Letters to Louis Wilkinson* will also note the great diversity of his interests in contemporary letters, and his awareness of scores of writers, known and unknown, about whom he makes wise, provocative or appreciative comments. It would be quite wrong to suppose that Theodore got along quite comfortably with Bunyan and the Bible, for in fact there is a wealth of literary allusion in his work, much of it less by direct quotation than by inference. And it would equally be wrong to suppose that Llewelyn's literary interests lay so closely with Lamb and Burton and Shakespeare and Arnold that he was unaware of recent literature, for he too quotes appositely on occasion from the moderns (he is a frequent quoter of John Cowper). But these two brothers betray no wide awareness of their contemporaries, and nothing like their brother's familiarity with the day-to-day give and take of the twentieth-century literary scene.

But he is like them in finding his deepest strength and nourishment in the classic writers: in Shakespeare, Wordsworth, Lamb, Dickens, Arnold, Hardy. In Whitman, Emerson, James. In Homer and Virgil and Dante and Cervantes and Rabelais. In Balzac and Dumas and Proust. In Goethe and Nietzsche; and in the great Russian novelists, though curiously enough he rarely mentions the Russian poets. He is at home among all the great philosophies and religions, and often some viewpoint is supported by reference to the sages of China, India, and Greece.

Inevitably, the book is stamped with his years of life in the United States, and it is amazing to me that the *Autobiography* is so little in the consciousness of the American reader. No Englishman of our time has written with such insight and sympathy of the American people and their country. In interpreting the Americans to others, probably in recent years Alistair Cooke has had no rival; but in interpreting them to themselves, probably no foreigner since de Tocqueville has rivalled John Cowper. Some of the finest passages in this extraordinary book are concerned with the American scene, page after page about life in Chicago, life in San Francisco, life in New York, in Boston, Los Angeles, Philadelphia. He discusses at length the average American man, the American Negro, the Jew, the priest, the tycoon, the bum. He speaks of their women, and of the relationship between the sexes. He evokes the wide plains, the high mountains. Here indeed is an anatomy of America in the early twentieth century which will be consulted long after the popularly superficial observations of such writers as Arnold Bennett, G. K. Chesterton and Ford Madox Ford are forgotten.

But, after all, in an autobiography it is the writer himself we have come to hear about. 'Did any man before ever paint so stark a portrait of himself?' asked J. D. Beresford, and there would seem to be but one answer. The self-portrait is stark enough, but it is not distorted: it is, indeed, wonderfully like. The man was not deceived, and here is his very voice. He speaks of all the principal elements that make up human life—religion, sex, love, friendship; all the factors that react upon these —experience, education, environment, opportunity; the preoccupations, of work, and war, and travel. Of his feelings about art and nature and literature and philosophy. Of ambition and disaster and illness and endurance and achievement and reaction; of happiness, too, of which he had a share.

On every one of these matters illustrative quotations could be made, but I am reluctant to quote for two reasons. First, the book is so supremely and superbly a book to read through, and the reader benefits enormously from the cumulative effect of doing this, especially as there are so many references back to what has been said on any particular issue before. And next, John Cowper is not best displayed by brief quotation (which is not to say he has not plenty of pregnant aphorisms if one seeks them). This book is a monologue, not to be interrupted. It is easy, colloquial, familiar, though never trivial. It does not carry the sustained lyrical eloquence which marks the novels. There are few set pieces and purple passages, nor do there need to be, for here least of any of his books is John Cowper concerned with putting over a message, or exercising the arts of persuasion. He is telling the reader *what he is like*, but he is not asking the reader to approve or disapprove.

When I was writing about *A Glastonbury Romance* I was conscious that that great book could not be displayed by any one-page, or by any twenty-page, quotation. I had promised myself that I would at least copy out the last paragraphs for the marvellous prose. But the passage was too long. The last page of the *Autobiography* is a long one too; but I cannot leave *both* of these major books without a valedictory quotation.

Looking back over these fifty years, since the days when I jeered so rudely at that 'Spanish Maiden' in the chestnut-walk at Dor-chester, I am inclined to think that the two great electric currents of my life, the currents that have gathered and gathered their momentum beneath all the changes and chances of circumstance have been first the gradual discovery and the gradual strengthen-ing of my inmost identity, till it can flow like water and petrify like a stone; and second the magic trick of losing myself in the continuity of the human generations. By this continuity I mean the way in which from father to son our life-sensations are handed down from the past creating a sort of 'eternal recurrence' of the poetic mystery of the *little-great* ritual, the daily acts by which we all must live.

These immemorial recurrences I have learnt how to appropriate to myself, just as if my soul had the actual trick of passing into the lives of the uncounted generations.

My father was an inarticulate man. I am an only too voluble one. My father was a man of rock. I am a worshipper of the wind. But now, when from this resting place, this ledge, this slab of

stone, in the wavering Indian trial of my migrations and rever-
sions, I look back at the path behind me and the path before me it
seems as if it had taken me half a century merely to learn with what
weapons, and with what surrender of weapons, *I am to begin to
live my life.*

The astronomical world is *not* all there is. We are in touch with
other dimensions, other levels of life. And from among the powers
that spring from these *other levels* there rises up one Power, all the
more terrible because it refuses to practise cruelty, a Power that is
neither Capitalist, nor Communist, nor Fascist, nor Democratic,
nor Nazi, a Power *not of this world at all,* but capable of inspiring
the individual soul with the wisdom of the serpent and the harm-
lessness of the dove.

And thus it comes to pass, even while we are still in life, that
when our soul loses itself in the long continuity of kindred lives,
it does not lose itself in any power less gentle, less magical, less
universal than itself, or less the enemy of cruelty; for what it finds
is what it brings, and what it sees is what it is; and though the
First Cause may be good and evil, a Power has risen out of it
against which all the evil in it and all the unthinkable atrocities
it brings to pass are fighting a losing battle.

23

J OHN COWPER POWYS wrote six novels during his years in America.
They were all novels of what was then the contemporary English
scene. When he finally returned home he wrote eight others—leaving
out the long stories of *Up and Out*—only one of which, *Maiden Castle*,
the first—was of the same kind. It was as though he was driven to write
of England only when in exile. The setting of *The Inmates*, though
recognizably English, might be anywhere for all the influence it exerts
on the story. The historical novels are too remote in time to be
'English'. With *Morwyn* he began to turn to landscapes remote in
time and place which led him farther and farther from home. We may
regret that he never gave us a huge panoramic novel of the city of New
York, which he knew 'far better than any other city in the world';
and we may regret the lack of a companion novel of the city of London,
the city abounding in whores, whose teeming street life he was so
familiar with in earlier years; but those novels will never be written.

We come now to the last great novels of Dorset, *Weymouth Sands*
and *Maiden Castle*. The first was completed, and indeed published,
before he left America. The other was his first major work on returning
home. They cover the same tract of country, but *Weymouth Sands*
looks towards the sea, and *Maiden Castle* is a story of fields and the
high hills, though its setting, around Dorchester, is but a half-day's
walk from Weymouth. There is nothing remotely like the Dorset
coast to be seen from the windows of Phudd Bottom, but it was in
High East Street, Dorchester, that John first lived on coming home,
and it is in a room high above the shops of the same noble street that
the action of *Maiden Castle* commences.

These are both novels of the interplay of personality and character.
In both there is, certainly, some influence exerted by the terrain—in
Weymouth Sands, of the Isle of Portland and the sea, in *Maiden Castle*

of the stupendous earthwork which gives the novel its name; but these influences pale beside that exerted in the earlier novel by the town and legend of Glastonbury. Here, the human figures are always in the foreground, the landscape in perspective, clear, but not predominant. The situations do not arise *because* they are happening in Dorchester or Weymouth, whereas the Glastonbury situations could have occurred nowhere else. Take away Glastonbury, and you have no central story.

In essence *Weymouth Sands* is a comedy, though not for those concerned. *Maiden Castle* is a tragedy of maladjustments and frustrations, the only one of the English novels in which there is no humour at all. But there have been great novels before, and there may be again, in which there is no humour; and this is a great novel. In *Maiden Castle* the author's faith that in any circumstances a person ought to be able to hold on, and reach a compromise with fate is not, as elsewhere (in *Wolf Solent*, notably), communicated to his characters. The frustrations in *Maiden Castle* are not resolved, and we are left doubting if the characters have even reached a means whereby they can go on living with them. But the novel is not the less interesting for that.

These two novels are both primarily love stories, and as always, not of one love affair, but of several, involving a fairly wide and fairly representative group of the townspeople, so that we are given a general view of life in the town. In *Weymouth Sands* there is a continuing undercurrent of violence, but in *Maiden Castle* the crises are more abstract, and go deeper. Jobber Skald carries a heavy stone in his pocket throughout the action of *Weymouth Sands*, with the declared intention of battering Dog Cattistock to death, and this seems to give a lead to the other characters: Sippy Ballard, officiously and callously trying to dispossess Gipsy May of her hovel; Sylvanus Cobbold, courting arrest in pursuance of his campaign against Dr Bush the vivisectionist; Captain Poxwell crazily hating his prospective son-in-law; James Loder in a subtler, more calculating way undermining his son's happiness; Curly Wix tormenting Magnus Muir, whom she is to marry. The *Weymouth Sands* situations are from the common stock of love's courses, which never run smooth: here are misunderstandings, infidelities, jiltings, family opposition and the like; and in more than one character the realization of loneliness which is the hardest situation to face of them all: to have love to give, and to receive none in return.

It would be too simple to say that any one of these stories is the book's main theme, although the story of Jobber Skald ties the whole together. In all these long English novels of John Cowper's it is as though we had entered part way through a play and the action is in full swing. Certainly, we arrive for the opening scene of the love affair between the Jobber and Perdita Wane; but his other affair, the feud with Cattistock (which weighs more than love with the Jobber), has progressed within sight of a climax before we arrive. The other main stories are well advanced when the story opens. At the end there is a rounding off whereby we can hazard a neat guess at how most of these affairs will turn out; but there is no 'finis' beyond which the action will not go, and these twenty or thirty citizens of the town of Weymouth are in full career, living their lives, when the last page is written. Every one of these English novels, as I may call them, could be taken up by the author and continued straight on from the place where he laid down his pen—'slices of life' from a gigantic and inexhaustible cake.

Coming as it did immediately after the writing of *A Glastonbury Romance*, some flagging in invention might have been looked for in *Weymouth Sands*. There is none, and the remarkable thing is that there is the least hint of flagging invention precisely in those places where it might first be looked for or expected: in situations and characters having parallels in the earlier book. The preacher Johnny Geard in *Glastonbury* is entirely a separate person from the preacher Sylvanus Cobbold in *Weymouth Sands*, although their fanatical approach and strongly individual faiths have so much in common. Philip Crow and Dog Cattistock are both pursuing commercial projects inimical to the interests of their towns, but they work in quite different ways, and are in themselves entirely different personalities. The memorable minor characters, like Morgan Nelly and Abel Twig of *Glastonbury*, are matched in *Weymouth Sands* by Larry Zed, Marret Jones and Dr Girondel, and in both books these characters and others like them perform in some sort the function of Chorus; except that in the later book they are somewhat more closely involved in the central action, perhaps because there is a smaller cast. A study might well be made of John Cowper's minor characters throughout, for they are alive and true: Larry Zed is beautifully developed within a restricted compass, and the scene where he gets Perdita Wane to lie on his bed has an ever-fresh poignance whether read for the first time or not; equally poignant is the scene where the young girl Marret is in bed with Sylvanus Cobbold, and her careful, anxious thought for him when she knows his 'other woman' is coming. John Cowper appears to get close inside

a young girl's thoughts, and time and again we are startled by the very
stamp of truth on some speech or action of one of them—be it Marret,
as here, or Wizzie Ravelston in *Maiden Castle*, or Gerda in *Wolf
Solent*. *Weymouth Sands* is full of such touches, and they are more
readily detachable and quotable than usual: here is a rich vignette, from
Chapter Eleven, 'Sylvanus Cobbold'. The two are lying in bed at
early morning, the old eccentric preacher and the very young 'punch-
and-judy girl'.

'What's the first thing you can remember in your whole life,
"Mart"?'
He called her 'Mart' because of the way she herself pronounced
her name, which was almost exactly the way young Zed pronounced it.
Marret was thinking to herself:
'That's the sun on the end of the bed! That's the sun on the
blanket over his raised-up knees! That's the sun on his forehead!
I must remember how *everything* looks, so I'll have something to
think about when it's all over,' but she replied to his question
without hesitation. 'The first thing I remember was Father
hitting Mother with a water-jug. He held it by its handle till it
broke. There was water in it and Mother's clothes got all wet.
She minded that more than being hit. Mother was never one for
water. She always said water were made for fishes, not persons.'
'Did your father kill her?'
'No, no, no!' cried Marret, while her little oval face—which,
when she had been asleep, had looked exactly like a small china
doll—puckered itself up into a number of anxious creases,
'Ermentrude, the Salvation Army woman, who lived under us,
came running in and she said to Mother, "did he hit you, dearie?"
and Mother said, "no, he didn't"; and she said to Mother, "did he
do anything to you, dearie?" and Mother said, "no, he didn't";
and she said to Mother, "was yer a-quarrelling, dearie?" and
Mother said "no, they wasn't"; and she never said another
word after that and when Ermentrude went to her she were gone
and her feet were cold. I knew they were cold, because when
Father camed in he said, "Mart, thee may feel her feet just once, if
thee likes, so as to say you've touched Death".'
'Did he say anything else before they put her in her coffin?'
enquired Sylvanus gravely.

Marret looked at him with a radiant face while the newly-risen sun turned her dusty-brown hair into the metallic shimmer of a copper-beech tree. It was wonderful to her that she could interest him by her conversation.

'He only said, when the parish-women came to lay her out, that he hoped they wouldn't wash her with water. "My wife," he said, for Father were one to talk high and mighty with strangers, "never were a 'ooman for the water; so let 'un be; do 'ee hear? let 'un bide in peace!"'

In *Weymouth Sands* we are constantly in the presence of the sea, which makes its first significant appearance in John Cowper's work since *Rodmoor*, nearly twenty years earlier. In fifty Atlantic crossings John must have seen the sea in all its moods and he describes them faithfully. The storm and wreck which make one of the book's turning points are vivid enough for anyone, but with extraordinary effect he keeps them subordinate to the human drama; the wind may howl, the sea roar, but attention is never diverted from the wet, staggering figures on the shore; whether the people in the doomed ship are saved or drowned is firmly irrelevant beside the drama being enacted among the rescuers, culminating in the calculated piece of melodrama in which Dog Cattistock vainly plunges into the sea to save a victim tossing in the waves off shore. And even whether or not this single and individual piece of rescue work is successful is irrelevant: what matters is that at that moment that particular person pulled off his boots and plunged into the sea. It is the climax between Cattistock and the Jobber, the moment of victory and defeat, characteristically with nothing said on either side.

These are nearly all studies in people who have to be content with life's second best. The Jobber has to be reconciled with his enemy's ascendancy over the commercial life of Portland, and is even forced to concede that perhaps Cattistock will not ruin the quarrymen after all. Sylvanus Cobbold's is a partial victory over the forces of vivisection, a local success in a local skirmish, no permanent decisive advance. Perhaps Magnus Muir will not be quite unhappy because Curly Wix has deserted him almost on the eve of their marriage, and perhaps Dog Cattistock will not be completely happy, after all, even though he has stolen her; and the irrepressible Sippy will find other girls; but we see Muir likely to be drier, and duller, and lonelier, after the book closes; and Cattistock, with all his busy interests, and the bright young

Curly beside him, will never, we know, forget his long-dead, irreplaceable first wife; and Sippy, most of all to be pitied, will go on placing reliance on casual loves and missing love's permanence and continuity: getting the glitter and missing the gold.

There are crowd scenes in *Weymouth Sands* akin to those in *Glastonbury*. The storm has been mentioned, with its leaping water, and the oilskinned, drenched figures struggling with the lifeboat, and the helpless, buffeted watchers on cliff and shore. The party at Mother Legge's in Glastonbury is matched in Weymouth by the gatherings at Dr Girondel's, and the disillusioned old abortionist and his disillusioned friend Jerry Cobbold the clown are as memorable in their way as the bawdy Mother Legge in hers. Another notable public occasion is the wedding that never takes place between Cattistock and Mrs Lily, with its excited onlookers and dramatic *dénouement*; but, much more than *Glastonbury*, this is a book of smaller, more personal encounters, and we remember most clearly the moments when one or two people only are on stage: Sylvanus walking on the cliffs, communing with his sunbeam, murmuring his strange and hopeless invocation, 'Caputanus!'. Magnus trying to establish a mood of sympathy with his difficult Curly, while Sippy Ballard keeps blowing his car horn in the road below. Jerry Cobbold desperately trying to keep Perdita from giving up her job as his wife's companion, and playing the piano badly to distract her thoughts from this intention. Perdita in bed with the Jobber, Perdita on the mad boy's bed—this perhaps most of all the most touching passage in a book full of insights and compassion. There are ten full pages I would wish to quote, to make the most effective illustration; I will try to convey something of their quality by quoting only one. It comes near the end of Chapter Five, 'Lodmoor':

. . . Larry's whole soul gleamed in his green eyes as he hung over her. His brain felt dizzy; but it seemed to him as though touching her so, and while she lay there prone and still beneath him, that a veritable consummation of his desire was already taking place. To his fervid imagination it was enough that their eyes clung together and that she knew he was ravishing her in his thought. Her bare hand, round which his fingers burned, was to him then her whole body. For this was the first time in his life that he had held a girl who knew what he felt and did not stop him. His green eyes, as they clung to her soft brown ones, kept saying to her: 'I'm taking you! I'm taking you!' and it seemed to him that she yielded more and more, as he bent forward, his body pressed against the side of the couch; and it seemed to him that it pleased her that he should be seeing her bare figure—as he *was* now seeing it in his intense imagination—and that it pleased her to lie so hushed and still, so that he could the more easily enjoy her; and it seemed to him that this strange passivity, she knowing that he was taking her, was the ultimate essence of her Being offered up to him; and that her lying so still, with her bare hand in his, while he enjoyed her, was the ultimate sign of what it meant to be a real, live, mysterious girl; and that this was the secret of all girls, that they could not know how exciting they were; and that this was their inmost nature that they stayed so quiet while they were loved.

How could he know that it was only possible for Perdita to remain so quiet, and to answer his impassioned gaze so calmly, because her own thoughts had once more grown so pitifully sad ? Weary and hopeless was her whole spirit, as she lay on Larry's bed; and all, all seemed futile to her. The fleeting quiver of response that the boy's beauty and passion had roused in her had been stricken cold by that image of the Jobber lowering above him. Perhaps it had been all the while her feeling for the Jobber— for not a night had passed, since she saw him, but she had gone to sleep thinking about him—that rendered her so sensitive to this boy's infatuation.

It was indeed peculiarly characteristic of Perdita, that fate's best way of making appealing the near and the pressing was to incarnate in them something belonging to the remote and the evasive. Thus while to the ecstatic sense of young Zed there lay exposed before him, yielding willingly up to him, two of the whitest, softest, young girl's breasts that the world contained, behind those breasts the girl's heart had substituted a full-grown man, dark and formidable and full of the magic of the sea, for the boy's red hair and burning fingers. But since such ecstasies, whether spiritual, or physical, after dipping their possessed in Eternity, toss them back all too soon into Time, the moment came when young Zed lowered his eyelids, removed his fingers, rose to his feet, and said in an abrupt jerky tone—

'Will 'ee bide quiet where'a be, while I fetches me seaweeds to show 'ee?'

If the principal characters in *Weymouth Sands* are left to make do with life's second best, those in *Maiden Castle* are left with nothing. It is almost as though we were meeting people we had known in earlier books, and finding them ten or twenty years older. There is a good deal of affinity between D. No-man and Wolf Solent, and between Enoch Quirm and *Glastonbury's* Mr Evans. Nancy Quirm might be Mary Crow, older and sadder. Something of this feeling was in the mind of the writer who composed the original 'blurb' for the jacket of the first edition, when he said, 'John Cowper Powys's new novel will in all probability be of greater interest to those over thirty years of age than any of his previous works. It is the story of men and women whose first love and first faith have gone. His subject is their struggle to readjust themselves to life . . .' This writer might have said more properly 'over forty years of age', but perhaps he did not want to discourage too many younger readers. With one exception, the main characters are well into middle age and they are disillusioned and settled into lethargic acquiescence. Nancy Quirm endures her dreadful old husband—loves him even—but her happiness lies with her dead son in his grave. Jenny Dearth makes do with 'platonic friendship' with Claudius Cask when she longs to be his wife. Thuella Wye is trapped into a loveless, friendless existence keeping her dull old father, with no hope of anything better, or even different. Dud No-man's arrival in Dorchester, like Wolf Solent's in Sherborne and Yeovil, stirs all these people up and alters all their lives; but it doesn't make any of them any happier, nor does it resolve any of No-man's problems. It changes a few directions, but the lesson is that men and women must endure, and endure, and endure.

No-man himself is one of John Cowper's best characters, like Wolf Solent in lots of ways, but no slavish copy of him; in fact, it is interesting to observe their reactions to similar situations and find them so individual. How would Wolf have taken it if Gerda had announced that she already had a child, after their marriage? Would he have dealt as No-man did with the blackmailing Urgan? Would Wolf have gone further, or not so far with Thuella, on the banks of the Scummy Pond?

Dud No-man is more certainly and positively the principal character of *Maiden Castle* than Jobber Skald was of *Weymouth Sands*. Here again he is like Wolf Solent, dominating the book, the story seen almost wholly through his eyes, his viewpoint the only one in every essential. In *Weymouth Sands* the several stories proceed independently of one another—that is to say, they would have happened individually as they did, if the parallel stories had not been told, or had happened differently. Points of contact there are, certainly, but Sylvanus would have suffered as he did if Perdita Wane had never come to Weymouth, and Cattistock would have jilted Mrs Lily if he had never known the Jobber—and so on. But *Maiden Castle*'s various sub-plots are inextricably intertwined and most of them depend for their development on the movements and actions of No-man and his girl. This girl, the circus waif, Wizzie, is far more complex than Gerda, and less beautiful. Surely few men could read of Gerda without wanting to take her to bed! But Wizzie arouses less clear-cut emotions. We sympathize with her, and disapprove of her at the same time. She is wilful and selfish and endearing and young and pathetic and a little absurd. She is twenty years younger than No-man, and of a completely different background and culture. From the moment he 'buys' her at the circus, paying old Urgan eighteen pounds for her, we know it can never be a satisfactory arrangement. One of the saddest short passages is where she returns to the circus later and is recognized by her old horse. To a girl like Wizzie No-man is incomprehensible; where she can sympathize she cannot understand, where she can understand she cannot sympathize. The happiness she brings him inevitably is brief, the unhappiness enduring. But Wizzie affects more lives than her own and No-man's: the whole 'circle' reacts to her, the households of Glymes, the house in Friary Lane, Quirm, Cask, Wye and all of them. If No-man's arrival in Dorchester is the spark, Wizzie's sojourn there provides the explosion. After her departure at the end, nothing is the same, nothing can ever be the same. The drama of this novel is not in the outward action, not in murder or shipwreck, but within the characters' hearts. There is one significant physical happening which works upon them all, the excavations and discoveries at Maiden Castle, and this plays a late but important part in the story; but the decisive crisis comes in every heart from within—Nancy's, dumbly to endure, Thuella's, impulsively to rebel, Wizzie's, somehow to get back all she has lost, Jenny's at last to give. Indeed, it is the women in this book who make the decisions, and abide by them. The men drift, and hesitate, are unsure and unstable. At the end, we are very close indeed to the mood and outcome in *Wolf Solent* as a comparison of the closing paragraphs of both books will show. So, *Wolf Solent*:

By God! He must be crafty in dealing with these modern inventions! He must slide under them, over them, round them, like air, like vapour, like water. *Endure or escape!* A good word, wherever it was he had picked it up.

Well, never mind the motors and the aeroplanes! King Æthelwolf was at rest, staring up at that fan tracery. It only needed an adjustment . . . and he could be as much at peace in life as that king was in death!

Was Carfax making love to Gerda now, all soft and yielding and relaxed, after her whistling?

Everyone had to *feel* according to the fatality of his nature; but who was he to make pompous moral scenes?

Alone! That was what he had learnt from the hard woman who had given him birth. That every soul was alone. Alone with that secret bestower of torture and pleasure, the horned snail behind the pigsty!

Endure or escape. He must spread the wisdom of that word over all the miserable moments that were to come.

Oh, Christie! Oh, Christie!

Well, he must go in and face those two now.

He took up his stick firmly and securely by its proper end, and for a few paces moved forward blinking, straight into the circle of the sun, as it aimed itself at him over the rim of the world. Then he swung round, scrambled through the gap, and hurried across the road.

'I wonder if he *is* still here?' he thought as he laid his hand on the latch of the gate. And then he thought, 'Well, I shall have a cup of tea.'

And *Maiden Castle*:

For a minute or two they stood hand in hand by the freshly turned mould. Then the woman whispered, 'I forgave him when he didn't know it. But he knows it now.' And Dud realized what was in her mind when, with a faint smile, she drew her hand from his and moved away to the grave of her son.

And an apathy, a numbness, a strange quiescence descended upon D. No-man; not the same apathy that had been weighing him down all these last days, but the apathy that comes on a person when his soul, removing itself to a distance from his body, faces without flinching but with an immense weariness the long ascending path up which it has to drag that mortal companion of its wayfaring. Which of those two—his mother, with her

inhuman egoism, or Mona, with her weird unselfishness—held
the secret that prevailed? Well! he must go on as best he could in
his own way. He must be decent to Nance. He must be faithful,
after his fashion, to Wizzie. He must hold fiercely to all those
'sensations' of his! It was no good. He could *not* live, as this
dead man had done, in a wild search for the life behind life.

One life at a time! But neither would he close one single cranny
or crevice of his mind to the 'intimations of immortality' that in
this place and in this hour were so thick about him. And then a
well-known sound in the air above him made him glance upwards. One of old Claudius's aeroplanes! 'Hold to the centre,' he
said to himself, 'as you move on. The future's *not* everything.'
And he dug his stick into the earth, with his eyes on his ground.
Then, pulling it out with a jerk, he went to meet Nance.

The similarities here are not simply verbal, the stick and the aero-
plane, but of mood. And the reading of both of these novels is en-
hanced and enriched when each is read in an awareness of the other.

There are memorable single scenes in *Maiden Castle*, as in all the
novels, from the first meeting of No-man and Nance in the cemetery
to the midsummer's eve walk through the fields to Maiden Castle.
The high drama of the circus scenes, when Dud No-man 'buys'
Wizzie. The several subsequent encounters with the sinister 'Old
Flunky'. The moment when Dud realizes that the filthy, erudite
Enoch Quirm is his own father. And there are memorable characters,
too, as always: Mrs Urgan, exerting an evil influence from the background, the ineffective, pathetic philosopher, Teucer Wye and his
strange, elemental daughter. And, much more than in *Weymouth
Sands*, we are conscious of the physical scene. In *Weymouth Sands* the
sea and the great storm take the stage momentarily, and the strange
beauty of Lodmoor is effectively conveyed, but as it were incidentally.
More superficially, the old town of Weymouth comes clearly to life,
but always as a backcloth. But in *Maiden Castle* the streets and
houses and environs of Dorchester play almost a central part, though
less 'consciously' than the part played in *Glastonbury* by that ancient
town. *Maiden Castle*, like *Wolf Solent*, is also a novel of the lanes and
fields, of clouds and winds and the light of heaven.

24

IN WRITING the life of one person it is not always possible to proceed chronologically; in discussing three lives, it is impossible. Some divergences are inevitable, but now a moment comes when we may see the three brothers together, for they all lived for a while as neighbours in Chaldon.

John Cowper left the United States early in 1934 and on first reaching England lived for a short time at Down Barn, or 'Rat Barn', as it was sometimes called, a remote dwelling in a fold of the hills about half way between Llewelyn's house and Theodore's. The barn was part of a range of buildings the others of which were still in use by the farmer; the dwelling itself being perhaps a conversion, perhaps part farmhouse cottage: without knowing the history of the building, it would be hard to tell. Willie Powys was the nominal tenant, although of course he lived in Africa and was almost never there. The place was available for the use of the family and friends, and Katie Powys used occasionally to spend a little time there as a change from Chydyok. John spent the summer and autumn there, after which he removed to Dorchester for a short time before going on to his chosen new home, in Wales. He was working on *Maiden Castle* (in speaking of which I have anticipated chronologically) and his latest published work was the *Autobiography*, which naturally was under discussion in the family. There are long passages in Llewelyn's letters at this time concerning the book, about which he had a number of reservations, and he speaks of a long letter about the book written by A. R. Powys, which perhaps one day may be put into print. A.R.P.'s views are always forthright and interesting, and have not been made available often enough. Undoubtedly there must also have been observations by Littleton Powys, although he can have had little sympathy with large parts of the book, the cast of his own mind being so different from John's. But, if the *Autobiography* provoked strong family reaction, this was nothing to what was to come, with the publication first of Louis Marlow's *Swan's Milk* in 1934, and of Marlow's *Welsh Ambassadors* and Richard Heron Ward's *The Powys Brothers*, just over a year later.

There have been no large occasions for reference to Louis Marlow in recent pages, but his influence within the 'Powys circle' had in no degree lessened over the years. He had returned to England from America in 1919, and after a very brief excursion into the world of commerce he had settled down to writing, lecturing and travelling. He spent a good deal of time in Europe. In the late twenties he returned to novel-writing, and began the series of sophisticated 'tragi-comedies' which so much impressed contemporaries like Arnold Bennett, Ralph Straus and Somerset Maugham. Maugham indeed wrote a preface for *Two Made their Bed* (1929) which was something very unusual for him. Marlow and Dr O'Neill were as always in constant touch with the Powys family, making regular rounds of visits and keeping up an extensive correspondence, and the writer of a detailed and comprehensive biography would find them at every turn, authorities for this statement or that. But Dr O'Neill can be consulted only in his letters, which have not yet been gathered and made available. Louis Marlow published several books in which the brothers figure.

Swan's Milk is the first of these. It is at first glance a novel. It is then seen to be a biography of Dexter Foothood, told within the framework of a novel. A little further scrutiny shows that Dexter is a figure for Louis Marlow himself (who appears in the book as narrator) and Louis Marlow was of course Louis Wilkinson. The hero is thus twice removed (like a sort of cousin) from Wilkinson, but so far as the facts go this is Wilkinson's autobiography: and by 'facts' I mean not only dates and events, but all material views, prejudices and opinions. Dexter is Louis as Louis saw himself, but presented with selection and art. The book can be read as a novel—and a very entertaining novel—but it is a little difficult to do this because many of the persons are represented under their real names—Oscar Wilde, Bernard Shaw, Maugham, Joyce, Bennett and the Powys family among others. Some important characters (important too for the reader in quest of Powys material) are disguised under fictitious names, for reasons perfectly sufficient at the time of publication. It may be hoped that in due course an edition will be published with a key and a few unobtrusive notes. Nothing less inviting than an annotated novel!—but perhaps a minimum of elucidation might be given discreetly at the back. Certainly, this book will long be consulted by students of English literary life in the nine-teen-twenties. The main thread of story does not come up to date, even to the date of publication; and in 1940 Louis Marlow added *Forth, Beast!* as a supplementary volume, and this also has passages concerning the Powys brothers. It is to be regretted that Louis Marlow did not return to the theme in the remaining years of his life.

Swan's Milk is too good a book to be cited only for what it contains on the Powyses—or on other contemporaries—and I hope many readers will continue to seek it out for its own sake. I will quote Llewelyn Powys, whose tribute appeared on the dust jacket:

> If an international, unmilitaristic civilization, happy and hedo-nistic, waits upon the dissolution of our more cowardly herd instincts, *Swan's Milk* is a book of the greatest cultural value. The moral energy latent in its shameless pages is enormous. Every topic that the 'right-minded' would wish to be left out is treated by Mr. Marlow with particular interest, vigour and veracity. Although I personally resented several of Mr. Marlow's references to my own family and was 'deeply hurt' by his malicious misrepresentation of my brother John, I scarcely remember ever having read a book with more relish and enter-tainment. It is utterly free of cant and utterly outrageous. I have no hesitation in saying that *Swan's Milk* is brilliant and out-standing and will remain for many years an important landmark in biographical-autobiographical writing.

Even the publication of this tribute could not be effected without some comings and goings. Originally, it was set with the deletion of the passage about Llewelyn being 'deeply hurt', and an impassioned letter of protest went to Louis; but the omission had not been made at his prompting, and before publication it was restored. If any collector has a copy of the jacket without the phrase, he has a rare piece of Powysiana.

The question of Louis's 'malice' towards John had been raised more than once, and not by Llewelyn only. It dates back certainly as far as *Blasphemy and Religion* and *The Buffoon*, and Louis Marlow said frankly again and again that there was much in John's character, and in his writings, that either repelled him, or evoked a response not in complete sympathy. I have never felt that these responses or their expression amounted to 'malice', and there can be no question of Louis's love for, and his loyalty to John, as shown by a hundred things; nor of John's love, and complete absence of resentment of Louis or his writings: the friendship revealed in the *Letters to Louis Wilkinson* sufficiently demonstrates that. *Because* they were opposite in so many fundamentals of character, the passages about John in *Swan's Milk* are among the best in the book, and moreover they do express a point of view many readers have shared. I do not share it, but I think such a passage as this an essential part of any attempt to come at the secret of John Cowper, to 'pluck out his mystery' as a phrase of his own expresses it:

'. . . Just look at this photograph.' He took it out of his breast pocket.

'Worn next to your heart,' I murmured.

'Look at it! Don't you see it's a fake face. Look at the mouth. Deliberately pulled about. And, oh, what spiritual intensity! What straining upward and onward! Golly, what a man of sorrows, how acquainted with grief. And how insanely far he carries it all. I met his train at Chicago once. He walked along the platform, head bowed, shoulders bent, carrying a suitcase in each hand, bearing his Cross.'

'But he often wasn't at all well in America. All that lecturing was a great strain. No doubt he really was tired.'

'He could at least have got a porter.'

'I don't expect that occurred to him.'

'No. No more than it "occurred to him" to buy thousand-mile tickets and save fifty per cent of his travel expenses. Although I told him about that time and time again. There never was a man with sillier extravagances. But it was all showing off. *He* couldn't do things like that, oh no, not he; much too ordinary, they were, much too undistinguished! He couldn't get a porter when he was being Jesus Christ. The awful thing about that time was that he didn't know I was meeting the train. It was just his daily crucified posture that he wanted *everyone* to see. Every place a stage, every passer-by one of the audience . . . And then the way he treats servants and social inferiors. The infatuated topsy-turvy snob! That exaggerated deference, you know it, it makes them horribly uncomfortable; of course makes them feel their position more than the most brutal and normally snobbish bullying possibly could. But he can't realize that. When it comes to real sensitive-ness—! It's all the same thing. Licking the sores of lepers, washing the beggars' dirty feet. Self-humiliation, exhibitionism, striking a sensational attitude and switching on the spotlight. You get it all in his writing, too.'

'Sometimes, a little——'

'In all of it, always.'

'No, no, you get a great deal else——'

'A pseudo-Dostoievski, a falsified *Wuthering Heights*. It's sheer Ouidaism, but much worse, with its intellectual and spiritual pretensions. Oh, intolerable! And he actually believes in "good and evil" in the old crass way. Does it on purpose, because he can't do without "sin" to whip him up. The "divine" and the "devilish"—you know—all that ridiculous tedious rubbish . . .'

So he went on.

'There are two subjects, Dexter,' I was able to say at last, 'on which your usual judgment completely deserts you. John Cowper Powys and the United States. The very two that gave you your chance in life, you ingrate!'

'He *likes* America!' That set Dexter off again. 'Actually lives there now. *Chooses* to. *Loves* it. You talk about "judgment". Judge him for that!'

In his own autobiography John Cowper several times mentions *Swan's Milk*—*The Buffoon* too—and he is careful to say that these books gave him no offence. Speaking of America, he remarks 'As my dear Louis laments, in a distressed and almost querulous tone, I "loved it".' As for Dexter Louis, elsewhere in *Swan's Milk*, after another outburst, he concludes, almost lamely, 'But I love him!', biting his lip.

With Theodore and Llewelyn his tone is much more sober, but the references are briefer; almost as if he were driven to write of John Cowper despite himself; and of course John's influence on Louis was profound, and not at all wholly along these lines of provoking antagonism. That he was in truth a terrifying genius, Louis never doubted.

His anecdotes of Theodore, grave and ironic, among a gay circle of Oxford men, like an owl among starlings, must not be stolen from their context, though I can't resist borrowing one. 'Church, Navy, Army, Bar,' Dexter had angrily declaimed. 'Liars, murderers and thieves,' was Theodore's tranquil comment. But how much must be lost by setting the words in print, without Theodore's voice to speak

them. In this book, as always, Louis speaks of Theodore's genius—
'The only man of full genius I have known.' And these are the words
of one who had known most of the greatest writers of his time, and
many other famous men.

Of Llewelyn's writings he says less, but of his personality much
more. His description of Llewelyn at Cambridge is loving and exact,
and—perhaps because they were more nearly of an age—these two
always wrote and spoke of one another with a special intimacy of
affection. Louis would seem almost to have stood in awe of Theodore,
and though always relaxed and at ease with John a little critical, a little
guarded. Of Llewelyn he says, in a short passage it is always a pleasure
to read:

Nearly all of the many Powyses have charm, but Llewelyn
abounds in it incomparably. His smile alone, with its broad
sudden light, is enough to win the stoniest heart. So is that air of
woodland simplicity and artlessness, which he can still wear,
although he is now as full of guile as the craftiest of all those
innumerable animals that his writings have invoked for metaphor
or simile. Like Carl, he gave an impression of naïvety often misleading; but there is no other point of comparison between the
two. In appearance as in nature they were quite dissimilar. The
young Llewelyn, with his crisp curly bright hair and fair com-
plexion, had a sunlike look; he was dazzlingly bright. He had light
eyes, eager and easily troubled, a rich unguarded mouth, a child's
soft mouth greedy of pleasure and sometimes sulky. His body was
hard and slight, with a hint of frailness, though one could not,
then, have anticipated that he was to be so soon consumptive.
Like Dexter, he had an unusually large head which seemed even
larger than it was because of its stiff woolly growth of light gold
curls. It was like a growth of the earth, 'crisp as a thicket of
thorns': like a vegetable growth stiff and resilient to the touch as
dry moss is in summer, or a cypress hedge. His hair by Dexter's
—Llewelyn's so natural, Dexter's so exotic—made a strange
contrast, one that took the eye.

From their first meeting the two were together almost every
day, going for long walks, as far even as Ely, quarrelling sometimes, when they would violently tussle and wrestle, each in
anger inflicting on the other physical pain. For some while
everyone but Llewelyn to Dexter, and everyone to Llewelyn but

Dexter, seemed irrelevant and dull. Dexter found every percep-
tion, every appreciation and emotion, heightened by the presence
and talk of his friend . . .
  'What days those were, what days!' Llewelyn would remind
him. 'Can we ever forget them? Not a moment of tedium, each
hour so new, so exciting. What savour, what zest!'

The appearance at this time of a full-length critical study of the three
brothers suggests how far they had journeyed since the days when
Llewelyn despaired of ever getting a start, and Theodore wrote his
stories and hid them in the cupboard, and John poured all his eloquence
into the air. One small pamphlet, William Hunter's *The Novels and
Stories of T. F. Powys*, published at Cambridge in 1931, represented
almost their only recognition outside the columns of the book reviews.
Richard Heron Ward's study, with the three portraits by Gertrude
Powys, appeared in 1935 under the title, *The Powys Brothers*. It was of
course incomplete, taking into account only what had then been
published and not discussing by any means all of that; but it is full of
shrewd comment and insight, and the promise which John Cowper
then saw in Mr Ward's writing has since been amply fulfilled, as his
later work—and especially his novels—may demonstrate. The longest
family comment we have on this book came from Littleton, and was
printed in his autobiography, *The Joy of It*, published just over a year
later. Littleton always took a keen interest in his brothers' writings and
in what was said about them, and he writes a long 'open letter' to Mr
Ward containing much praise and some criticism. But his main
observations and strictures are reserved for Louis Marlow's *Welsh
Ambassadors*, which came out in 1936 (*The Joy of It* appeared in
autumn, 1937).
  Welsh Ambassadors, like so much of Louis Marlow's writing, is
calculated to upset the conventional reader; Llewelyn's adjectives
applied to *Swan's Milk* apply equally happily here—'shameless, outrageous, free of cant, brilliant'. It was a book with which Littleton
Powys could feel no sympathy. It must be agreed that his brother
Llewelyn (who loved him) understood Littleton very well, and
Llewelyn wrote a long letter to him about his limitations—limitations
calculated to stand between him and Louis Marlow's book. It is in *The
Letters of Llewelyn Powys*, letter 269; and among others there is a
notable discussion of their opposite attitudes to sex in letter 225. As for
Littleton's strictures on *Welsh Ambassadors*, these appear to me to be

based on a complete misunderstanding of his own family. He takes literally Louis's observations about the 'sadism' of the Rev. C. F. Powys, and the 'masochism' of Mrs Powys, as though Mr Powys made a practice of beating young girls to death, or Mrs Powys had herself tied to the bedpost and scourged. Perhaps those are two words people fight shy of when applied to their fathers and mothers, and perhaps Louis Marlow could have said what he had in mind by a circumlocution.[1] But in the overall context his meaning is quite clearly something more subtle than Littleton's interpretation, and it would be assented to by many readers who have no desire to call other people's parents horrid names. Littleton also objects to Louis's assessment of John Cowper's character—as Llewelyn did, on this and other occasions. Loyalty here dictated a bias, I think, for, as I have said, no one could doubt the affection of these two for each other over almost sixty years. Llewelyn always jumps to John's defence with a forthright oath or two and gives Louis a drubbing; but Littleton assumes an air of more-in-sorrow-than-in-anger, and affects humility and seems to speak with sweet reason, except when a weak sarcasm escapes him; and the resulting passages make uncomfortable reading. It will be seen that in this I too have a bias, and I will agree that I find this brother at all times entirely unsympathetic; the reader must remember this when I have occasion to mention him.

Louis Marlow's book is an essential source book for any student of the Powys brothers, and a rare entertainment for all. It is subtitled 'Powys lives and letters', but this description is not quite accurate, for the 'lives' are far from complete, even in the light of the book's date— 1936. John Cowper's biography is not taken past the year 1911—except by occasional passing references—and Llewelyn's not past 1925. Theodore, it is true, is 'brought up to date', but this is not difficult with Theodore, who seldom stirred beyond the fields around Chaldon, and had no 'biography' in any wide sense of events, alarums, and comings and goings.

But biography is not the main purpose of the book, and it is in any case strong in biographical detail of their early lives. The main purpose is to display a large body of correspondence, with linking commentary, and by means of this to furnish portraits of the three brothers. There is no book, and there cannot soon be one, in which this purpose is better

[1] As Mr George D. Painter has remarked of 'sadism' and 'masochism', 'if there were other words for these supremely important fuels of creative imagination, I would gladly use them'.

achieved. The intimacy between Louis Marlow and the three brothers gives him an advantage over all later commentators, and the freedom with which they write to him makes this book the most revealing document about them outside their own books.

Littleton Powys wrote two volumes of autobiography. Both contain material relating to his brothers, and something of the family and its background. *The Joy of It* is 'straight autobiography', his life from birth until the time of writing. *Still the Joy of It* [1] (1956) is a collection of papers and lectures, with some new chapters of autobiography and a number of interesting photographs. After his first wife's death Littleton Powys married the novelist Elizabeth Myers, and he writes an account of their life together until her untimely death. I find the book embarrassing to read—it makes me uncomfortable.

---

[1] Littleton Powys died in 1955 while his book was in the press.

25

SHORTLY after John Cowper's return to England the English publishers of *A Glastonbury Romance* were threatened with a libel action by a Somerset landowner who believed himself to be represented by one of the characters. The action was settled out of court, but it cost a good deal of money and effectively swallowed up John Cowper's royalties. Some reform of the law in this particular is long overdue, for writers of fiction have frequently suffered by their use of a name, or a situation, or a characteristic, which some reader has claimed represented him and did him injury. But a novelist has to give his characters names; has to involve them in situations; has to give them characteristics. Are we to give them numbers (·008, perhaps?) and cause them to play out their dramas in the town of 'Blakesmoor', in H—shire? The law could easily be made to give protection against a true libel, without penalizing writers who inadvertently tread on some tender corn; and a demonstration that the writer did not know, and had never heard of, the person alleged to be libelled, at least ought to be a good basis for defence.

This action, apart from inflicting a severe hardship financially, led to the publication of *Weymouth Sands* in England in a severely modified form in which every trace of the town of Weymouth was eliminated. The result was *Jobber Skald*, published in 1935. As Mr E. R. H. Harvey has said, in introducing the restored text for the 1963 English edition of *Weymouth Sands*, there are authors whose connection with a locality gives a special significance to their work. The removal of real place names and real scenery upset the balance of *Jobber Skald*, and it is good that it has now appeared in England in the original text. This threatened action also exerted an influence on John Cowper's later work. Writing to Louis Wilkinson about *Maiden Castle* in 1930 he speaks of the special care he has taken to make nothing and nobody

'identifiable'. '. . . fear of libel has been—I grudge to confess it but it
seems to me true—one of the directing forces—& not the smallest—
in the actual form, line, matter, method of the story'. The reader of
this novel will notice several passages in which the author says 'this
house no longer exists' or 'that locality has been swept away'; and it
may not be entirely fanciful to suppose that the very name 'No-man'
for his principal character is designed to make it hard for anyone to see
himself reflected. In his same letter John Cowper expresses some
apprehension that his English publishers will be shy of a book with
'real names', and this apprehension was justified, for the book was
rejected by John Lane the Bodley Head, and also by several others,
before being accepted by Cassell at the instigation of Mrs Thomas
Hardy. These considerations may have weighed with John Cowper
when he turned (as he did in his very next novel) away from a recognizable English scene to the landscapes of Hell.

Theodore never encountered this difficulty, although his people are
some of them much more despicable than anyone in *Glastonbury*, and
although nobody ever doubted that East Chaldon was the centre of
the Theodorian world. This is puzzling, but it is so, and we must bow
to it. It is puzzling, because there were people in the area quite willing
to bring libel actions if they saw need, and in 1934-35 Llewelyn
became involved in one, which he lost. The result was an even severer
financial blow to him than the Glastonbury affair had been to John
Cowper. The matter is fully discussed in Malcolm Elwin's *Life* of
Llewelyn. It provides further evidence that the law is in need of some
revision, as Mr Elwin shows. Llewelyn naturally did not enjoy losing
money, but he put a good face on it, and his letters to James Cobb at
this time are illuminating as well as doing him great credit. (Mr Cobb
was also prosecuted, with Valentine Ackland and Sylvia Townsend
Warner.) The stimulus of the court proceedings themselves was
evident. There is the photograph of him on his way to the court, hat
set firmly and somewhat jauntily, flower defiant in buttonhole; and his
letters. One to Arthur Davison Ficke sets the mood—'. . . I am to be
carried over the downs in an armchair placed in a dog-cart like some
—— Buddha for the populace to bawl after and the seagulls to molest
—a "proper guy"—swaying this way and that above the heads of all.'
This was hardly the 'dying author' the Sunday newspapers featured so
dramatically in reporting the case; although at that time (January 1935)
he had been in poor health for a long time, recovering very slowly
from a severe haemorrhage of the previous July.

It was to this court case that I owed my own good fortune in making Llewelyn Powys's acquaintance, and through him in due course I was able to meet John Cowper. How much these meetings, and my correspondence with these two brothers, meant in my life is hardly relevant to this book, but I cannot pass over it in complete silence. In 1935 I was in my twenty-first year, living at Bournemouth, and just beginning to take seriously the possibility that I might become a writer. I had left school at the age of fourteen, and as a working-class lad in a provincial town (a veritable fortress of unpoetical prosperity, Llewelyn Powys once called it) I had few opportunities of meeting writers or young men interested in writing. Accordingly, when I realized that a real writer lived not very far away—and I first learned this from the newspaper accounts of the libel action—I wrote to Llewelyn Powys asking if I might visit him. This I did some months after the court case, but the matter had been in my mind from first hearing that he lived at East Chaldon. Our subsequent intercourse is fully and sympathetically described by Dr R. L. Blackmore in his edition of the letters Llewelyn Powys and I exchanged, and is touched on in the introduction to my own volume of *Selections* from Llewelyn Powys. I think it would be supererogatory to enlarge upon it here.

Llewelyn's life in England was now drawing to its close. Since his severe attack in August 1933 he had been obliged to live as an invalid, he was unable to get about very much, and spent a good deal of time confined to his garden shelter. But he did not write or think like an invalid. No man was ever freer of self-pity. Some of his sunniest affirmations were made in these years. And the remote cottage on the downs was by no means remote from rewarding visitors. When he was able he saw his family, and many friends—Louis Wilkinson was at Chaldon for several months, writing *Welsh Ambassadors*. He was visited by Mrs Thomas Hardy, Edwin Muir, H. M. Tomlinson, Middleton Murry, Robert Gibbings, H. J. Massingham, Edna St Vincent Millay and others, old friends and new; and he was engaged in advising and encouraging a number of correspondents of the younger generation, including John Wallis, John Rowland, Clifford Musgrave, May Chesshire, Richard Heron Ward, Benjamin de Casseres, Gamel Woolsey, Gerald Brenan, and Andrew Wordsworth and others whose names are not recorded in the published letters. He took great trouble and gave much time in these matters, in contrast to the attitude of many prominent writers of the twentieth century whose names I had better not mention, writers whom one might describe under the graphic phrase 'enemies of promise'; but it is encouraging to know that he was not alone. John Cowper Powys also carried on a wide correspondence with young people needing help and encouragement, and so have many: scores of young people must recall the generous responses of Walter de la Mare, to name one other example. Llewelyn Powys also replied carefully to inquiries about his own books, or his attitude to various matters of philosophy, religion and the craft of writing, as a number of his published letters show.

In the autumn of 1936 Llewelyn was again very ill, and when he was sufficiently recovered to travel it was decided that he should make trial again of a visit to Switzerland, where he could consult the doctor who had treated him all those years before, when he had so nearly been cured. He left England on 2nd December and was soon established in the house of another old friend, Lisaly Güjer, at Clavadel, Davos-Platz. Dr Frey thought his case might yet respond to treatment and the disease was kept at bay, although not defeated; and it was not directly under its attacks that he died. For three years he continued writing, and he was employed almost until the end; and no one reading his letters and essays of these years can doubt that they were happy ones.

Llewelyn Powys had begun the 'imaginary autobiography' of *Love and Death* in 1933, but the work proceeded slowly, and was sometimes laid aside. In 1937 it was taken up for revision and completion, and it was published in England in spring 1939. The American edition did not appear until after the author's death, and in writing to Arthur Ficke he expressed some regret that this, which he considered his best book, had not found an American publisher. He had not met with much success with American publishers since returning to England, unlike John and Theodore, almost all of whose books were appearing in American editions at this time—their turn for neglect was to come later. The book was met with some hostility from the 'fashionable' English reviewers, and Mr Elwin's account of these may make a few of them blush, if this is something they are capable of. There is always a gulf between the critics and the creative writers, and speaking of contemporary critics Mr C. Day Lewis has recently noted their 'supercilious or brash bumptiousness of tone, the complacence, the lack of humility, which can be heard in the utterances of the more mediocre nineteenth-century scientists'.[1] The reader wishing for a word of

[1] *The Lyric Impulse* by C. Day Lewis (Chatto & Windus, 1965).

introduction before setting forth on Llewelyn's last book may ignore
the reviewers (whose words are long since scattered, anyway) and
read Alyse Gregory's 'magnanimous tribute'—for so the author
called it.

> Is it too much to prophesy [Miss Gregory concludes] that this
> volume of my husband's with its timeless ballad-like quality, its
> innocent classic truths, its passionate spiritual sincerity, and its
> rich exuberant store of natural poetry will be read and enjoyed by
> men and women long after his bones have come to dust, will be
> honoured, indeed, by all those people whose interest in litera-
> ture is firmly grounded upon an ardent and philosophic love
> of life?

'Love and Death . . . the two realities of life,' Theodore had called
them in *Innocent Birds*, and they were two realities ever present in
Llewelyn Powys's thought. In this book they are present on every
page. Miss Gregory, in her introduction, remarks that it is not easy to
be sure how far the story is true, and how far 'imaginary' autobiography; certainly, all that appertains to the present is true except
the concluding pages. The book begins with the summer of 1933, in
which, after feeling quite well, Llewelyn unexpectedly had a dangerous
haemorrhage, so severe that he thought he would die. He describes the
pleasant summer weather, and this contrasts with the abrupt interruption when he wakes at night with his mouth full of blood. He then,
as he lies desperately ill in the slow weeks that follow, sets himself to
remember the story of his first love, his love for Marion Linton—the
book's 'Dittany Stone'. This story he tells, alternating it with the
story of his illness, which for the purpose of the book he supposes to be
fatal: the last pages are very moving, both for themselves and for the
consciousness we may have that so soon after publication they were to
come true. The love story keeps close to truth in many particulars, but
he allows Dittany to be won by a rival, where Marion was lost to him
for a reason he must have regretted much more keenly, her giving up
of the world to enter a nunnery.

But neither the story of his first love, nor the story of his last illness,
is responsible for the book's unique value. It is for the eloquence with
which he expresses his views on these matters of love and death that
Llewelyn's *Love and Death* will be read: the eloquence, the compassion, the insight, the resignation and the exultation. On love and
death and religion and sex and nature and friendship: his ripest and

maturest conclusions are gathered here, and the prose in which he expresses them reaches an excellence even he never surpassed elsewhere. It is as though he really felt that the life whose closing hours he chronicled so poignantly was, in fact, coming to a close. Whatever he wished to say, he must now say or leave unsaid for ever.

26

THEODORE's last full-length work was *Unclay*, published in 1931. For ten years thereafter he continued to write short stories, though these became fewer as the years passed. His publications were fewer, too; between 1923 and 1932 he issued twenty-five separate books, a large total even if in some cases they were limited editions of single stories. In the period 1932 until his death in 1953 he published only four books, and the last of these was a selection from his earlier books; and the whole content of them all consisted of short stories. It was as if he felt he had said all that he wished to say, in the major works; and as if, in these later years of authorship, he wanted only to add here a footnote, and there a minor emendation.

Moreover, in his last twelve or fifteen years he gave up writing altogether, and would seem never to have put pen to paper, beyond writing occasional letters, after his removal to Mappowder in 1940. In part this may be explained by failing health. He suffered a stroke shortly before leaving East Chaldon, and although he recovered largely from this he had to take great care in the future. The small Civil List pension he had been granted some years previously, with what other modest resources he could command, served to keep him and his household from need; but a whole series of Christmas letters to Louis Wilkinson, thanking his old friend for gifts of money, show that in England in the twentieth century a great writer can be glad to lay hands on a pound. No doubt Shakespeare's countrymen are proud of their magnificent literature; but equally without doubt they are not prepared to pay for it. This has been demonstrated in recent years by the impassioned refusals of the public at large to consider a modest charge for authors' benefit at their free public libraries. How such people can read the letters of John Cowper to Louis Wilkinson, in which he speaks—time and again—of having next to nothing in the

bank, and not feel the flush of shame passes my comprehension—
especially as there is a good chance they are reading the book without
having paid a penny piece for the privilege. No one, it may be pre-
sumed, will have reached the present page of the present book unless
he has been reading it with enjoyment; he may now pause to reflect
that my income as a professional writer is rather less than I might enjoy
if I went out road-sweeping.

With the removal of T. F. Powys in 1940, East Chaldon ceased to
be a literary centre, although that distinction may come to the village
again. About the same time, Miss Sylvia Townsend Warner and Miss
Valentine Ackland gave up their cottage over the way from Theodore
and moved to Frome Vauchurch—not very far from Mappowder—
and Llewelyn Powys and Alyse Gregory had of course already gone.
The 'circle', as John Cowper would have called it, now centred on
north-west Dorset, and over the years several members of the Powys
family and their friends settled in or around Mappowder, which is
itself a village as small and remote as East Chaldon, though much
farther from the sea.

Of Theodore's life in Mappowder we hear little, nor could there be
much to hear. It seems appropriate that he should live in a house 'by
the churchyard'—a small, low house, 'The Lodge', which had formerly
been a school-house in which Theodore's grandfather had studied.
The house is set almost as much 'under' as 'by' the churchyard, for
the old church of St Peter and St Paul stands on a slight slope. Mr
Francis Powys tells us that his father gave up reading the lessons in
church, as his habit was at Chaldon, and no longer attended on Sundays. But he would ring the bell daily for Compline, and then slip into
the dark nave and listen, perhaps the only person there except for the
vicar. He preferred the quiet of an empty church to the movement of a
full service; he also liked to please 'old Frank', who was the vicar. He
would linger in the churchyard, ready to point to the place where his
grave was to be. He walked the lanes and fields, thinking; and was of
course a familiar figure in the village, held for his simplicity and kindness in the same kind of esteem that the dalesfolk felt for Hartley
Coleridge. There is a story of an old countryman in Cumberland who
remarked on the number of visitors to Wordsworth's grave and added,
'. . . for my part I'd walk twice distance over Fells to see where
Hartley lies'. This chimes with the comment by a Dorset man on
Theodore: 'There baint no more like he—not nowadays. He was the
last. They be all gone now.'

The books of those later years may be noticed together. The three
curious long-short stories of 'God', 'In Good Earth' and 'The Two
Thieves', published under the title of the last, in 1932, take us back to
the mood of *The Left Leg*. 'In Good Earth' is a tale of unrelieved
gloom. Thomas Gidden and his son John farm a barren stretch of
downland near the village of Adams Folly. They are careful, skilful
and conscientious, but their care and skill go unrewarded: nothing
grows, nothing prospers. Nor is this unlikely, in parts of the fair
county of Dorset. Not very many miles from East Chaldon there is a
real property with the picturesque but not encouraging name of
Labour-in-Vain Farm.

Close to the Giddens, however, there is a fine farm with rich fields
and sturdy bartons—Church Farm. When the tenant dies, John
Gidden—with several others—hopes to receive the tenancy. His old,
defeated father is fretful: where will the money come from to pay old
debts and take on new? How can they hope with their restricted labour
to cultivate so large a farm? And so on. But his son is hopeful and
determined.

But, 'to him that hath shall be given', and the prize goes to Farmer
Pillar, who already has the second best farm in the district. John
Gidden's enemy in this is Squire Yollop's agent, James Cupper.

John has a faithful lover among the village maidens, Ivy Mitten.
But just as he is dissatisfied with his poor farm, so he looks beyond the
pleasant but unspectacular Ivy to the voluptuous 'good earth' of
Nancy Yollop, the squire's daughter. He becomes an intimate of the
Squire's circle, hunts beside Lord Bullman himself, and at last feels
himself sufficiently in the Squire's favour to ask for his daughter. But
just at that moment her engagement to James Cupper is announced.

Again John is driven back to his 'second best'—to Ivy and the child
he has given her. For a little while he is satisfied, they all live in har-
mony, and the old father is content after years of disquietude. But the
ambition in John Gidden comes again to the surface: he must possess
himself of 'good earth'. He has a conversation with the sexton, who
tells him that the churchyard earth is the best in the village, and he is
about to begin buryings in the best part of it. That evening John kisses
his baby, takes his gun and goes out.

'God' is a notable study in childhood, initially; Johnnie Chew has
heard God mentioned very often, but he is not clear who or what God
is, although he knows this to be something very important. Finally, in
his six-year-old mind, he fixes his attention on his father's Sunday hat,

and finds plausible arguments to support the notion that this indeed is God. From this day forward the hat is a potent influence in Johnnie's affairs, right up till the end when the parson is obliged to preach against God the hat in favour of his own God, who is in Heaven. Reluctantly, John—now married, and not doing well—agrees that his God may be sacrificed; but when God is torn open for the sacrifice, he is found to be stuffed with five-pound notes. . . .

The third of these stories, 'The Two Thieves', concerns God and the Devil—the two thieves. It is a study in evil; the idle George Douce decides that the only soft life is the life of a thief, who takes what he wants. There is the Theodorian *naïveté* here, the stripping of an idea to essentials. No mention of law, police, counter measures. It is assumed that if a man wants to be a thief nothing will hinder him.

Unfortunately, George Douce steals from the Devil. He steals four bottles, curiously shaped, and drinks their contents: Greed, Anger, Pride and Cruelty. Under their influence we see him embarking on a life dominated by these four qualities.

But there is another thief in the village—Tinker Jar. One by one he robs George Douce of Greed, Anger, Pride and Cruelty; and the farmer hangs himself, having nothing left.

These stories are allegorical, much more so than the short stories in general are; and they abound in symbolism. They are to be read slowly, and more than once. They afford a strong contrast with the three stories of *The Left Leg*. In 'The Left Leg' itself we have the cruel, acquisitive Farmer Mew, whose fortunes are so exactly the opposite of John Gidden's in 'In Good Earth', though his end, like all men's good or evil, is the grave. The story 'God' may be contrasted with 'Abraham Men'—studies in aspects of simplicity, Luke Bird preaching to the sheep, John Chew ordering his life by a hat, and both men finding a happiness their faiths have not brought them to. And 'Hester Dominy', another contrasting study: Hester shown a momentary happiness only to have it taken from her, and George Douce brought to his own kind of happiness by another road, and led in the same circle back to nothing. It is as though Theodore were saying, neither by good nor evil shall a man or woman find rest in earth.

The two collections of short stories, *Captain Patch* (1935) and *Bottle's Path* (1946), complete the tale of Theodore's books, for *Goat Green*, a long story separately published in 1937, was introduced under its second title, 'The Better Gift', into *Bottle's Path*, and the other single publications were short tales subsequently collected—except

Make Thyself Many, which somehow escaped and remains available only in the long out-of-print limited edition of 1935.

The stories of *Captain Patch* reflect all Theodore's moods, and among them are two fables which might, perhaps, at some time be incorporated with the original collection of *Fables* in a new edition. 'The Hill and The Book' shows what happens to a God-fearing man who throws away his Bible and takes to modern novels. He prospers and rejoices at first, but afterwards he finds that true happiness must be looked for in the Bible. But the Bible also has its ups and downs, and finishes up once more forsaken and rejected, on the bare side of Madder Hill. In 'The Cat and the Rooks' we see once again how a plausible tongue can bring simple creatures to disaster; the cat persuades the rooks to build in Miss Pettifer's tree, and we who already know Miss Pettifer can foresee that no good will come of this. Inevitably, the rooks die. One last fable is to be found in *Bottle's Path*—'The Dove and the Eagle', in some respects the most fabulous of them all. Something like a golden age has arrived on earth—but a very Theodorian golden age, in which the gold is not all it appears, and God looking down decides that earth was better in the old days. So he sends the Holy Dove down to make a disturbance. Unfortunately, the Dove is intercepted *en route* by an Eagle—the very Eagle which in the ordinary course stands in Madder church to support the Holy Bible which the vicar reads the lesson from. Fortunately for the Dove, the Eagle is not hungry immediately, and the two birds enter into conversation, in the course of which the Dove explains his mission—to start a quarrel among the people so that 'Babes will immediately be outraged, old men will be starved or kicked to death, and in a little while a million harmless people will be rotting upon a field of battle.—And then we shall have again some good poetry to read in Heaven—'

The Eagle remarks that things are very dull and the two concoct a plan whereby a fifty-pound pumpkin which is in the church for Harvest Festival shall fall upon the head of the preacher, who happens to be our old acquaintance Dean Ashbourne. This misadventure duly befalls, and at once everyone begins fighting. 'Every sin was committed—and the Holy Dove returned to Heaven.'

In *Captain Patch* we seem to take leave of Mr Dottery and Sexton Truggin, and with them of Theodore's comedy, for *Bottle's Path* is a collection carrying a graver burden. There are fewer stories here, and those longer and sadder; but at the end—and perhaps this fact also carries its burden of symbolism—the gentle vicar and his wily sexton

reappear in the little idyll of 'Circe Truggin' as though the author
after all wished to part from his readers leaving a smile upon their lips;
and—so that more solemn matters may not be forgotten—the last
sound he leaves with us is that of a thieving farmer being roundly
thrashed.

Theodore deliberately 'went out of business', but there was no
question of this with Llewelyn, who continued writing until within a
few days of his death, and who sent for paper in his last hours to leave
one final message behind, reaffirming the faith he had held and ex-
pounded for so long: 'Love Life! Love every moment of life that you
experience *without pain.*'

The essays of his Swiss years make, in the collected volume called
Swiss Essays (1947), a sort of anthology of all Llewelyn's beliefs and
interests. Here are autobiography, criticism, his love of nature, his
interest in people, his controversial and polemical views, his delight in
quaint or picturesque customs among the country people, and his ever-
present consciousness of the desperate nature of our tenure on earth.
The photographs, many of them by his friend H. Rivers Pollock, are
a satisfying accompaniment.

The last book Llewelyn himself saw through the press was *A Baker's
Dozen*, which appeared immediately after his death in a limited, signed
edition issued at Herrin, Illinois, by the Trovillion Private Press. This
edition (of 493 copies) has an introduction by Lloyd Emerson Siberell,
and engravings by Nicholas Noheimer. The English edition was not
published until 1941, with an introduction by J. C. Powys and decora-
tions by Gertrude Powys. In both cases the illustrations take the form
of chapter headings and it is interesting to compare them; the American
artist is the more factual, the English more interpretative; but because
Miss Powys knew the scenes depicted, and Noheimer had never seen
them, her drawings are sometimes closer to objective truth as well—
her 'herring gulls', for example, shows the Dorset coast looking west
towards White Nose, while his circle over two small ships in the open
sea which look more like the Cape Ann vessels of Connecticut than
our Dorset fishing smacks. All the same, Noheimer's work is not
alien to the author's spirit, and indeed Llewelyn was fortunate in his
illustrators. Lynd Ward in *Impassioned Clay* and *Now that the Gods
are Dead* provided dramatic interpretative engravings to march
with Llewelyn's philosophy, and the engravings by Robert Gibbings
for *Glory of Life* and *The Twelve Months* are among that artist's
best work.

Almost Llewelyn's last task as an author was to complete his essay on Paracelsus (now in *Swiss Essays*) and to pass proofs and sign the colophon for *A Baker's Dozen*. He was taken suddenly ill as he was dressing on the morning of 19 November 1939, and had to return to bed. His digestion had been disordered for some time, and now a stomach ulcer was diagnosed. Blood transfusions were given, and somewhat revived him, but only temporarily. It was decided that perhaps an operation would be advisable, but he was not convinced, and agreed to an operation only if a second doctor advised it; and the second doctor did not. Moreover, it was found after Llewelyn's death that such an operation could not have succeeded. Early in the morning of 2 December he died.

I do not wish to paraphrase Miss Gregory's account of his last days, which may be found in her introduction to *The Letters of Llewelyn Powys*, nor to tell again the story as Mr Elwin tells it in his biography. I don't want to take readers away from those earlier books, but to send readers to them. Miss Gregory's words cannot be bettered: simple, few and moving. She prints in full the paper I have quoted, in which her husband wrote his last affirmation of faith. She tells of his resolution and courage; of his thoughts turning to his childhood, of how, once, he said as the end was seen to be inevitable, 'I am a *little* disconsolate'. It was a small reproach against fate for taking him from the sunshine.

Miss Gregory tells how he expressed a wish that no service should be said over him. She and Lisaly Güjer alone followed the body to the crematorium, and she chose a plain metal box to receive his ashes until these could be brought to England. Later they would lie under Elizabeth Muntz's big carved stone, on the cliff above Chydyok.

Llewelyn Powys wrote many letters, of which only a selection have yet been published. *The Letters of Llewelyn Powys* were selected and edited by Louis Wilkinson in 1943, with an introduction by Alyse Gregory which is of particular interest and value for its insight into his character as his wife saw it. The 366 letters represent, of course, only a fraction of those he wrote; and it will be an excellent day when more can be published. His letters to me, under the title *Advice to a Young Poet*, were published in 1946, and have recently been re-edited with the addition of some of my letters and a commentary by Robert L. Blackmore.

Collections of letters are naturally autobiographical, and the reader of Llewelyn's will learn a great deal about the circumstances of his life, and about his family. Indeed, they are a source of prime importance for this purpose. But if letters are to be read for their own sake, to be read as literature, they have need to be something more. We may go to the letters of Matthew Arnold for information, but they afford very little else: it may be doubted if anybody ever kept those two blue volumes as a bedside book. But Llewelyn Powys was a letter writer of another order, and these wise, forthright, headlong, perverse and racy letters bring us very close to the man. This is his very voice, we may reflect, turning the pages; here is his philosophy, here are his loves and hates. His observations on books and authors and the trade of an author are of great interest, and some of his most mature thought has gone into them.

> A writer's work should be a direct expression or flowering of his own life [he writes to John Rowland]. It should be as close to his personal life as marrow to bone. It should be an unstudied, a radiant and random reflection of his deepest thoughts and his deepest feelings. Man's peculiar prerogative is consciousness, and if there is any reward to be had out of his ephemeral days it comes from a heightened awareness of his existence during his scanted years.
>
> . . . good writing has nothing to do with lamps. It uses a grey goose's feather for its mechanical expression, but its true inspiration is derived from the bed, the ladle, the crib, and the coffin. . . . It is not the brain that makes a great writer, it is the temper of his whole being in its approach to life as he finds it on the green earth under the golden sun.

But such a passage as this, and long passages on his views about religion and ethics and affairs, valuable as they are, do not represent the letters' real value; for such passages can, after all, be paralleled in his more formal writings. The great value of these letters, as of all good letters, is in bringing us close to the writer. What was he like to know, to live with, to talk with, to be with? Let us see him off guard now and again, see him in a phrase of his own, 'whimsical, wise and wanton'. Is there any reader of these short random samples who would not wish to take the book up and read on from there?

> . . . Willie has turned up on a week's leave. He captured six Germans a few days ago, the bullets whizzed round him but he did not care, when he got to their camp he ate a Hovis loaf and a

great fat sausage. We ride about together, he looking like Uncle
Littleton in his soldier's clothes. Last night a lion killed a stray
camel within 300 yards of my house. Willie set a trap for it as if it
was a coal-house rat, however the lion evaded the trap and simply
carried the camel to a safer place.

(Letter 69; 1917)

We went to Weymouth one day and came upon Theodore and
Violet and Francis seated on corporation chairs in the most
crowded part of the front. Theodore looked very benevolent,
though he was eager to dissociate himself from 'our party',
saying to Bernie when he met him in St. Mary's, 'there go your
friends', and a little later told Alyse that he had just seen 'her
husband'.

(Letter 108; 1925)

. . . my nephew, the young Littleton, has decided to take Holy
orders . . . Think of this Golden youth of whom I am so proud
becoming a mincing Priest . . . I had rather he had been a beggar
on the road to Framlingham, rather he had manufactured motor
cars than come to this. The news sticks in my gullet. I cannot
stomach it. Yet how unphilosophic we are! In a hundred years
what will it matter whether we have a piece of brass with the
words Clerk in Holy Orders engraved upon it hanging by a loose
screw to a coffin 6 foot underground? It is nothing. Everything
cancels everything and naught remains. I killed a snared rabbit
this afternoon. Its eyes were sticking out of its head. I suppose
priests are like peppercorns in a good pudding. They add a
certain flavour to life. But God bless me what an upshot, and he is
a charming boy!

(Letter 110; 1925)

We have two girls next door with a gramophone and cars. The
place is not the same. The girl is attractive though and for this
reason I cannot be as splenetic as I wish to be. She hangs up on the
line little silken meshes for supporting her little breasts which are
as pleasantly shaped as any William pears on your garden
wall . . .

(Letter 145; 1929)

I have never been so ill . . . I feel ill still. I found my spirit remained firm and I was not afraid. I used to watch the cows on the downs with their religious heads bowed and their tails indifferently flicking and presently my plight would seem inconsequential. Did not every living thing have to pass through its hour of Trial?

(Letter 176; 1933)

And the last he ever wrote, a postcard:

I shall be delighted, my dear John Rowland, to be associated with anything you write, whether of roguery, poetry, or philosophy. I believe with you that the present desolations will pass and you and your children will live in a better age with simplicity and gaiety. Dust is soft, secret, and silent. I am not so well, but have had a happy life for half a century in sunshine.—Bless you

Llewelyn Powys

27

JOHN COWPER, of all the brothers and sisters, was the one most conscious of the family connection with Wales, and the identity of name with the ancient princes of Powysland. A. R. Powys spoke of Jack's 'nonsense' about being Celtic and Welsh, and Littleton asserted that the family had been English for at least four hundred years; this was when discussions were going back and forth about Louis Marlow's proposed title, *Welsh Ambassadors*. But John wasn't compiling family trees, he was responding to a poetry and a temperamental affinity, when he identified himself with Wales. In the early winter of 1934 he found a small but convenient house in Corwen, Merionethshire, and there he settled for the next twenty years—the longest he was ever in one place. In May 1955 he removed to Blaenau-ffestiniog, where he remained until his death, so that he lived in Wales almost thirty years.

John Cowper lived in separation from his wife for a long time and his last years in America and his life in Wales were shared by Phyllis Playter, daughter of his old friend Franklin Playter, a sturdy native of Kansas who died at a great age shortly before John Cowper returned to England. It was with three ladies that he made the move to Wales, for Franklin Playter's widow and her sister accompanied Phyllis, and set up an establishment next door. The houses were new, and neat, part of a small estate on the hillside west of the ancient little town of Corwen, with its intimate associations with the old Welsh Powys legends, and with ancient legends older far than these, and as old almost as the world—legends going back into remote regions of time and space, as a reading of *Morwyn* shows. There was nothing of this romance about the houses on the hillside—new, red-brick, ordinary; but they looked across the valley of the sacred river to the mountains of Snowdonia, and romance lay all about them. It was James Hanley who helped to find this place for John Cowper to live, and Hanley himself lived a few miles away and has written memorably about life in this corner of Wales. Nearer at hand, in rooms over a shop in the main square at Corwen, John Redwood-Anderson settled for a number of years, and would discourse with John Cowper almost daily. Anderson said to me once, 'His ideas were always interesting, but they were always wrong!'

The arrival in Wales marks a change in the work of John Cowper Powys. The last novel written in England, and about England, *Maiden Castle*, was the last with a conventional and present-day setting; and although conventional is an odd word to use of this author's novels, it can be used of *Maiden Castle* and the novels that went before, but never of any that came after. It is as though from the Corwen hillside John decided to give himself his head, and write to please himself, in whatever way he chose. Llewelyn Powys quotes a saying which seems to apply: 'The older the Welshman, the more madman!' John's later novels are reckless, extravagant, headlong, perverse, shameless—all words he would approve of.

The first of this later series of novels was published in 1937: *Morwyn, or The Vengeance of God*. There is an old-fashioned flavour about the device of a subtitle, and about the device of the narrator retailing these events in a long letter to his son. The whole framework of the story has something of this leisurely, nineteenth-century convention, and that serves to highlight the appalling events described— no less than a descent into Hell. Writing to Boyne Grainger a few weeks before publication, he says 'My new book is a wild and savage tale of adventures *in Hell*—adventures there of myself and my dog and Phyllis (as a Welsh girl).' Certainly, so far as the dog is concerned, *Morwyn* gives a pretty close picture of 'The Old', John Cowper's black spaniel, whose engaging habits and personality are minutely described. This book met with a certain amount of critical ridicule from reviewers not prepared to meet the author half way—reviewers unable to assess something outside their small terms of reference. One facetiously discussed the adventures of 'Mr Powys and party' as though this were a Cook's tour of the shades, and another used a rather nice phrase and called the book 'a farrago of wordy nonsense'. Well, I suppose so is the *Inferno* of Dante. All works of imaginative literature must be approached with a certain suspension of disbelief, and Mr Powys and party are entitled to this benefit like any other group of travellers in strange foreign parts.

The central theme is cruelty, how to endure it, how to fight it, how to destroy it. And the great cruelties are branches of Sadism, which we see under practice in the novel: man's inhumanity to man, and to animals. Here is John Cowper's most sustained attack upon the evils of vivisection, his views upon which he had expressed more briefly in *Weymouth Sands*, and occasionally (again briefly) in other books. But now he prepared a full-scale attack, and the horrors of his hell are almost all linked with this theme. He puts the indictment into the mouth of the Welsh bard Taliessin:

'You hold your licence! And the moaning of your victims goes up to the Creator night and day. You're the plague spot at the heart of your accurst civilization! And let me tell you this. Your science may torture all it likes with your precious licence, but the vengeance of Heaven will fall on your race! More will perish because of science than will live because of it. You can't mock God forever. The lives you save—if you *do* save them—by this unspeakable wrong, will survive to curse you and your diabolical science. The law of the universe is righteousness and justice and mercy and pity; and not all the Science in your laboratories can make wrong right! The moan that rises from your places of torment will return upon you and upon your children—yea! it is doing so already!—with a vengeance that will shake the world. It is the pity of God that lies bound upon your tables; it is the justice of God that lies helpless under your racks. But it will be the *vengeance* of God that will descend on your children's children. . . .'

But the scientist has already given his answer: 'You laymen know nothing about it. I am a privileged person. I hold a licence from the Home Office. No society can touch me—no pity can affect me. My Research Laboratory is beyond good and evil. *I am Science*—holy and sacrosanct.'

Many people turn a blind eye to any evil done in the name of science, and they will do well to read this book and reflect. *Is* Science holy and sacrosanct? Since 1937 we have come many steps nearer the truth of John's prophecy, that more will perish because of Science than will benefit from it.

The setting of *Morwyn*, the descent into and the sojourn in Hell, are something more than 'a farrago of wordy nonsense'. This is a magnificent feat of imaginative writing, and so are the conversations and encounters with some of Hell's notable inhabitants, particularly

Torquemada, the Marquis de Sade and the Emperor Nero. Other great figures from the past enter the story, including Socrates, Rabelais, Taliessin, as already mentioned, and Merlin. There are ancient gods, too, deep at the still centre of the universe into which the travellers are led at last. Rhadamanthus sits in judgment, Cronos waits in immemorial sleep the return of the Golden Age.

Of course, the book is a tract; but it is as exciting as a western, told with unfailing narrative power which compels acceptance in any candid reader, so that even the incongruities, like television in Hell, appear inevitable. And despite the horrors, whether experienced or imagined, there is a constant play of humour. This is the only novel of John's told in the first person, and the narrator is something of a Dr Watson—not very bright, not at all sure of himself most of the time, but a man of strong feelings and convictions, rather out of his depth (as who would not be when the earth opens beneath his feet and deposits him in Hell with a girl, a dog and the corpse of a vivisector?), but obstinately determined to see the affair through.

This was no easy book to get published, and the author records that it was rejected in America and only published in England by the intervention of Mrs Thomas Hardy, who recommended John's agent to go to Cassell's. He records this in a letter to Louis Marlow (12 March 1944) which, looking back nearly ten years, may not be strictly accurate, for Cassell's had already published *Maiden Castle*, and any new novel would automatically be an 'option book'. But John goes on to say he visited Sir Newman Flower, the head of the firm, and said, 'I'm writing a novel against vivisection which may be hard to get published', and Flower's reply was: 'Opposition to vivisection is my strongest opinion—I will take it, I will *take* it, I *will* take it!'

At this time, and for several years, John Cowper had difficulty in finding publishers. He was rejected by The Bodley Head over *Maiden Castle*, and returned to them with *Owen Glendower*. His New York publishers made a number of objections to various books, rejecting some and requiring revision in others. Indeed, only a few of his later books were published in America, sometimes in small imported editions by small, specialist publishers; and it is only now, after his death, that a revival of interest is beginning there, fostered by the action of Colgate University Press in issuing or reissuing thirteen titles almost simultaneously in the autumn of 1965. He reached calmer publishing waters in 1951 when Macdonald's published *Porius*; and thereafter they not only brought out his new books, ten in all up to the time of his death, but they put in hand a series of reprints of his major novels which continues. The days when important writers could expect an elaborate 'Collected Edition' in their later years, or at least after their death, have gone and may never return; they were extinguished by the war of 1939–45, and a generation older than the Powys brothers—the generation of Hardy, Kipling, Conrad and Shaw—was the last to enjoy this crowning achievement as of right. A uniform edition of Llewelyn Powys, issued by The Bodley Head, had to be suspended after only three volumes had appeared. These Macdonald reissues of John Cowper are the nearest we can hope to get in our lifetime to a Collected Works of John Cowper; perhaps of the less voluminous Theodore something may be possible, but there is no hope of it yet.

With the death of Llewelyn Powys and the virtual silence of Theodore, it may now be best to modify the biographical framework of this book. Some biographical details are to be added, but they may conveniently be gathered together later. John Cowper became as permanent a feature of the Corwen scene, and afterwards of the scene at Blaenau, as ever Theodore was at Chaldon. In those years—small accidents apart—his biography lay in the successive appearances of his books. The need for a chronological appraisal of these is not urgent, and it seems better to examine them in groups—the historical novels, the later 'science-fiction' tales, and the philosophical and critical works. A 'sport', at once unlike any of them, and (because of its author) having affinity with them all, is the curious novel *The Inmates* (1952), which may conveniently be noticed here, along with *Morwyn*. The link is tenuous, but important. Like Dr Brush in *Weymouth Sands*, the sinister Dr Echetus conducts an asylum and a vivisection laboratory; but the horrors of 'Hell's Museum' are much stronger than those at Glint in *The Inmates*; because, after the early references, vivisection ceases to be a main topic in the book's development. It is almost as though, for the time being, he had written himself out on this subject, in *Morwyn*.

The Inmates is provided with a prefatory note in which the author explains the ideas that prompted him to write. He wanted to invent a group of 'really mad' people, and display their 'fantastic and grotesquely humorous extravagance' in facing life with what he calls 'the Philosophy of the Demented'. The book is in fact a long conversation piece, for of action or event there is a minimum, except at the end where the inmates make a mass exodus, and even this is recorded mainly by inference. There is a broad basic resemblance between this book and the satirical novels of Peacock; in the queer names—Mr Frogcastle, Father Toby Tickle, Mr Pantamount, Dr Echetus and a dozen others, all Peacockian; in the talk, and especially in the device under which prominent characters expound their philosophies and the others listen and comment; and in the ironic humour. This resemblance is probably unconscious, and may indeed be quite coincidental; for I don't recall that John Cowper anywhere betrays any wide awareness of Peacock and his work.

But what makes *The Inmates* a unique *tour de force* is the essential madness of the book—its convincing madness. One feels that only a madman could have written it. Long since, John Cowper had said, talking of his work as a lecturer, that he *became* the person he lectured on; and here in the same way he gets under the skins and into the minds of his lunatics in a remarkable way, so that the reader never stops to say, 'That's crazy!' but sympathizes, understands and acquiesces. These inmates, on the whole, appear more sane than their keepers. As for the author being 'mad', he speaks in his *Autobiography* of being rather less than wholly sane, and I have myself no doubt that he was in certain moods to madness near allied—why not? John Cowper says in the prefatory note to *The Inmates* that 'the genius of great artists has always been in their unearthly and startling imaginations allied to madness'. He is speaking specifically of painters; but the precept may be applied to all the arts, and certainly not least to his own and his practice of it.

The story is of no place or time—'time, the present' might be the direction if it were a play. It is located in our own day, we know, if only for the helicopter which comes at the end—but this helicopter, incidentally, is a great deal bigger than any that were flying in 1952 when the book was published. This is a point worth noting because John Cowper increasingly turned away from conventions of time and place in his later books and in particular, as already indicated, he gave up writing about the contemporary scene in any conventional sense. The curious tale of *Up and Out*, for example, happens 'in the present year of our Christian era', we are told in Chapter One; and the book was published in 1957. But no tale ever written was less firmly rooted in the mid twentieth century, and the people and places may or may not live 'on the borders of Somerset and Dorset'—we can only say that if they do they keep well out of sight; the village of Foghorn is not in the least like any west country village; Brobdingnag is another matter. So, in *The Inmates*, the contemporary setting is immaterial, the landscape ideal and almost illusory. We are concerned strictly with people, in the timeless situations of loving and hating, thinking and feeling, and, most nearly and most fully, with the 'love at first sight' of John Hush, newly certified, and Tenna Sheer, already an inmate. John Hush, we feel, is not *very* mad; he simply has a mania for cutting off locks of young girls' hair. Tenna has tried to murder her father, and is inclined to attempt the murder of any elderly man when the mood is upon her, but in all else she is sane. The love of these two is told tenderly and engagingly, and holds the framework of the book together while the isolated conversations develop between groups of the patients putting severally their interpretations of the 'Philosophy of the Demented'. The mass escape at the end introduces a tincture of farce into the affair. Most of the inmates are recaptured—and probably are glad to be back inside. But John and Tenna get clear away.

These two novels, *Morwyn* and *The Inmates*, have not provoked much critical attention as yet, and they will repay closer study. They bear something of the same relation to *Owen Glendower* and *Atlantis* that *Rodmoor* and *Ducdame* do to the later English novels. The later books surpass them, but they are not discredited.

28

A T FIRST sight, the long row of John Cowper Powys's books offers comparatively little in literary criticism, and this would seem curious in view of his many years as a lecturer and 'interpreter' of the great classics. It might be expected that from time to time a man so employed would collect his lectures and essays into book form. But we know why he did not do this—he had no formal, prepared lectures. Every lecture was impromptu and unique—when he stood up to speak he had usually no more idea what he meant to say than his audience had. He must have sent millions of words of criticism into the air over a period of almost forty years in lecturing, but he wrote very few of them down. He lacked the frugal instinct to rescue his occasional essays and papers from magazines and journals which is necessarily a part of the make-up of most writers, and accordingly some of his significant work—the long early essay on Joyce, for example—is virtually unavailable now, although no doubt it will eventually be collected.[1] He wrote long introductions to a number of books, and these alone would make an attractive volume of essays if gathered together.

In 1938 he published *The Pleasures of Literature* (in the United States this book was called *The Enjoyment of Literature*). It is a big book, and it records his mature conclusions on a score of the greatest writers of the world, from Homer to Hardy. Each essay is about as long as a lecture, and the reader who never had the good fortune to hear John Cowper lecture may take these essays as the best available substitute. They are eloquent, but informal—often colloquial, as if here indeed were the living voice. The book might be called 'talking about literature', but that is not to say that these are the cosy, relaxed

[1] A later essay on *Finnegans Wake was* collected—in *Obstinate Cymric*.

familiar essays about books we associate with such names as Augustine
Birrell or Edmund Gosse (I am not suggesting that such essays do not
have their value). No: these essays carry heavier metal, for all their
ease and familiarity; the reader may think rather of Coleridge as he
turns these pages; for Coleridge, like John Cowper, saw new and surprising things even in texts which had been the subject of commentary
for a thousand years. The book is interpretative rather than empirical,
and this is a point of some importance because it means that the reader
who has never opened (say) the essays of Montaigne may be stimulated
and entertained by John Cowper's remarks on Montaigne—and,
doubtless, sent to his writings—whereas so much contemporary
criticism can be understood only in the light of a prior knowledge of
the subject. If ever there were a book of criticism for the general
reader, this is it; and how much some of the writers under discussion
need it!—undoubtedly, hundreds of readers have hesitated before
embarking upon Proust, or Nietzsche, or Dante, or Dostoievsky,
deterred by their bulk, or complexity, or strangeness; and for such
readers *The Pleasures of Literature* offers here a starting point, there a
short cut, somewhere else a clue. But this is not all, nor is it perhaps the
book's principal value. The reader who has been a life-long lover of
Shakespeare, or Milton, or Matthew Arnold, may turn to the essays
here and find an illumination, a new viewpoint, which will give
excitement and strangeness again to the most familiar text.

The Pleasures of Literature was, despite its division into chapters
with specific titles—Dante, Goethe, Whitman—a long celebration of
the pleasures and rewards of reading. It was everywhere a relation of
literature to life, and it may be that John Cowper felt this to be a final
word to which he had nothing to add—a hail and farewell to his lifetime's task of interpreting the world's literature. There were still some
big romances of his own he wanted to write, and he could not tell how
many years remained in which to write them. But he owed special
allegiance to two great writers about whom he wanted to say something further, and he produced his long essay on Dostoievsky in 1946,
his life and interpretation of Rabelais in 1948.

The book on Dostoievsky reverses what I have said about *The
Pleasures of Literature*. This commentary does call for some prior
knowledge in the reader, and he will benefit by having Dostoievsky's
major novels at his elbow while he reads. There are also a good many
references to leading authorities—to the opinions of D. S. Mirsky, for
example, and to the *Life* by E. H. Carr. In some degree this book is a

defence; there are elements of special pleading in it, and this may possibly have influenced the publishers for whom it was originally written—Staples & Staples—for they never brought it out. It also explains the rather odd length of the book, longer than an essay but shorter than a normal book-length study; for it was designed as a half-crown paperback. *Dostoievsky* was finished in 1942, but did not appear in book form (published eventually by The Bodley Head) until 1946.

A reader seeking an 'introduction' to Dostoievsky would probably not find John Cowper's book the best initial approach, and the Dostoievsky essay in *The Pleasures of Literature* is short and in a sense perfunctory; it is almost as though this writer who meant so much to John Cowper Powys somehow stood between him and his readers when he came to write. The early essay, in *Visions and Revisions*, is the most likely to convey Dostoievsky's essence to a reader coming newly to him; but *Dostoievsky*, the book, contains insights and observations which will delight the converted reader.

With *Rabelais*, however, the case is altered. Here is a book which makes the ideal introduction, and moreover an introduction to Rabelais was badly wanted, for his greatness—and it is significant that John Cowper ranks him with Homer and Shakespeare—has never received in England the general recognition it merits, despite the excellence of Sir Thomas Urquhart, the original translator. Although his name gives a popular adjective to the language, Rabelais, the most readable of the great foreign classics, is among the least read. Yet he is not a poet—that stumbling block of the general reader—and he tells a story far less discouraging than does, for example, Tolstoy. But the sombre Russian is more widely read in this country today, and more widely read are Balzac, Cervantes and probably Dostoievsky. Perhaps the perspective is wrong: Rabelais is too big to be seen, his huge exaggerated book having every power except the power to beckon inside a reader newly and tentatively adventuring. Certainly Rabelais is not lightly to be entered upon, or lightly to be interpreted. No great writer may be summed up so easily—or so wrongly—if a superficial acquaintance is to be the basis of criticism. His seeming faults of prolixity, exaggeration, grossness, are so apparent that it is easy to overlook his humanity, his wisdom and his sanity. He is the most earthy of humorists, and the most wholesome—one of the morning stars of thought, a 'maker' who contributes something unique and irreplaceable to the record of human experience.

He afforded, of course, a splendid subject for John Cowper, in whom so many of Rabelais's qualities are paralleled. The gusto, the depth and the idiosyncrasy of John's appreciations of literature are themselves unashamedly Gargantuan, and the comic passages in his novels owe as much to Rabelais as to anyone. Moreover, he came to Rabelais as his biographer and interpreter fifty years after first reading him, and after re-reading him many times in the interval.

The book is of particular interest, its subject apart, for several reasons. It offers John's only essay in biography, and as the reader of *Henry Hudson* might say that in Llewelyn a born biographer was lost when he wrote no more in this *genre*, so the reader of *Rabelais* might argue of John Cowper. The biographical essay runs to ninety pages, and in it the author subjects himself to a rare discipline by 'keeping his eye on the ball'. He never forgets that biography ideally is a connected, coherent, chronological narrative. In the life of Rabelais, as in any life of the Renaissance period, there are gaps, uncertainties, lacunae; but what is known, or can reasonably be inferred, he gives us, together with a lively commentary on the background of Rabelais's times. As a biographical essay it could hardly be bettered within its scale.

The second part of the book is also a *tour de force*, and especially so for John: a summary or précis of Rabelais's work in some forty pages. If John Cowper Powys was indeed 'one of the great sprawlers of literature' he performed a difficult feat here in reducing that other great sprawler to so narrow a compass; but a feat of considerable value, for an awareness of 'the story' is of service to the reader embarking upon Rabelais for the first time, and certainly it is not readily come at in the original.

Next comes a long and generous section of 'newly translated' passages from Rabelais. In the book's preface the author has a number of observations about Sir Thomas Urquhart's translation, and some about later versions, and about the business of translation in general. The preface indeed is one of the most interesting parts of the book. And as the 'Life of Rabelais' is his sole sustained essay in biography, so in these passages 'newly translated' we get our only chance to see John Cowper as a translator, except for very occasional very brief passages from the Welsh or the Greek which arise incidentally in his other writings. He discusses the various ways of translating, whether literally or by paraphrase, and sums up his own preference: 'What we want therefore from a translation is not a display of a fellow countryman's gifts for turning foreign classics into English classics, but a real *initiation*, at any cost to our comfort in reading, into the actual psychic *smell*, if I may say so, and the intimate *physical taste*, of a new and foreign approach to the *universally human*.' Now, many will sympathize with the suggestion that merely to translate is not enough: Pope's Homer is a splendid English poem, but it isn't Homer's Homer. There should be a certain strangeness in a translation, underlining its foreign origin, conveying its foreign flavour, retaining what the author himself would have recognized as its quintessence. Rabelais has been swamped by Urquhart, so that it is hard to think of him in any other English version; but more than one commentator has pointed out the disservice Urquhart did to his original by being more Rabelaisian than Rabelais. John Cowper's specimen translations will hardly correct this, for they represent too small a part of the whole; but they may serve to encourage another translator working along similar and sympathetic lines to attempt a new complete translation. My own rudimentary French makes it impossible for me to attempt an assessment of John Cowper's success as a translator; but clearly and frequently I hear his own voice in these passages, so that however he may have succeeded in interpreting Rabelais he never did so to the complete exclusion of himself.

Perhaps the translations, because of their comparative brevity, must remain matters mainly of academic interest; after all, when it comes to reading Rabelais, most people will have to be content with Urquhart and Motteux. Here is where part four of John's book comes into its own—'An Interpretation of Rabelais, consisting of an Analysis of his Genius and Religion, and a Re-Valuation of his true place as a World-Genius.' This section is about the same length as the book on Dostoievsky, and affords an interesting contrast. There can be no doubt of John Cowper Powys's understanding of the Russian, or of his astonishing insight into the novels; and of their affinities as writers and thinkers John's own novels offer sufficient proofs. But somehow his writing about Dostoievsky is not completely satisfying: there lacketh something still. It is quite otherwise with *Rabelais*. This book is written with a sure touch, an effortless touch, throughout. It has an assured authority. We feel too that the author was never extended, that he always had something in reserve. A reader ignorant of Greek, Latin, German, French, as I am, must read the classics of world literature in translation, and must come to his understanding of them by the help of commentaries such as this one on Rabelais. This gives him one small advantage over more informed readers: he best knows which commentaries have served him best. I have never encountered a better book in this field than this *Rabelais*. It should be at the elbow of every reader setting out for the first time to enter the world of Gargantua and Friar John, Panurge and Pantagruel.

These three books, the latest of them published in 1948, represent John's farewell to interpretative criticism, except for occasional detached short essays, a very few lectures, and some introductions. This may seem a biggish list of exceptions, but it means none the less that for the last fifteen years of his life he concentrated almost solely on writing fiction. The essays of *In Spite Of* (1953), although new, are a restatement of his former positions in regard to these several subjects of 'Loneliness', 'Insecurity', 'Pride' and so on, 'in spite of' which he formulates his 'Philosophy for Everyman'. His other 'non-fiction' book of this time was *Obstinate Cymric* (1947) a gathering of essays. I said some pages above that the gathering of essays was just what he did *not* do ... and in the ordinary way, he did not. These essays were in some degree a special case. They are largely, though not entirely, auto-biographical; and largely, though not entirely, about Wales. They were published at Carmarthen by a Welsh publisher, and had, I suppose, a restricted circulation, though I hope not. At all events the reader's attention is invited to them now for their autobiographical content. They make, with the essay on life in upper New York State recently published in Colgate University's *Philobiblon*, the too brief, too few footnotes to his *Autobiography* which are all we have of a 'sequel' to that book—and he lived nearly thirty years after writing it. In particular these essays give us much insight into his feelings about Wales, and a view of his final personal philosophy which is of particular interest as showing how far he modified his views at the close of his life on the great absolutes of speculative philosophy, God, morality, immortality and the rest.

—— 29 ——

WHEN John Cowper settled at Corwen he at once began studying all things Welsh—her language, her legends, her history, customs, traditions, poetry. Half humorously, perhaps, perhaps half seriously, he began to think and speak and write of himself as a Welshman. He referred to the 'land of my fathers'; the very first words of *Obstinate Cymric* speak of 'we Welsh people'. A man rarely learns well or rapidly in middle or later life when he embarks upon a new study. But John Cowper became genuinely learned in Welsh lore, and this interest brought him new friendships and a new reputation in his last years. It would be too much to say he became a national figure in Wales, but it would not be too much to say that his presence was a source of pride and delight to his adopted countrymen, and nothing certainly could be more proper than for his portrait to hang in the National Museum of Wales. The painting is by his sister Gertrude, and seems to me more successful than her earlier drawings as reproduced in Richard Heron Ward's *The Powys Brothers*.

The fruits of his Welsh residence and studies were soon apparent, in his first and perhaps finest historical novel, *Owen Glendower*, published in New York in 1940 and in England the year following. Owen Glendower is the greatest national hero in Welsh history; his campaigns to free Wales of English domination were very successful and came close to complete fulfilment, and his dream of independence was not an idle one. As a central figure for an historical romance he could hardly be bettered. John Cowper, following established convention, tells Owen's story through its impact upon a group of his followers, and in particular on Rhisiart ab Owen, the chieftain's cousin and secretary. But the book is Rhisiart's story, too, and as in any of John's big novels, there are a dozen lesser plots and threads which are resolved often in enough detail to furnish out a full novel. Rhisiart himself is one of the most complex of John Cowper's characters, the first really *young* hero in any of the novels, and consequently the least immediately identifiable with his creator, although as the story develops we find him thinking and behaving from time to time in a manner reminiscent of Wolf Solent or Dud No-man, though more decisively, as though the difference of twenty or more years in age gave the younger character a greater freedom of action.

This is in fact a novel of youth, the more impressive because it is the work of a man already close to old age. Insurrections, alarums and expeditions call naturally enough for youth in outlook and leadership, even if graver counsels lie behind them, and in making his principal hero one close to the centre of events, but not primarily concerned in ordering them, John Cowper is able to give a detached view of the rebellion. The reader does not feel personally involved in taking sides, beyond a natural sympathy for the people through whose eyes he sees the tale unfolded. The advantage here is that as we do not see the characters primarily as warriors taking a part in history, we do not see them dressed up in a tapestry-stiffness, and we meet them on common ground as human beings. Most of the time these people are talking, eating, making love, walking in the fields, looking out to see if it will rain, tying their shoe laces—just as we all are. The war is an element in their lives, but it isn't in the same room with them, and those of us who have seen war know that it goes on mostly in the background, and ordinary life goes on parallel with it but in the foreground.

In *Owen Glendower* the balance between ordinary people living ordinary lives, and the influence of the coming of public disorder upon them is delicately maintained. The reader forgets that he is reading an historical novel, for the history never takes precedence; in a tale of conquest and intrigue, the reader is led on eagerly to wonder what will happen next, but in this book his interest is less in the event than in how the people will react to it. *Owen* as much as any other of the novels of John Cowper Powys is concerned with character, and the interplay of character upon character. And what a wealth of contrasting characters the book affords! Owen himself, brought by pressures of circumstance and fatality to a rebellion that cannot succeed, and yet nearly does succeed: a man of indecision forced into action, the action often enough having to be directed against his own headstrong and incautious commanders, who will lose the war for him quicker than he would himself. For Owen almost all of the fighting is within the Welsh council chamber, where ambition clashes with prudence, religion with blood-lust, policy with impatience. We have also the turbulent priests, the mad Friar Huw with his delusion that King Richard is still alive, the scheming Prior Bevan, the cynical Father Pascentius, the saintly Abbot Cust, and Father Rheinalt whose daughter Tegolin is the rebellion's Joan of Arc. We have the knights and chieftains, men of recorded history like Harry Hotspur, Lord Grey of Ruthin, Walter Brut the Hereford Lollard, Don of Kidwelly, Gam of Brecon; and significant figures created to fill the gaps history has left unfilled, like the sinister and sadistic Lowri ferch Ffraid, Philip Sparrow the champion of the peasantry, and Denis Burnell, the sturdy Constable of Dinas Brān—a great gallery as usual, some fifty major characters, all rounded, all plausible, all convincing, all alive. These characters are so individual that if any one of them spoke or acted 'out of character' the reader would notice it, would say to himself, 'That's not like Simon the Hog!' or 'That's not like Mistress Sibli!'—but they never do.

There is no attempt in *Owen Glendower* to write a connected and chronological narrative of external events. The confused clashes and encounters of those first years of the fifteenth century are not readily disentangled, and there was no major decisive battle between the main opposing armies which makes a natural climax to the story. Many incidents of prime importance in the history of the rebellion are hardly mentioned, or are recorded as happening 'off stage', and the only time we take the field with Owen at the head of his army it is for the abortive siege of Worcester. But the sense of history going on all around is strong; the reader is living in history in the making and as in real life, history being made is confused, not fully recorded and not fully understood. The characters react in the light of what they know, without help from the author's hindsight even indirectly, and this strengthens the reader's illusion of being among the people to whom these things are happening.

But, if the overall history of Owen is not directly narrated, this is not to say there is no movement, no crisis, no climax, in the novel. There is constant movement, several masterly crowd scenes, battle and crisis and confrontation and treason and disaster in plenty. Nowhere is the author's huge grasp of a crowded narrative more confidently exercised than in this novel. One of his great crowd scenes, comparable with the pageant chapter in *Glastonbury*, comes right at the start, when Mad Huw is dragged to the stake and the drunken, blaspheming, out-of-control mob of peasants and soldiers swirls and lurches about the funeral pyre in the twilight, and their opposing leaders argue the pros and the cons and the Maid clings to the Friar's pinioned body: a rushing, confused, obscure, irrational tableau, and suddenly, in a great silence, on his old horse, the boy Rhisiart moves forward to the centre of the stage, with drawn sword, and everything is still. This is a moment in fiction when one really feels it would be possible to hear a pin drop. Another such sudden calm in the midst of confusion comes when Owen arms the Maid and sets her at the head of his army, and again for a moment all is still.

Professor G. Wilson Knight has written an eloquent essay on *Owen Glendower*, in which he comments on the historical learning the book displays. It is not only—as he points out—the learning that knows about battles and events. The author has created the world and the society in which his characters move by a hundred small touches whose authenticity may go unnoticed individually, but which add up to an overall authenticity which is very impressive. Such touches, for example, as a reference to the 'new-fangled' chimney with which a great house was furnished, a casual reminder that the use of these was only then beginning to come in; or the incidental touches about fashion in clothes, changing manners and customs—matters the general reader will accept in passing, but which the student may check if he will, and will always find accurate and informed.

This story, for all its fringing upon great events, is a simple domestic tale, too. It is a picture of how folks lived. We are taken down the draughty corridors, into the smoky dining-halls, into the dim sleeping chambers, the dark latrines. There is hardly any privacy, hardly any quiet: life is lived in public, among others: so people are born, and so die. The fumes of the torches catch in our throat as we read.

A simple domestic tale, I call it. For, essentially, whatever the press of occasion and diplomacy, this is the story of Rhisiart ab Owen. It is a study of character, and the development of character, and nowhere in all John Cowper's novels is a character more skilfully developed and displayed. Rhisiart enters the story in the first sentence of Chapter One, a raw lad who, for all his Oxford training, is innocent and unsophisticated. But he learns from the start, and profits from his learning; and he learns not from books but from people. At the close he is a formidable and successful man, a Judge, one of the few men about Owen's court who gain in fortune and reputation, when the battles are over. And, parallel with this material education, we watch the maturing of Rhisiart's character. He would be a key figure in any extended essay on the influence of sex on John Cowper Powys's characters. His love affairs do not depend for their interest in any direct sexual description, but for the influence we see in them on his character; and indeed in all fiction there can be few young men whose reaction to sex is shown to be so integral in the forming of their character.

The emphasis is on Rhisiart, but there are other important threads in the story, some personal and human, like the tender relationship between Mad Huw and the Maid, and others tending to illustrate the changing manners and times—tending to establish within the novel a recognizable 'portrait of the age'. The picture of Walter Brut well illustrates this. The Lollard is a sympathetic and noble character, a shining light among the many motivated by self-interest. But he is also a symbol, and in the account of his actions and beliefs we learn a great deal about the religious turbulence of the time. Between them Philip Sparrow and Father Pascentius, Griffith Young and Sir John Oldcastle, and the knights and priests, give us a picture of the changing political scene and of individual viewpoints. The astonishing relationship between Mistress Lowri and Simon the Hog is one of the darkest and most complex in all John Cowper's novels, and the dwarf Sibli is a creation worthy of Dickens or Dumas. Indeed, if famous names are to be invoked, *Owen Glendower* will bring a score of them to mind: there are scenes and passages here that would not discredit Chaucer, or Rabelais, or Shakespeare, or Scott, or Hardy, or Henry James.

The action of *Owen Glendower* ranges pretty widely over Wales, and for a time into England, but most of it is set in the area of Corwen, and one can imagine the author propped up on his couch with his writing board on his knee, looking across the valley to the hills of Snowdonia, peopling the ancient castles with serving-men and men-at-arms, and maids and lords and ladies. He was always conscious that he was now living in the heart of the land he wrote about, in a manner the exact opposite of that which obtained during the writing of his English novels. I remember his writing to me, when I was journeying into Wales, to say that his hero was exactly of my age and at that moment at the Abbey of Valle Crucis; as if in my visit to the ruins I might easily encounter him.

Between *Owen Glendower* and *Porius*, the novel that followed, there is an interval of almost ten years, the longest time that ever passed during John's active writing career between the appearances of his novels. There was, of course, no complete silence during this time, for he published half a dozen books, including the important study of Rabelais, and the philosophic essay on growing old. There would be several reasons for the delay between novels. First, historical novels are not written so quickly as others, because of the research necessary in establishing the background, and in the case of *Porius* with its setting in the Dark Ages this research was not easily conducted. Next, John Cowper was writing his *Rabelais* during part of the same time—he writes to Louis Wilkinson that he works on the two books on alternate days; and *Rabelais* also entailed research in greater measure than most of John's books. Further, we hear of the manuscript being 'revised', which as Louis Wilkinson points out, is something new with John. He certainly took enormous trouble over the book, and it is a tremendous feat of creation, for he lays a living world before us where recorded history is silent, or nearly so. It must also be remembered that *Porius* was written during the period when its author was having difficulty with publishers. The Americans rejected *Porius* out of hand and in England it was published neither by Cassell's, Cape nor The Bodley Head, the three principal houses with whom he was then associated. Instead, it appeared under the imprint of Macdonald, the first complete book of John Cowper's they published, although his association with the firm began with the publication of his introduction to the 'Macdonald Illustrated Classics' edition of Sterne's *Sentimental Journey* in 1948. This he had undertaken at the request of Malcolm Elwin, general editor of the series, to whom John Cowper Powys and his admirers owe a considerable debt. From this time until the end of his life he had no further difficulty in getting his work published, and moreover, as previously mentioned, Macdonald's gradually put back into print a number of major works which had long been unavailable.

Porius is a magnificent piece of imaginative reconstruction. The action takes place in the year A.D. 499, mainly in that same area around Corwen which is the setting for *Owen*. This was indeed the middle of the Dark Ages, so far as our knowledge is concerned, and as G. M. Trevelyan says, 'The past is inexorable in its silence'. So far as records go, John Cowper had a blank page to write on. He creates a court in Wales, and shows the factions that divide it—loyalty to the overall emperor of Britain, King Arthur, loyalty to the lost Roman ideal, loyalty to the ancient religion that is older than Rome, loyalty to the Saxon invader—all loyalties tugging at one another and dividing the people. In this savage border country we find the worship of Mithras going along beside the Christian religion, and we find great Merlin in the flesh, and the bard Taliessin and Ninue the enchantress, and Galahad and Arthur. The high tragedy of *Owen* was in its action—a rebellion that came to nothing; the tragedy in *Porius* is inaction: here we have a rudderless country, drifting, a people without purpose or unity. The Roman civilization has collapsed in Britain, but the Saxon conquest has not been consolidated. All is hesitation, speculation and confusion.

In *Owen* there is a constant tension—battle imminent, councils gathering, messengers arriving and departing; even while Owen sits at dinner in his great hall there is a man behind him in the flickering fire-light sharpening weapons. But in *Porius* an enormous silence lies over the empty land. The contrast between the two landscapes is striking, for their locality is the same. In *Owen* we have castles, towns, abbeys; defined roads, cultivated fields. In *Porius* we move through thick forest, across valleys sparsely peopled: we meet hardly a soul. Only, lurking in the thickets, the sinister Cewri, aboriginal giants, waiting to take a revenge on any interloper, be he Roman, Briton or Saxon. Life is less complex, lived more in blacks and whites; the law, which so exercises Rhisiart, hardly exists for Prince Porius, for whom a sword is law enough. But love and religion and politics go on, as in any com-munity in any age, and these furnish out the five days' plot. As so often in John Cowper's novels, there are public events and movements and controversies, and we approach these through the effect they have on ordinary people, rather than on the principals; although in Prince Porius we have a man close to the centre. Porius, however, is not the policy maker, and it is his relationship with a group of representative people—what now would be called a cross section of the community —rather than his high position as prince, which makes the core of his part in the story. In this respect, *Porius* is more closely knit than most of the novels and Porius is almost continuously at the centre of the stage, although there are supporting parts of nearly comparable importance. Another difference between this and the other major novels is the relatively smaller part played by the women—smaller, that is, in terms of their presence physically; for their influence is as always in John's books broad and decisive. Some great scenes there are involving women, but the story is told much less from their point of view than in (for example) the novel that came next, *The Brazen Head*, and much less than in any of those with a twentieth-century setting. But towards the end, and particularly in Chapters Twenty-six and Twenty-seven, there is a subtle analysis of Princess Morfydd's confrontation with her sad destiny, and of the measures she adopts to endure it. This is in a degree the human climax to the book, for thereafter the crisis is super-natural: we are in the presence of portents and intimations too mon-strous to comprehend, too mysterious to fathom. The dying Merlin—

if he is dying—leads Porius to the edge of those great cracks which strike down to the centre of the world, where Cronos lies asleep; and brings *Porius* into communion with *Morwyn*.

There is no modern author more difficult to illustrate by direct quotation than John Cowper Powys. He recognized this himself, and expressed strong disapproval of any ideas of 'anthologies' or 'extracts' to represent his work. The customary illustrative passage which with most authors will serve a reviewer or critic trying to display in little the essence of a novel cannot begin to serve with such a book as *Porius*—least with *Porius*, I think, of all John Cowper's novels. Every paragraph tells, and tells significantly, in the overall context, but no quotation of manageable proportions can give any idea of the book's splendid vigour and complexity. A reviewer of T. F. Powys once wrote, 'Mr. Powys creates a society; and that, I think, is genius'. Theodore deserves the tribute, but he would not mind lending it to John, for he too creates a society, and in no book more triumphantly and convincingly and definitively than in *Porius*. For the last word on *Porius* one may borrow again, and say in the illuminating phrase of Christopher Smart, it is a thing determined, dared and done.

30

THE most nearly conventional of John's historical novels was the first, *Owen Glendower*, dealing as it did with a defined period and based as it was on actual events—although, of course, with a good deal of imaginative matter too. *Porius*, which followed, had a much less factual basis, because of the almost complete absence of authentic historical record to draw upon; but this novel also was concerned with events which must have happened, if not in the way narrated, at least in some comparable manner: the Romans did withdraw from Britain, and the Saxons did invade. In *The Brazen Head* and *Atlantis* John Cowper Powys moved away from a strictly historical position, in the first to what might be called 'half-history' and in the second to pure imagination; so that *Atlantis* is really not an historical novel, but because Homer's work had impressed itself so firmly in the world's consciousness, his characters *seem* historical, and it is convenient to consider *Atlantis* along with *The Brazen Head*.

The 'half-history' of *The Brazen Head* (published in 1956) may be noticed first, although *Atlantis* appeared in 1954, because the story of Roger Bacon lies in English history, and that of Odysseus in Greek myth; and *Atlantis* also has affinities with *Homer and the Aether* (1959).

Roger Bacon was born near Ilchester, in Somerset, a town which is the subject of one of Llewelyn's lively essays. It lies within walking distance of the Powys childhood home of Montacute—lies therefore in what we may call the 'Wolf Solent country'. But in setting his tale here in the thirteenth century John sweeps away the twentieth-century fields and hedgerows, and substitutes a wilder landscape such as it undoubtedly exhibited seven centuries ago, the marshes marshier, the forests denser, the roads fewer and muddier. In these melancholy surroundings he erects the fortress of Roque, solid and secure, but not inviting; and nearby the sinister Lost Towers. Around these opposing castles, and at the adjacent Bumset Priory, the principal action takes place. At Bumset Friar Roger Bacon is held prisoner—a willing prisoner, for he has no desire to go anywhere, and his work is not interfered with. To Bumset come various persons having business with the Friar, and in particular having an interest to destroy or preserve his work on the remarkable invention of 'the Brazen Head', which has been given the power of speech, and is expected to make a pronouncement of formidable weight. The house of Abyssum, lords of Roque, is behind Roger Bacon; Baron Maldung of Lost Towers is opposed to him, and to Roque. The Priory authorities try to preserve a secular neutrality, looking towards higher authority in the Church— and the issue here is confused, for the late Pope was a friend and protector of Roger Bacon, and his successor the new Pope has yet to make his position clear. So, if the central struggle of *Owen Glendower* was political, and that of *Porius* diplomatic, here in *The Brazen Head* it is religious; but of course in none of them is it definable in terms so simple. *Owen* presents the age-old and ever-present problems of self-determination and self-government opposed to an alien, centralized authority. *Porius*, the clash of systems, an old order giving place to a new, and again under an old law, the weakest going to the wall. In both the two Welsh novels we see the old religions fighting Christianity. *The Brazen Head* shows us Christianity fighting itself.

I call *The Brazen Head* 'half-history' because only the barest skeleton of it is based on historic fact; some of the characters are real, but virtually none of the events, and only an outline of the setting. Moreover, as in *Owen*, the central historical character is not the principal character in the story. Roger Bacon's presence at the Priory is an aggravation which sets events in motion, but the main story could then proceed quite independently of him, although in fact it doesn't quite do that. Roger Bacon is often in the picture, but he is seldom at its centre or in the direct foreground, alone: here, as in the other two novels under notice, the public event is seen through the eyes of ordinary people, or is shown in the effect it has upon their lives. Gradually, but unmistakably, the central hero is disappearing—the middle-aged man who so closely resembles John Cowper Powys in appearance, character, temperament and the rest; he hardly survives the change from contemporary to historical in the novels. True, in Rhisiart (*Owen Glendower*) we have a character around whom the novel is built; and in Porius we have a hero always present in the narrative, or never far away—but Prince Porius is less centrally the character about whom the book is written. Now, in *The Brazen Head*, we have a dozen or more characters of almost equal importance, and none whose affairs take precedence or demand a special prominence. The author is no longer personally involved, no longer speaking through one mouth, looking through one pair of eyes more than another. It is as if his preaching were over, and he now invites us to sit back and enjoy a comedy we are not to be actors in.

'Enjoyment' is perhaps the key word for *The Brazen Head*. There is a Chaucerian gusto about the book which is especially apparent to the reader who takes it up after *Porius*, a slower, gloomier, weightier story, 'big with the fate of empire, and of Rome'. Over *Porius* hangs an oppressive atmosphere through which light never breaks; the people in the book seem always to be embarked upon hopeless errands through dark paths beneath dripping trees, under the watch of hidden, hostile eyes. But in *The Brazen Head*, though blood flows and voices are raised, there is no gloom but rather a sort of genial give-and-take, and a pleasure-in-life-itself which the *Porius* characters never have leisure to cultivate.

Everywhere in John Cowper's novels there are memorable queer characters, people who are in the colloquial sense 'characters'—eccentrics, madmen, old crones, originals. But *The Brazen Head* marks the division (though *The Inmates* gave intimations) between people like (say) 'Number One' and 'Number Two' in *Glastonbury*, who are odd but entirely human, and some of the people who begin to appear increasingly in the later stories who are either human but not in perspective, or sub-human or non-human or indeed of very tenuous standing like, for example, the Cerne Giant. In *The Brazen Head* certain characters who are in themselves ordinary human beings are portrayed in caricature, or foreshortened, or distorted: Heber Sygerius the elderly Roque armourer, and Peleg the giant Tartar, and Lilith of Lost Towers—they purport to be human, there is nothing about their appearance or movements specifically less or more than human, and yet they do not convince us that they are 'normal'. They foreshadow the extraordinary people of *All or Nothing* and *Up and Out*.

Another way in which the later novels differ from the earlier is in the degree to which the supernatural enters them. Before *Morwyn*, in 1937, it plays a significant part only in *A Glastonbury Romance*, but from *Morwyn* onwards marvels abound, the descent into hell, the magic of Merlin, the magic of Roger Bacon, the immortals of *Atlantis*, and all the queer gallery of folk in the 'science fiction' stories that close the list. In *The Brazen Head* there are two major forces at work, the mysterious 'Lodestone' by virtue of which Peter Peregrinus imposes his will upon others, and the Brazen Head itself, so potent and so reticent, giving of its wisdom too late. The bounds of time and space cease to have a definition by the time we get to *All or Nothing*, and people pass from earth to the stars and back again as though taking the bus to Oxford Circus.

The Brazen Head is the least formal of the three historical novels, and this is reflected in the more relaxed prose; the great set-pieces are lacking, the story proceeds rather as comedy than as tragedy, even though tragedy enters in; and the drama is often close to melodrama, as at the very end, when Lost Towers crashes in ruin and Lilith and Peter destroy themselves and the Brazen Head. For all its many beauties, this novel must take its place behind the two novels of Welsh history, and behind *Atlantis*; but, this said and agreed, what a splendid, ripe, engaging narrative it is, leading the reader on from the first page intent to know *what happens next*, and keeping his attention thus engaged until the very last sentence in the book.

For John Cowper Powys's last novel in the grand manner we must turn back from *The Brazen Head* to *Atlantis* (for *Homer and the Aether* is a special case). *Atlantis* is as remarkable for its inventive element as *Morwyn* or *Porius*, and the prose is not surpassed by any of John's earlier books. He re-creates the Homeric landscape and characters and adds to them. The reader of Homer may feel he has got to know Odysseus pretty well, and yet here he may think he has come to know the old hero even better, as though Powys's own insight into Homer had enabled him to look beyond the end of the *Odyssey* and divine what happens next. *Atlantis* employs the very apparatus of Homer, men and gods jostling and coming and going, magic in the very air, fate and destiny taking a palpable part in the action. John Cowper's awareness of the influence of the inanimate upon men's lives finds its strongest expression here. Rocks and trees are sentient and involved; weapons think, moths and flies talk, the stones of the house cry out their startling intelligence, and crowds are carried from place to place by the great immortal horse, Pegasus. The extraordinary spell of this book begins to work upon the reader with the opening paragraph:

There had been an unusual tension all that Spring night in the air of the arched corridor that led into the royal dwelling. It was a weird, hushed, premonitory tension, the sort of tension that implies a secret fore-knowledge shared among a number of so-called inanimate things. It was the sort of tension that strikes human beings as ominous, and from which all sub-human creatures instinctively shrink.

So, at the outset, we have the 'so-called inanimate' and the sub-human being called to our attention, and thereafter we are never unaware of them. The Fly and the Moth, the Club and the Pillar, act as Chorus, and as more than Chorus, for whereas a chorus functions as commentator these 'inanimates and sub-humans' influence and at times direct events. The first chapter of *Atlantis* is the author's most sustained statement of his belief that in the diurnal course of nature rocks and stones and trees have a consciousness, and an understanding, of what takes place around them, and that they feel something of the pleasure, and the pity and the terror, which there is in life itself. He gives an identity and a dignity to these things which few would expect or detect in them, but he does this so subtly that we accept the olive stump and the sixth pillar at their own valuation of themselves as rational and informed intelligences. This is the triumph: not to imagine that a stone may speak, or a moth reason, or a club *enjoy the thought of being a club*; but so to write these things as to carry the reader with him, not simply persuaded, not merely convinced, but taking the fly and the olive branch and the pillar for granted, and admitting them as characters on equal terms with the humans, and without question. I think, too, that I find in these entities elements of separate and non-human identity, so that when the club speaks or thinks, it employs human speech to express the feeling or the reasoning of a club: the point of view of a great, old, smoothed, mature lump of wood. Little enough has been written anywhere of the parallel dilemma of the creatures and objects by which men are surrounded, but *Atlantis* makes its contribution. A man going to his death in battle may carry body-lice to their death with him. A chariot plunging over a cliff may destroy rabbits and weasels in its path. 'There are pensioners and dependants everywhere,' and John Cowper Powys is fully aware of this.

The story of *Atlantis* may easily be outlined, but it is the least important part of the affair. Odysseus, tired of a humdrum life in his small island kingdom, plans a last voyage into the unknown. While his new ship is building, rumours begin to come in that the ancient continent of Atlantis has been overwhelmed and lost in the sea, and the king determines to sail over the place of the disaster, and then onwards into the unknown western seas where no man has ventured. This he accomplishes in the last chapters, and lands finally in north America, where he burns his ship and determines to settle for what remains of his life. This plan, and its fruition, shows the king's character closely allied to that of Tennyson's Ulysses—restless, frustrated, aware of the onset of age, and determined to dare greatly yet once before the end.

There are forces in Ithaca, men and gods, who do not share the hopes of Odysseus—some will seek to usurp his throne, others will sabotage his ship, yet others again will be revenged on him, or seek to use him for their private ends. Two women struggle for his love. He is old, not so skilful, not so cunning, not so wise as he once was; and his success in overcoming the obstacles, and in setting his prow to the west, is brought about largely by luck, and largely by the aid of faithful younger hearts, and friendly gods. Much of the story unfolds through the eyes, and by the commentary, of the fly and the moth, hidden as they are in a crack of the great club which the king carries; and much is seen through the eyes, and influenced by the actions, of Nisos, the young prince who is of the house which seeks to overthrow the king, but whose own loyalties are with Odysseus. But here, as in *The Brazen Head*, there is no one central paramount figure through whose consciousness alone we follow the story, and although the fate of Odysseus serves as the central pivot many other threads of action are unravelled. I say the story is the least important part of the affair for this reason: that *Atlantis* is a comedy without beginning and without end, concerned not with particular events as such, but with the springs of action that lie behind them—with human nature, human behaviour, human emotions, and with the extensions of these that motivate the immortals and everything animate or inanimate that comes into contact with the life of men.

To say this, however, is to forget John Cowper's extraordinary narrative gift. The story may not be of first importance compared with the insights into character, and the explorations into new frontiers of consciousness which distinguish this novel. But that is not to say that the reader ever loses interest in the secular event. There is a consistent progression towards the climax, and the way is marked by scenes as splendidly managed as any in John's work, like for instance the confrontation of Odysseus with the priest Enorches at the farm of Zeuks, when the immortal horses Pegasus and Arion pass into the king's hands; or the tremendous moments under the surface of the sea when

Odysseus and Nisos engage in their weird exploration of the drowned city of Atlantis,[1] and their encounters with the terrifying entities that sojourn there; this passage, comparatively brief as it is, is paralleled in modern fiction only by the ecstasy and horror of the climax of E. H. Visiak's *Medusa*.

With *Atlantis* it is natural to associate *Homer and the Aether*, for both are steeped in the spirit of Homer, whom John Cowper held to be the supreme poet of the world. In *Atlantis* the Homeric characters live again, and not unworthily of their creator; and Homeric echoes abound in turns of phrase and lines of thought. But the work goes on from where the *Odyssey* leaves off. *Homer and the Aether* is much more closely allied to the *Iliad*, of which it is a paraphrase with commentary. More than once, John Cowper Powys has said that the essence of such great foreign poems as Homer's and Dante's must be looked for in a prose translation: not a literal or word-for-word and word-by-word translation, but what he himself calls a *walking commentary*. He paraphrases the story, keeping close to his original, but he adds through the asides and interjections of 'the immortal Aether' here elucidation, there amplification, somewhere else judgment upon what is going on. His preface is a stimulating introduction to the reading of Homer, and the whole book (as he says he hopes it may) offers an ideal text and interpretation, especially for younger readers. Not, I hasten to add, a 'children's book': but a book to delight and amaze and enchant readers in their early teens, just discovering literature for themselves. It is interesting, and amusing, to note here, as in the translations from Rabelais, that no matter with what adroitness the spirit of the original is retained and displayed, the voice of John Cowper Powys sounds, time and again, behind the voice of Rabelais, or of Homer, in a turn of phrase or an inflexion or a single characteristic word deftly used.

The Homeric quality of *Atlantis* may be seen in a comparatively brief quotation; and the imposition of a Powysian essence upon the *Iliad* may be detected in another, from *Homer and the Aether*.

> . . . at that very second they arrived at the end of the wood. There, before them, lay the salt waves with their islands and ships and rocky reefs and wide-stretching curving bays. And there, beyond all these, in far-away, vision-fulfilling, story-ending, mystery-resolving, resting places for the imagination,

---

[1] Some readers may remember the splendid passages of underwater horror in Southey's *The Curse of Kehama*, a poem now too seldom read.

the eyes of those three human beings were led further and yet further, to the vast horizons of the encircling sea.

And the great Club of Herakles ceased its rudder-like quiverings as impelled by an irresistible impulse Odysseus lifted the great weapon high above his head and shook it in the air as if he, a man among men, were taking it on himself to challenge that golden sun-path which, originating behind him, was now flowing across the darkening waters!

Yes! and to challenge the divine ether itself he lifted it up, the ether under which the sea-spaces before him extended beyond the ships, beyond the islands, beyond the main-land, beyond those far-away Asiatic mountains, on the Eastern verge of the world, where from the image of Niobe, the mother of mankind, fell no longer that ceaseless torrent of tears, and finally to challenge the very trident of Poseidon himself as he strove to dominate the multitudinous waves.

The two men, the now one-winged horse, the Heraklean club, the two insects, and our young friend Nisos, they were all silent; they were all gazing in front of them. What they saw as they gazed was the ruin of a building so colossal in its pre-historic enormity that the first impression Nisos had of it was that it ought to have sunk down by its own weight thousands of years ago to the very centre of the earth.

But what else did the boy see that made him even forget, as he looked, Eione's danger from the shaggy lasciviousness of the Goat-foot from Arcadia? He distinctly saw, erect on a huge flat stone under a cyclopean arch, the figure of a young girl, a young girl of about the same age as Eione, though she may have been a little taller, and it seemed to him as if, with an outstretched arm, that figure was waving to him; not to the others, but to him—to him alone.

The passage from *Homer and the Aether* is from Book Seven:

But it was not only of their mortal foes that these daring Greeks should have taken thought. They ought to have remembered that immortal eyes were also looking down upon them and that Troy had allies in Heaven. Indeed it was very soon when none other than Poseidon himself, god of the ocean and shaker of the earth, resting at one moment by one side of Zeus the Father of them all, burst out in a rage.

'Look, Father Zeus, look what these confounded Greeks have gone and done! I tell you the news of this performance of theirs will soon be resounding over the whole earth, whereas the much more wonderful wall which Apollo and I erected for Laomedon, the father of King Priam, is now totally forgotten!'

Seldom had cloud-assembling Zeus felt more teased and aggrieved than he felt at this moment.

'Shaker of the earth, is it for you to talk like this? How can you utter such a ridiculous absurdity? Of course your glory goes as far as the light of the morning! Up with you, you old silly! Can't you see that when these precious Greeks have gone home in their ships, you'll be free to sweep your great billows over the whole business, bank, rampart, ditch and all, and then when you've covered their work with sand from the depths of the ocean, lo! every sign of their tinkerings and clinkerings will be as if it had never been!'

Neither Greeks nor Trojans that night had the faintest notion why, when on both sides there was such a pleasant sound of revelry, there should suddenly have burst out above their heads terrifying rumblings and rollings and rattlings of thunder. The bravest of them turned pale as they listened, and their hands trembled so much that the wine they were drinking fell splashing to the ground. It was indeed not until they had bethought themselves to pour out a supplicatory libation to the Father of all, that they were able to lie down that night in peace of mind and sink quietly to sleep.

31

IN THE last ten years of his life John Cowper Powys was freed from the financial worries, and the worries about whether or not he could get his books published, which had dogged him for the ten years before the appearance of *Porius*. This he owed to the enlightened treatment he received from his new publishers, Macdonald, who not only took books which could not be expected to meet with a wide success or an extensive sale, but also restored to print many of the earlier works; and this enabled John Cowper in these last years to write to please himself, and to produce such extraordinary tales as *Up and Out* and *All or Nothing*. It enabled him to see splendidly produced the long poem *Lucifer*, written half a century earlier, which he says in his preface is 'the only poem of my own that I feel any temptation to pray that posterity may read'. And it enabled him to write those several prefaces to *A Glastonbury Romance*, *Wolf Solent*, *Visions and Revisions*, and *Lucifer*, which are so revealing of his attitude to his work, and so interesting as supplementary to his *Autobiography*.

The fantastic stories of *Up and Out*, *All or Nothing*, and *You and Me* (which has yet to be published) may be dismissed by some readers as their author's dotages. Dreams, are they, or fairy stories, or fables, or allegories? Just what they are is not wholly clear, and every reader may reach his own conclusion. But they are stimulating, and provoking, and alive, fancy following hot-foot upon fancy, fantasy giving place to ever wilder fantasy, mystification alternating with revelation. Many readers will find the extraordinary names a stumbling block; certainly I do myself. Woom-o-Rim, Gor Goginog, Oom, John o' Dreams, Grumble Nu and the rest are not easy to identify with; and most readers look for some normal thing, even in the most fantastic of tales, to lay a hold on as guide or rudder. It is often hard to feel a reciprocal sympathy with these Bogs and Wugs and Zugs, with these Oms and

Yooms and Asms. Swift sets up a similar hazard for his readers with the unpronounceable and inhuman Houyhnhnms and Struldbrugs, and elsewhere among the Utopias there are names whose strangeness seems their only purpose and end. Perhaps John Cowper took a pleasure in the invention and bestowal of outlandish names, as indeed I believe others have done—Robert Southey, for one, and Charles Dickens for another. Among recent writers the curious inventions of Brian Aldiss come to mind, and no doubt this strangeness is imposed upon the writer of science fiction—and it must be remembered that these late stories of John Cowper Powys may be so defined—by the necessity of differentiating between humans from earth and the inhabitants of outer space; it would be even stranger if the traveller to Mars arrived to be greeted by a creature called George. As for John Cowper, he was here only indulging to its limit an impulse which had been with him throughout his writing career, for there are oddly named characters from Mr Lickwit and Mrs Seldom, in *Wood and Stone*, to Teucer Wye and Claudius Cask, with the rest of the protagonists of *Maiden Castle*, not forgetting Dud No-man, who was given 'no *proper* name at all'. It seems that the reader must indulge the author, and take what names *Up and Out* and *All for Nothing* afford him.

The title-story of *Up and Out* is followed by 'The Mountains of the Moon', described as 'a lunar love story'. 'Up and Out' is concerned with the handful of survivors of an atomic holocaust: but hardly with such practical matters as determining the extent of the destruction, or providing shelter and medical treatment and food, or taking precautions against fall-out or disease. For the atomic explosions open up rifts in Time and Space themselves, and the adventurers are led into depths of experience never sustained by mortals before, until finally they talk face to face with both the Devil and God—without receiving any very satisfactory answers to their obstinate questionings. This is the most nearly an allegory of the stories, as 'The Mountains of the Moon' is the most nearly a fable, and *All or Nothing* the most nearly a fantasy. There is an unexpected and endearing tenderness in the loves of the Moon-creatures Yoom and Lorlt, Helia and Rorlt, and a rich fanstastic humour in the unfolding of their tale. The crazy drama of the relics is surely one of John's most original inventions, as he brings successively on to the stage to dance and posture, the core of the apple that Eve ate, the mortal heel of Achilles, a string of Nero's fiddle, a feather of the dove that flew out from the Ark, and a group of other bygones as pregnant and unique.

But *All or Nothing* is the longest and craziest and fullest and pro-foundest of these stories, with its philosophy that one must accept of life 'all' or 'nothing', and in the end, 'all the same for that', all is nothing and nothing, all. But because of this identity between oppo-sites neither is obliteratingly the other, and 'both of them have one home-star, where they can sink to eternal quiescence, or mount to everlasting activity, and that home-star, my children, is the heart in every one of us'.

The restless, ceaseless comings and goings of *All or Nothing*, the accumulating wonders of 'Up and Out', the breathless arguments of 'The Mountains of the Moon' beguile the reader into reading on so eagerly, and at the same time often with so much bewilderment, that he doesn't follow half what is said, or goes on. These three stories deserve close study, more study than a first reading, however disciplined, will exhaust; for they express the latest conclusions of a mind which has pondered upon life and death and love and birth for over eighty years.

Among these later books, the one which received the most attention was the *Letters to Louis Wilkinson*, published in 1958. It was widely agreed among reviewers that these are unique among twentieth-century letters for their frankness, their unselfconscious revelations of the writer's character and personality, and their lively judgments on a score of matters, personal, literary, political, religious, ethical and what you will. A large, solid book, formidable to take up, impossible to put down: a headstrong, headlong, tumbling cataract of words, a great bubbling largesse of wisdom, satire, wit, perversity, prejudice, and knockabout fun. Too large a volume would have been called for if this correspondence had been printed entire, either as the whole cor-respondence between the two friends, or as the complete letters to Louis Wilkinson from John Cowper; and so all the earlier letters from John to Louis, as represented (though not there printed in full) in *Welsh Ambassadors*, are omitted; and so too are the letters written by Louis to John, a necessity much to be regretted, for in exchanges of this kind Louis Wilkinson was entirely capable of giving as good as he got, and the whole correspondence must certainly one day be reunited in print.

In the meantime, this volume is of particular value because it opens with letters dated mid 1935, which come close on the heels of the final chapters of the *Autobiography*; and it goes on until the end of 1956, which although it is some years before his death yet may represent as far as a more formal autobiography would have gone—for naturally in those closing years the pace of life slowed down, not very much of material importance happened, and there was not very much for letters or biography to record.

The range of subject-matter in these letters is as wide and diverse as life itself: where one can buy back collar-studs, what exactly is a kipper—trivial day-to-day minutiae—mixed with observations about the way to deal with Hitler, the value of Henry Miller's novels, the bother of having no money in the bank, and the for-and-against of immortality. When he is serious, he gives us some of the profoundest of his thinking. When he jests, the gusto and relish are Gargantuan. His generous appreciation of other writers, and especially of younger writers, is constant and endearing. The anecdotes and observations about the Powys family are invaluable to the student, and full of interest to the general reader. The whole book leaves the reader eager for further volumes, and there must be material for a dozen such volumes, when the proper time has come. Perhaps it will be a long time before the complete surviving letters can be published—there are thousands of Powys letters extant, of which John's make the greatest bulk and number—but the publication of them is as much a necessary service to be done for the student of twentieth-century letters as was that of Horace Walpole's for the eighteenth- or Byron's for the nineteenth-century student.

The publication of *Lucifer* in 1956, and of the *Selected Poems* in 1964, reintroduced John Cowper as a poet. His previous last book of poems was *Samphire*, in 1922, published only in the United States, and he had in fact not published a volume of poems in England for nearly sixty years. Many of his readers and admirers were hearing of him as a poet for the first time. I have said something of his poetry in Chapter Six, above, and elsewhere, and I will not add to those observations at any length here. But I will say again that whatever John's standing as a poet among poets (and a small group of his poems I rate highly) his verse will always have great interest to readers of his other work— which is admittedly his major contribution to literature—because of the way it underlines and supplements the principal turns of his philosophy. *Lucifer* itself is a young man's poem, full of echoes; but they are majestic echoes, of Milton, Keats and Arnold, nor do these echoes drown the still small original voice of the author entirely, although they make a background diapason. It is easy to overlook the fact that, although first published in 1956, the poem was written in 1905; and if it had been published at that time, the slightly old-fashioned air it presented to readers coming to it as a new work first published would not have been so apparent. Such a reader in 1956, or now, would review the poem not beside contemporary work from which it differs in form, technique and impulse, but in the light of the work of such poets as were active when it was composed, and were of an age with John Cowper: T. Sturge Moore, for example, and R. C. Trevelyan, and Gordon Bottomley, poets all under a cloud now, neglected or forgotten, but all solid enough and virile enough to return to critical favour in due time. There will eventually be a secure place among his peers for the poems of John Cowper, and no doubt when that time comes a complete edition of his poetry will be possible. My own volume of selections was restricted to published work for several reasons, but enough unpublished or uncollected verse remains to fill a volume at least as large. When that volume is published, and hardly till then, it will be possible to form a final judgment upon his stature as a poet.

It had been Llewelyn Powys's wish to be buried on the Dorset downs near his home, but the possibility of this was frustrated when he died abroad and war-time conditions made it impossible to return his body at once to England. Accordingly, he was cremated; but after the war his ashes were brought home and buried at the top of the cliff south of Chydyok under a large block of Portland stone, carved by Elizabeth Muntz:

LLEWELYN POWYS

13 AUGUST 1884

2 DECEMBER 1939

THE LIVING THE LIVING HE SHALL PRAISE THEE

The Powys connection with East Chaldon was coming to a close. T. F. Powys removed to Mappowder, Gertrude Powys died, and Alyse Gregory and Philippa Powys left Chydyok, Miss Gregory for Devon and Miss Powys for Buckland Newton. The sturdy cottages still stand in which they lived, but the one truly personal monument to the long Powys association with this part of Dorset is the memorial stone to Llewelyn, and this may be expected to endure for centuries in its place by the Roman road; and it is here, as much as anywhere on earth, that a wayfarer might feel closest to the mighty spirits of the two brothers who formerly so often walked here, Theodore and Llewelyn.

John Cowper's footprints lie here too, but perhaps his spirit waits more certainly on the mountain paths above the River Dee, where it bends round the ancient town of Corwen.

I have spoken of Theodore's last years, but not of his death. After his illness in 1939 he was never fully well, but his quiet way of life was not greatly disturbed by an increasing disinclination to go far, or do much: he had never wished to go far, or do much. The years at Mappowder were tranquil, with the monotony he liked. In the spring of 1953 he was found to have cancer, and on 27th November he died. Theodore had refused the expedient of an operation; it would have prolonged his life, if at all, only temporarily, and he was content if his time had come, to die.

He was buried in the churchyard beside his house, where his grave may be seen marked by a headstone inscribed:

In loving memory of

Theodore Francis Powys

At Rest

27 November 1953

Aged 77 years

John, the eldest, was to live longest of these three brothers. He had settled in Wales in 1935, and he remained at Corwen until 1955, when he removed to Blaenau-ffestiniog. Like Theodore, these last years for John were tranquil, his life simple and unvaried. He made one or two brief excursions, but the reader of the *Letters to Louis Wilkinson* forms a picture of one sitting quietly at home, reading, thinking, writing. Now and again he was interviewed by a journalist, or received visitors from the big literary world of London; and he was also occasionally visited by an artist to do a drawing, or sketches for a sculpture; his encounters with Augustus John are inimitably recounted in the Wilkinson *Letters*. Now and again the outside world remembered him more officially, as when in 1957 the Free Academy of Arts in Hamburg awarded its Plaque to him in recognition of his outstanding services to Literature and Philosophy. It never occurred to any British authority or learned society to honour him, although there seems never to be any shortage of honours for footballers, singers, and senior local government officials with a blameless political record. It must always be a reproach to the Royal Society of Literature that it refused to make him a Companion of Literature. Belatedly, a single academic honour, the degree of Honorary Doctor of Letters, was conferred on him by the University of Wales. Some striking tributes were paid on the occasion of his ninetieth birthday, but it is hard on these occasions not to feel that the British honour a man for his great weight of years rather than for the weight of his achievement.

John Cowper's ninetieth birthday fell on 13 October 1962. He died some eight months later, on 17 June 1963, of no specific disease but quietly, of old age. He was cremated, and his ashes scattered on the waters of the Channel at Chesil Beach.

I shall not attempt a postscript, or a summing-up, or any last general assessment of these three remarkable brothers and writers. Almost the whole of their work has been passed in review in these pages, not with the intention of reaching a settled, final judgment, but rather with the hope of stimulating interest and sending readers back to the original texts. This body of more than a hundred books represents the most original family contribution to English literature in our time, and for bulk, variety, and its general high level of excellence, perhaps the most remarkable in the whole range of our literature. Its importance will become increasingly apparent as the lesser talents of the period fall away into perspective; for it will be remembered that very rarely to later generations are the most esteemed writers of any period those who enjoyed the greatest contemporary acclaim: in the time of Milton the acknowledged genius was Abraham Cowley, in that of Blake it was William Hayley; when Wordsworth hardly found a reader the poems of Robert Montgomery were selling by the tens of thousands.

The books remain, the writers of them are gone. And my last thought must be, as I write finis to this book, and turn to begin upon another, that never again shall I pass the little gate of Beth Car and see old Theodore sitting at the window; never again climb the narrow stair to the room in which Llewelyn sat in Edward Fitzgerald's shawl, reading the essays of Montaigne; never hear again the voice of my friend and master, wise old John Cowper. Never, never, never, never, never!

PRINCIPAL PUBLICATIONS BY OR CONCERNING
THE POWYS BROTHERS

This is a chronological list, not a bibliography, to give a quick reference for titles mentioned in the foregoing text. Some pamphlets are omitted where their contents reappear in collected volumes.

1896   *Odes and other Poems:* J.C.P.

1899   *Poems:* J.C.P.

1907   *An Interpretation of Genesis:* T.F.P.

1914   *The War and Culture:* J.C.P.
       (*The Menace of German Culture,* 1915)

1915   *Visions and Revisions:* J.C.P.
      Wood and Stone: J.C.P.

1916   *Confessions of Two Brothers:* J.C.P. and Ll.P.
      Wolf's Bane: Rhymes: J.C.P.
      One Hundred Best Books: J.C.P.
      Rodmoor: J.C.P.
      Suspended Judgments: J.C.P.
      The Soliloquy of a Hermit: T.F.P.
        (*Soliloquies of a Hermit,* 1918)
      Blasphemy and Religion: L.W.
      The Buffoon: L.W.

1917   *Mandragora:* J.C.P.

1920   *The Complex Vision:* J.C.P.

1922   *Samphire:* J.C.P.

1923   *Psychoanalysis and Morality:* J.C.P.
      The Left Leg: T.F.P.
      Black Bryony: T.F.P.
      Ebony and Ivory: Ll.P.
      Thirteen Worthies: Ll.P.

1924   *Mark Only:* T.F.P.
      Mr. Tasker's Gods: T.F.P.
      Honey and Gall: Ll.P.
      Cup Bearers of Wine and Hellebore: Ll.P.
      Black Laughter: Ll.P.

1925   *The Art of Happiness:* J.C.P.
        The Religion of a Sceptic: J.C.P.
        Ducdame: J.C.P.
        Mockery Gap: T.F.P.
        Skin for Skin: Ll.P.

1926   *The Secret of Self-Development:* J.C.P.
        Innocent Birds: T.F.P.
        The Verdict of Bridlegoose: Ll.P.

1927   *Mr. Weston's Good Wine:* T.F.P.
        Henry Hudson: Ll.P.
        Bibliography of T.F.P.: Muir & van Thal

1928   *The Art of Forgetting the Unpleasant:* J.C.P.
        The House with the Echo: T.F.P.

1929   *Wolf Solent:* J.C.P.
        The Meaning of Culture: J.C.P.
        Fables: T.F.P.
          (*No Painted Plumage,* 1934)
        The Cradle of God: Ll.P.
        The English House: A.R.P.
        Repair of Ancient Buildings: A.R.P.

1930   *In Defence of Sensuality:* J.C.P.
        The Owl, The Duck, and—Miss Rowe! Miss Rowe!: J.C.P.
        Debate: Is Modern Marriage a Failure?: J.C.P. with Bertrand Russell
        Kindness in a Corner: T.F.P.
        The White Paternoster: T.F.P.
        An Hour on Christianity: Ll.P.
          (*The Pathetic Fallacy,* 1930)
        Apples be Ripe: Ll.P.
        The English Parish Church: A.R.P.
        Driftwood: Philippa P.
        The Blackthorn Winter: Philippa P.
        The Novels and Stories of T. F. Powys: William Hunter

1931   *Dorothy M. Richardson:* J.C.P.
        Unclay: T.F.P.
        A Pagan's Pilgrimage: Ll.P.
        Impassioned Clay: Ll.P.
        Origins of Bad Architecture: A.R.P.

1932   *A Glastonbury Romance:* J.C.P.
        The Two Thieves: T.F.P.
        Now that the Gods are Dead: Ll.P.
        Life and Times of Anthony à Wood: Ll.P.

1933   *A Philosophy of Solitude:* J.C.P.

1934 *Weymouth Sands:* J.C.P.
    (*Jobber Skald,* 1935)
    Autobiography: J.C.P.
    Glory of Life: Ll.P.
    Earth's Memories: Ll.P.
    Swan's Milk: L.W.*
    Bibliography of the First Editions of John Cowper Powys: L. E. Siberell

1935 *The Art of Happiness:* J.C.P.
    Captain Patch: T.F.P.
    Make Thyself Many: T.F.P.
    Dorset Essays: Ll.P.
    Damnable Opinions: Ll.P.
    The Powys Brothers: R. H. Ward

1936 *Maiden Castle:* J.C.P.
    The Twelve Months: Ll.P.
    Welsh Ambassadors: L.W.*

1937 *Morwyn:* J.C.P.
    Goat Green: T.F.P.
    Somerset Essays: Ll.P.
    Rats in the Sacristy: Ll.P.
    From the Ground Up: A.R.P.
    The Joy of It: L.C.P.

1938 *The Pleasures of Literature:* J.C.P.

1939 *Love and Death:* Ll.P.
    A Baker's Dozen: Ll.P.

1940 *Owen Glendower:* J.C.P.

1941 *Mortal Strife:* J.C.P.

1943 *Letters of Llewelyn Powys:* edited L.W.

1944 *The Art of Growing Old:* J.C.P.

1946 *Dostoievsky:* J.C.P.
    Bottle's Path: T.F.P.
    Life of Llewelyn Powys: Malcolm Elwin
    Forth, Beast: L.W.*

1947 *Obstinate Cymric:* J.C.P.
    Swiss Essays: Ll.P.
    God's Eyes A-Twinkle: T.F.P., edited Charles Prentice

1948 *Rabelais:* J.C.P.

1949 *Advice to a Young Poet:* Ll.P.

1951 *Porius:* J.C.P.

1952   *The Inmates:* J.C.P.
       The Powys Family: L.C.P.
       Llewelyn Powys: A Selection: edited Kenneth Hopkins

1953   *In Spite Of:* J.C.P.

1954   *Atlantis:* J.C.P.

1956   *The Brazen Head:* J.C.P.
       Lucifer: J.C.P.
       Still the Joy of It: L.C.P.

1957   *Up and Out:* J.C.P.

1958   *Letters of John Cowper Powys to Louis Wilkinson:* edited L.W.

1959   *Homer and the Aether:* J.C.P.

1960   *All or Nothing:* J.C.P.
       T. F. Powys: H. Coombes

1964   *Selected Poems of John Cowper Powys:* edited Kenneth Hopkins
       Theodore: Essays on T. F. Powys: a symposium, edited Fr. Brocard
          Sewell
       The Saturnian Quest: G. Wilson Knight (on J.C.P.)

1965   *John Cowper Powys: old earth man:* H. P. Collins

1966   *Rosie Plum:* T.F.P., edited Francis Powys
       John Cowper Powys: a record of achievement: Derek Langridge

In the press: *Advice to a Young Poet: Letters between Llewelyn Powys and
    Kenneth Hopkins,* edited by R. L. Blackmore

Abbreviations: J.C.P.: John Cowper Powys; T.F.P., T. F. Powys;
              Ll.P.: Llewelyn Powys; L.C.P.: Littleton Charles Powys;
              A.R.P.: Albert Reginald Powys; L.W.: Louis Wilkinson
              (with asterisk, under pen name Louis Marlow)

INDEX

ABRAMS, Dr, treats Ll. P. success-
fully, 69
Ackland, Valentine, 22, 205, 211
Across the Plains (Stevenson), 67
Aethelwolf, King, 193
Aids to Reflection (Coleridge), 10
Alaska, 134 n.
Albany (New York), 97, 138
Aldeburgh (Suffolk), 9, 18
Aldington, Richard, 100
Aldiss, Brian, 251
American Library Service (pub-
lishers), 73
American Patriotism (Münsterberg),
36
American Society for the Extension
of University Teaching, The, 28
American Traits (Münsterberg), 36
Amsterdam, Ll. P. at, 121
Anacapri, Ll. P. at, 117, 139
Animal Farm (Orwell), 125
Antony and Cleopatra (Shakespeare),
28
Arcimbaldo, Giuseppe, 107
Arimathea, Joseph of, Ll. P. at the
tomb of, 139
Arnold, Matthew, 2, 135, 180, 181,
217, 228, 253
Arnold, Thomas, 2
Aryan Path, Ll. P. writes for, 169
Ashbourne (Derbyshire), 1
At the Harlot's Burial (Ll. Powys),
147
Atlantic City, 41
Austerlitz (New York), 133, 144–5
Austria, Ll. P. visits, 117

Babylon, 105
Bacon, Roger, 241–3
Baltimore, 134
Balzac, Honoré de, 38, 181, 239
Barents, William, 121

Barnes, William, 15, 74; acquainted
with the Powys family, 5; quoted,
75
Bates, H. E., 96, 100
Beaumont Press, 100
Belley (France), Ll. P. at, 121
Belloc, Hilaire, 172
Benn Brothers (publishers), 85
Bennett, Arnold, 100, 181, 196
Beresford, J. D., 161, 181
Bewick, Thomas, 3, 74, 118
Bible, 3, 8, 104, 140, 214
Birrell, Augustine, 50, 115, 228
Black Archer Press, 152
Blackmore, Robert L., 138, 206, 216
Blaenau-ffestiniog (Merionethshire),
220, 224, 255
Blake, William, 68, 228; quoted, 115
Blue Moon Press, 153
Boissevain, Eugen, 133, 144
Book of Days, The (Chambers), 176
Boston (Massachusetts), 91, 138, 181
Bottomley, Gordon, 253
Bournemouth (Hampshire), 22, 51,
121, 206
Bradford Abbas (Dorset), 1
Bragdon, Claude, 46
Brecon, Gam of, 235
Brenan, Gerald, 206
Brighton (Sussex), 13, 73, 179
Bristol, 73, 99
Broadstairs (Kent), Ll. P. teaches at,
25
Bromsgrove (Worcestershire), Ll. P.
teaches at, 26
Brooks, Van Wyck, 72; writes
preface to *Ebony and Ivory*, 74
Browne, Sir Thomas, 56
Browning, Robert, 56
Brut, Walter, 235, 237
Bryant, Sir Arthur, 119
Buckland Newton (Dorset), 254

Bunyan, John, 125, 180
Burpham (Sussex), J. C. P. at, 14, 30
Burton, Robert, 74, 118, 180
Byron, Lord, 253
Byron (Marchand), 119

Calne (Wiltshire), Ll. P. a private tutor at, 26
Cambridge, Powys brothers at University, 11, 12, 25, 26, 33, 179, 191; L. W. at, 18; T. F. P. visits, 20, 21
Canterbury Tales (Chaucer), 105
Cape, Jonathan (publisher), 121, 238
Capri, Ll. P. at, 117, 142, 175
Carmarthen, J. C. P. published at, 232
Carr, E. H., 228
Cassell & Company (publishers), 205, 223, 238
Casseres, Benjamin de, 206
Century Magazine, J. C. P. writes for, quoted, 84–8
Cervantes, Miguel de, 38, 56, 181, 229
Chaldon Boys or West Chaldon (Dorset), 51–2
Chaldon Herring or East Chaldon (Dorset), 22, 63, 77, 91, 101, 102, 105, 121, 145, 167, 169, 176, 195, 202, 205, 206, 210, 224, 254; described, 51–2
Chambers, W. and R., 176
Charles I, 130
Charles II, 163
Chatto & Windus (publishers), 23, 77, 77 n.
Chatto & Windus Miscellany, A (1928), 128; quoted, 129–31
Chaucer, Geoffrey, 107, 110, 161, 237
Cheslea, 70, 73
Chesshire, May, 206
Chesterton, G. K., 172, 181
Chicago, 94, 97, 198
Chilon of Sparta, 129
Chiswick, 17
Chronicle of Ancient Sunlight, A (Williamson), 157

Churchill, Sir Winston, 98
Clark, Andrew, 119
Clavadel (Switzerland), Ll. P. at, 31, 207
Cleverdon, Douglas, 99, 153
Cobb, James, 175, 205
Cole, Hon. Galbraith, 41
Coleridge, Hartley, 211
Coleridge, S. T., 10, 37, 228
Colgate University, 75, 97–8
Colgate University Press, 223
Colum, Padraic, 72
Conrad, Joseph, 223
Cooke, Alistair, 181
Coombes, H., 43, 113, 114
Cooper, Nancy, 175, 176
Coppard, A. E., 96, 100
Coriolanus (Shakespeare), 28
Corpus Christi College, Cambridge, 11
Corvinus Press, 100
Corvo, Frederick Rolfe, Baron, 34
Corwen (Merionethshire), J. C. P. settles at, 220–1, 233; background for *Owen Glendower* and *Porius*, 237–8
Coryate, Thomas, 74, 118
Cowley, Abraham, 256
Cowper, William, 163; in Powys ancestry, 1–2, 4
Crewkerne (Somerset), 85
Crowley, Aleister, 23
Culpeper, Nicholas, 74, 83
cummings, e. e., 152

Daily Herald, Ll. P. writes for, 169, 176
Dante Alighieri, 50, 181, 221, 228, 247
Davos-Platz (Switzerland), Ll. P. at, 31; described in *Skin for Skin*, 103
Day-Lewis, C., 207
De Kantzow, Alfred, 16–17, 19, 38, 48, 55, 179; his poems quoted, 16–17
De La Mare, Walter, 28, 207
De Quincey, Thomas, 102
De Sade, Marquis, 223

Deloney, Thomas, 74
Dent, J. M. & Sons (publishers), 85
Detroit, 134
Devoe, Alan, 133
Dial, The, 90, 91, 92, 94; Ll. P. writes for, 63; J. C. P. writes for, 71; Alyse Gregory becomes Managing Editor, 72
Dickens, Charles, 96, 97, 98, 107, 110, 181, 237, 251
Dodd, Mead & Company (publishers), 75
Dodds, Violet Rosalie. *See* Powys, Mrs T. F.
Donne, John, in Powys ancestry, 1–2
Donne, John (the younger), 2
Donne's Satyr (J. Donne the younger), 2
Dorchester (Dorset), 2, 4, 15, 35, 55, 101, 105, 129, 136, 182, 191, 192, 194; Ll. P. born at, 5; setting for *Maiden Castle*, 184; J. C. P. at, 195
Dostoievsky, Feodor M., 38, 50, 77, 120, 198, 228
Dounce, Harry, 67
Dreiser, Theodore, 71, 180; J. C. P. assists, 55; Ll. P. meets, 68; writes preface for *Thirteen Worthies*, 73
Dresden, 36
Dryden, John, 56, 84, 161, 163
Dugdale, Giles, 4
Dumas, Alexandre, *père*, 96, 181, 237
Durweston (Dorset), 175
Dynasts, The (Hardy), 158

Eastbourne (Sussex), 122; T. F. P. lectures at, 22
Edel, Leon, 119
'Elijah the Tishbite' (de Kantzow), quoted, 16–17
Eliot, T. S., 157
Elwin, Malcolm, 33, 63, 95, 105, 118, 145, 205, 207, 216, 238
Emerson, R. W., 181
Epicurus, 142, 143

Ethelbald, King, 10
Ethelbert, King, 10
Evening Post (New York), Ll. P. writes for, 67

Faerie Queene (Spencer), 125
Farson, Negley, on *Black Laughter*, 92
Ferrers, the Earls, 1
Ficke, Arthur Davison, 72, 133, 145, 180, 205, 207
Field, Sarah Bard, 68
Finnegans Wake (Joyce), 227 n.
Fitzgerald, Edward, 256
Fitzgerald, Scott, 72
Flecker, James Elroy, 31
Flower, Sir Newman, 223
Ford, Ford Madox, 181
Fort, Charles, 180
Framlingham (Suffolk), 218
France, Ll. P. in, 117
Franzen, Walter, 91, 120, 148, 172
Fraser, Gordon, 153
Freeman, The, J. C. P. writes for, 94
Frey, Dr, 207
Frome Vauchurch (Dorset), 211

Gabbitas and Thring, scholastic agency, 25
Galsworthy, John, 100
Galton (Dorset), 95
Garnett, David, 22, 83, 100; assists T. F. P. in publishing, 77 n., 78
Geneva, 121
Genius, The (Dreiser), J. C. P. and, 55 n.
Genoa, 34
Genuine Epistles of the Apostolical Fathers, The (Wake), 56
Gibbings, Robert, 22, 144, 176, 206, 215
Gilgil (Africa), Ll. P. at, 35, 41–2
Gill, Eric, 99
Girard (Kansas), 65, 75
Glastonbury (Somerset), 136, 185, 189, 194; setting of *A Glastonbury Romance*, 157–9
Glendower, Owen, 233–7

Goethe, J. W. von, 50, 181, 228
Golden Cockerel Press, 99, 100, 153
Gosse, Edmund, 50, 228
Grainger, Boyne, 221
Gray, Thomas, 21
Greening & Company (publishers), 27
Greenwich Village, New York, Powys residence in, 70–3, 152
Gregg, Frances (first Mrs Louis Wilkinson), 34, 53
Gregory, Alyse (Mrs Llewelyn Powys), 52, 117, 118, 121, 139, 142, 144, 145, 148, 152, 169, 211, 216, 218, 254; meets Ll. P. 72; marries, 90; quoted on life at Montoma, 91; quoted on *Love and Death*, 208
Gregory, Dr, treats Ll. P., 91
Grey of Ruthin, Lord, 235
Güjer, Lisaly, 207, 216
Gulliver's Travels (Swift), 125

Hamburg, 36
Hamburg, Free Academy of Arts, honours J. C. P., 255
Hamilton, Cosmo, 27
Hanley, James, assists J. C. P., 220–1
Hannah, Ian Campbell, 43
Hardin, Rev. Henry, 175
Hardy, Mrs (the first), 15
Hardy, Mrs Florence, 205, 206, 223
Hardy, Thomas, 4, 5, 22, 38, 50, 57, 75, 83, 100, 101, 113, 130, 136, 158, 180, 181, 223, 227, 237; visits Montacute, 15
Harington, Sir John, 175
Harris, Frank, his 'Contemporary Portrait' of L. U. W., 49
Harvard University, 36
Harvey, E. R. H., 134, 205
Hawaii, 134 n.
Hayley, William, 256
Hazelbury Bryan (Dorset), 86
Heinemann, William, & Company (publishers), 38, 77
Henry James (Edel), 119

Herbert, George, 168
Herrin (Illinois), 215
Hillsdale (New York), J. C. P. settles at, 132–3, 169
History of British Birds, A (Bewick), 3
History of the Christian Church, 10
Hitler, Adolf, 253
Holborn, L. B. Stoughton, 43
Holland, Ll. P. visits, 117, 121
Home Chat, 26
Homer, 56, 181, 227, 231, 241, 244, 247
Hotspur, Harry, 235
Hove (Sussex), J. C. P. teaches at, 13
Hudson, Henry, 118, 121
Huebsch, B. W. (publisher), 53
Hunter, William, 113, 201
Huxley, Aldous, 100

Ilchester (Somerset), 241
Iliad (Homer), 247
In the South Seas (Stevenson), 118
Inferno (Dante), 221
Italy, Ll. P. and J. C. P. in, 34; Ll. P. visits, 117

James, Henry, 70, 180, 181, 237
James, William, 180
John, Augustus, 255
John Lane The Bodley Head (publishers), 205, 223, 224, 229, 238
Johnson family, of Norfolk, 9
Johnson, Father Hamilton Cowper, 91
Johnson, Rev. John, 2
Johnson, Mary Cowper. *See* Powys, Mary Cowper
Johnson, Samuel, 102, 176, 178
Joiner & Steele (publishers), 157
Jones, Tom, 48, 49, 180
Joyce, James, 75, 180, 196, 227; J. C. P. supports, 55

Keats, John, 2 n., 56, 97, 253
Kensington, 73
Kenya, 12, 41, 132

Kingston (New York), Ll. P. married at, 90

Kipling, Rudyard, 100, 223

Kirchner, Ernst Ludwig, Ll. P.'s essay on, 121

Knight, G. Wilson, 161, 236

Knopf, Alfred (publisher), 53, 77

Krick, Albert, 133

Kwang-tze, 152

La Rochefoucauld, 168

Lamb, Charles, 50, 87, 176, 180, 181

Langdon, Rev. W., 175

Lao-tze, 152

Lawrence, D. H., 117, 148, 180

Le Gallienne, Richard, 72, 90

Leipzig, 36

Lewes (Sussex), 13

Life and Times of Anthony Wood, The (Clark), 119

Lilford, Barony of, a Powys connection, 1

Limited Editions Club, 100

Lindsay, Vachel, 180

Linton, Marion, 4, 30; engaged to Ll. P., 33, 34; engagement broken, 41–2; 'Dittany Stone' of *Love and Death*, 208

Little Review, J. C. P. at trial of, 55

Liverpool, 180

London, 31, 84, 118, 136, 184

London Mercury, The, A. R. Powys writes for, 90

Longmans, Green & Company (publishers), 75, 121

Los Angeles, 68, 181

Lowell, Amy, 72

Lubbock, Sir John (1st Baron Avebury), 56

Lucas, E. V., 172

Lucretius, 143

Lulworth (Dorset), 174

Lynd, Robert, 172

Lyon, Margaret Alice. *See* Powys, Margaret Alice

Lyon, Thomas Henry, 18, 19, 48

Lyons, 121

Lyric Impulse, The (Day Lewis), 207

Macaulay, Rose, 91

Macaulay, Thomas Babington, 119

Macbeth (Shakespeare), 8

Macdonald & Company (publishers), 58, 223, 224, 238, 250

Malory, Sir Thomas, 145

Manas Press, 46

Manchester, 16

Mansfield, Katherine, 96

Mappowder (Dorset), Philippa Powys dies at, 147; T. F. P. settles at, 210–11; T. F. P. dies at, 254–5

Marchand, Leslie A., 119

Marlow, Louis. *See* Wilkinson, Louis Umfreville

Marvell, Andrew, 176

Massingham, H. J., 206

Masters, Edgar Lee, 180

Matthews, Canon Norman A., 161

Maugham, W. Somerset, 49, 196

Maupassant, Guy de, 87

Mayor of Casterbridge, The (Hardy), 4

Medal, The (Dryden), 163

Medusa (Visiak), 247

'Melancholia' (de Kantzow), quoted, 16

Melville, Herman, 38

Merchant of Venice, The (Shakespeare), 8

Merriman, Henry Seton, 27, 49

Meynell, Alice, 176

Milan, 34

Millay, Edna St Vincent, 22, 72, 133, 206; Ll. P. visits at Austerlitz, 121; her estate described, 144–5; assists Ll. P. financially, 145

Miller, Henry, 253

Milton, John, 50, 174, 228, 253, 256

Mirsky, D. S., 253

Mitchison, Naomi, 139

'Modern Thinker, The', J. C. P. quoted from, 151

Monmouth, Duke of, 176

Montacute (Somerset), 2, 4, 8, 9, 10, 11, 15, 33, 34, 51, 61, 62, 101,

103, 136, 147, 148, 174–5; described, 5–6; setting for *Wood and Stone*, 39

Montaigne, Michel de, 228, 256

Montgomery, Robert, 256

Montoma (New York), Ll. P. at, 90; Alyse Gregory quoted on, 91; *Skin for Skin* written at, 102, 104

Moore, Marianne, 72, 139

Moore, T. Sturge, 253

More, Hannah, her *Works* buried in Augustine Birrell's garden, 115

Morning Post, 36

Mornings in Mexico (Lawrence), 118

Motteux, Peter, 231

Mr. Perrin and Mr. Traill (Walpole), 26

Muir, Edwin, 206

Münsterberg, Hugo von, 36, 66

Muntz, Elizabeth, 22, 216; carves Ll. P.'s memorial stone, 254

Murry, Middleton, 206

Musgrave, Clifford, 206

Myers, Elizabeth (second Mrs Littleton Powys), 203

Nation, T. F. P. writes for, 98, 110

National Trust, 5

Nero, 223, 251

New Age, Ll. P. writes for, 33, 63

New English Weekly, Ll. P. writes for, 169

New Leader, T. F. P. writes for, 98, 110

New Orleans, 94

New Statesman, Ll. P. writes for, 33, 63

New York, 26, 38, 41, 55, 66–7, 69, 70–4, 75, 89–91, 94, 105, 121, 133, 152, 181, 184

New York Herald Tribune, Ll. P. visiting critic for, 117, 121

New York Times, Professor Münsterberg quoted from, 36

Nietzsche, F. W., 20, 56, 228

Noctis Sussuri (de Kantzow), 16

Noheimer, Nicholas, 215

Nonesuch Press, 100

Norfolk, Henry Fitzalan Howard, 15th Duke of, 14

North American, J. C. P. writes for, 94

Norwalk (Connecticut), 91

Novaya Zemlya, 121

Novels and Stories of T. F. Powys, The (Hunter), 201

Odyssey (Homer), 157, 244

O'Flaherty, Liam, 100; on *Mr. Tasker's Gods*, 110

Oklahoma City, 134

Oldcastle, Sir John, 237

O'Neill, Bernard Price, 17, 18, 19, 20, 34, 48, 103, 196, 218

O'Neill, Mrs B. P., 18

Orage, A. R., 33

One Hundred Best Books (Lubbock), 56

Orczy, Baroness, 27

Osborne, Rev. Sidney, 175

Osmington Mills (Dorset), 113, 175

Owermoigne (Dorset), 101, 130

Oxford, 18

Painter, George D., 202

Palestine, Ll. P. visits, 117, 121, 123, 139

Paracelsus, 216

Paradise Lost (Milton), 124

Paris, 70; Gertrude Powys studies art at, 89

Parker, Herbert, 175

Pater, Walter, 87

Peacock, Thomas Love, 225

Pembroke College (Oxford), 18

Pepys (Bryant), 119

Phelips family, of Montacute, 6, 8

Phillpotts, Eden, 82, 136

Philobiblon, essay by J. C. P. in, 232

Pickwick Papers (Dickens), 78, 154

Pilgrimage (Richardson), 156, 157

Pilgrim's Progress (Bunyan), 125

Plato, 56, 76

Playter, Franklin, 220

Playter, Mrs F., 220

Playter, Phyllis, 220, 222

Pleasure Ground, The (Elwin), Ll. P.
'A Voyage to the West Indies' in,
145; and quoted, 146
Plucknet, Sir Allan, 85
Plymouth (Devon), 68
Poe, Edgar Allan, 57
Pollock, H. Rivers, 121, 139, 215
Poole (Dorset), 22
Pope, Alexander, 56, 231
Portrait of the Artist as a Young Man, A (Joyce), 79
Portslade (Sussex), 16
Powys, Albert Reginald ('Bertie'), 2, 4, 18, 20, 29, 30, 33, 34, 35, 52, 88, 90, 121, 147, 195, 218, 220; his career and writings discussed, 84–6; *From the Ground Up* quoted, 84–5; *The English Parish Church* quoted, 85–6; *Repair of Ancient Buildings*, 85; *The English House*, 85
Powys Brothers, The (Ward), 196, 201
Powys, Rev. Charles Francis, 9, 10, 11, 13, 14, 17, 20, 24, 25, 30, 33, 38, 62, 89, 91, 175, 179, 182, 201; parentage and early career, 1–5; becomes Vicar of Montacute, 5–6; Littleton Powys on his father's character, 7; death of, 88; character sketch of, in *Apples be Ripe*, 122; Ll. P.'s essay on, 172
Powys, Eleanor, 2, 2 n.
Powys, Francis (son of T. F. P.), 124, 147, 211, 218
Powys, Gertrude Mary, 2, 3, 22, 52, 62, 89, 201, 215, 254; her drawings of her brothers in *The Powys Brothers*, and her portrait of J. C. P., 233
Powys, John Cowper, 3, 4, 5, 6, 8, 20, 21, 22, 23, 25, 30, 31, 33, 34, 43, 44, 45, 46, 47, 51, 52, 53, 62, 77, 78, 89, 90, 99, 100, 101, 103, 104, 105, 142, 147, 148, 149, 166, 169, 170, 174, 175, 195, 197, 201, 202, 207, 210, 211; ancestry, 1–2; birth, 2; at Sherborne

School, 9–11; at Corpus Christi College, 11–12; takes up lecturing, 13; early poems published and quoted, 14–17; early influences, 17–19; marriage, birth of only son, 19; first visit to United States, 27–9; war activities, 35–6; war-time publications (1914–16), 36–41; character sketch of, in *The Buffoon*, 48–9; early literary criticism, 50; growing reputation in United States, and activities there (1917–19), 55–61; with Ll. P. in United States, 63–72; on his brothers' writings, 84–8; his work in the early twenties, 94–8; his methods contrasted with T. F. P.'s, 106–8; his method as a biographer, 120; settles at Hillsdale, 132–3; *Wolf Solent*, 133–8; books of philosophy, 150–2; *A Glastonbury Romance*, 156–61; *Autobiography*, 177–83; *Weymouth Sands* and *Maiden Castle*, 184–94; character sketch of, in *The Buffoon*, quoted, 198–9; *Glastonbury* libel threat, 204–5; settles in Wales, 220–1; *Morwyn*, 221–3; *The Inmates*, 224–6; later critical writings, 227–32; *Owen Glendower*, 233–7; *Porius*, 237–240; *The Brazen Head*, 241–3; *Atlantis*, 244–8, (quoted), 247–8; *Homer and the Aether*, 247–9, (quoted), 248–9; the 'science fiction' stories, 250–2; last publications, 252–4; last years and death, 255–6
WORKS
All or Nothing, 243, 244, 250–2
Art of Forgetting the Unpleasant, The, 65
Art of Growing Old, The, 64, 150
Art of Happiness, The (1925), 65, 75
Art of Happiness, The (1935), 150; quoted, 151

WORKS—*continued*

Atlantis, 152, 166, 226, 241; discussed and quoted, 244–8

Autobiography, 2 n., 4, 10, 11, 17, 35, 46, 48, 49, 52, 94, 97, 136, 137, 159, 195, 196, 225, 232, 250, 252; on his early years, 12–16; discussed and quoted, 177–83

Brazen Head, The, 239, 246; discussed, 241–4

Carlyle, Ruskin and Tennyson: six lectures (syllabus), 28

Complex Vision, The, 66, 94; discussed and quoted, 63–5

Confessions of Two Brothers (with Ll. P.), 11 n.; quoted, 25–6, 54; circumstances of publication, 46–7

Dostoievsky, 120; discussed, 228–9

Ducdame, 39, 52, 75, 132, 226; discussed, 94–7

Enjoyment of Literature. See Pleasures of Literature

Glastonbury Romance, A, 9, 39, 94, 96, 99–100, 136, 137, 177, 182, 186, 189, 191, 204, 235, 243, 250; discussed, 156–61

Homer and the Aether, 241, 244; discussed and quoted, 247–9

In Defence of Sensuality, 64, 149–50; quoted, 151

In Spite Of, 64, 151, 232

Inmates, The, 184, 243; discussed, 224–6

Is Modern Marriage a Failure? (with Bertrand Russell), 156

Jobber Skald. See Weymouth Sands

Letters to Louis Wilkinson, 178, 198, 252, 255

Life of Keats (unpublished), 29–30, 37

Lucifer, 250, 253

Maiden Castle, 4, 39, 52, 136, 184–5, 187, 195, 221, 223, 250; discussed and quoted, 191–4; fear of libel in writing of, 204–5

Mandragora, 59, 63; Ll. P. on, 60

Meaning of Culture, The, 150

Mortal Strife, 66, 150

Morwyn, 177, 184, 220, 224, 226, 240, 243, 244; discussed and quoted, 221–3

Obstinate Cymric, 227 n., 232, 233

Odes and Other Poems, 6, 18; discussed and quoted, 14–15

One Hundred Best Books, discussed and quoted, 56–7

Owen Glendower, 161, 223, 226, 238, 239, 241, 242; discussed, 233–7

Owl, The Duck, and—Miss Rowe! Miss Rowe! The, 96, 157; discussed, 152

Philosophy of Solitude, A, 150; quoted, 151

Pleasures of Literature, The, discussed, 227–9

Poems (1899), 14, 15–16, 18; circumstances of publication, 17

Porius, 241, 242, 243, 244, 250; discussed, 237–40

Psychoanalysis and Morality, 65, 66, 75

Rabelais, 18, 120, 238; discussed, 229–32

Religion of a Sceptic, The, 65, 75

Rodmoor, 9, 39, 65, 188, 226; J. C. P. on, 60; discussed and quoted, 60–1

Samphire, 75; Ll. P.'s editorial work on, 57, 60

Secret of Self Development, The, quoted, 65–6

Selected Poems, 58, 253

Six Lectures on Shakespeare's Historical Plays, quoted, 28 n.

WORKS—*continued*

Suspended Judgments, 18, 49–50

Up and Out, 184, 225, 243, 250, 251. *See also* 'Up and Out', below

Visions and Revisions, 37–8, 49, 250; kept at Hardy's bedside, 15

War and Culture, The, discussed and quoted, 35–7

Weymouth Sands, 39, 52, 61, 134, 136, 138, 159, 177, 191–2, 194, 222, 224; discussed and quoted, 184–90; published in England as *Jobber Skald*, 204

Wood and Stone, 5, 45, 52, 60–1, 251; discussed and quoted, 38–41; contrasted with T. F. P.'s *Soliloquy*, 43–4

Wolf's Bane, discussed and quoted, 57–9

Wolf Solent, 5, 39, 40, 52, 96, 97, 100, 101, 107, 185, 187, 241, 250; discussed and quoted, 132–8, 192

You and Me (unpublished), 250

OTHER WRITINGS

'The Death Birds' (*Wolf's Bane*), quoted, 58

'Four Brothers: A Family Confession' (*Century Magazine*), 84, 90; quotations from, 86–8

'Knowledge' (*Wolf's Bane*), quoted, 58–9

'Metaphysic' (*Samphire*), 60

'Mountains of The Moon, The' (*Up and Out*), discussed, 251–2

'Ode to Proserpine' (*Odes and Other Poems*), passage from, 14

'The Old Pier Post' (*Samphire*), 60

'Sonnet Written in Sweffling Churchyard' (*Poems*), 9

'They Say' (*Mandragora*), 59

'To Montacute' (*Odes and Other Poems*), 6

'The Ultimate' (*Samphire*), 60

'Up and Out' discussed, 251–2

Powys, Littleton Albert, 2, 218

Powys, Littleton Alfred (son of J. C. P.), 18, 19, 33, 218

Powys, Rev. Littleton Charles, 2, 211

Powys, Littleton Charles, 2, 5, 12, 29, 30, 33, 35, 63, 101, 147, 179, 195; at Sherborne School, 9–10; headmaster of Sherborne Prep., 26; death of, 203; *The Joy of it*, 4, (quoted), 7–8, 11, (discussed), 201–2; *Still the Joy of it*, 203

Powys, Llewelyn, 3, 4, 6, 8, 9, 10, 13, 14, 15, 18, 19, 20, 21, 22, 38, 39, 43, 45, 51, 52, 53, 88, 89, 90, 94, 99–100, 132, 147, 150, 151, 152, 179, 180, 195, 202, 211, 221, 224, 230, 241, 256; ancestry, 1–2; birth, 5; at Sherborne School, 9–11; at Corpus Christi College, 11–12; schoolmastering, 25–7; first trip to United States, 27, 29; first attack of consumption, 30–2; in England and Europe, 33–5; in Kenya, 41–2, 54–5; on J. C. P.'s poems, 57, 59–60; returns to U.S.A., 62–3; travels in America, 66–9; in New York, becoming established as a writer, 70–5; J. C. P.'s opinion of his style, 86–7; marriage and residence in New York State, 89–93; and *Ducdame*, 95–6; returns to England, 101; *Skin for Skin* and *The Verdict of Bridlegoose*, 102–5; in Europe and America, 117–23; writing philosophical books, 139–144; visiting Edna St Vincent Millay, 145–6; *Apples be Ripe* compared with *The Blackthorn Winter* and quoted, 148–9; suggests the idea of *Fables* to T. F. P.,

163; five years' work at East
Chaldon, 169–76; quoted on
Swan's Milk, 197; L. U. W. on,
in *Swan's Milk*, 199–201; in libel
action, 205; author's first meeting
with, 206; goes to Switzerland,
207; writing *Love and Death*,
207–9; last works, and death,
215–19; memorial stone erected,
254

WORKS

Advice to a Young Poet, 216

Apples be Ripe, 11, 87, 148;
discussed and quoted, 121–3,
149

Baker's Dozen, A, 172, 215, 216

Black Laughter, discussed, 91–
92

Confessions of Two Brothers
(with J. C. P.). *See* entry
under Powys, John Cowper

Cradle of God, The, discussed
and quoted, 139–41

*Cup Bearers of Wine and
Hellebore*, 72

Damnable Opinions, 169; discussed and quoted, 170–1

Dorset Essays, 89, 169, 170,
175

Earth Memories, 11 n., 19, 89,
91, 169, 170, 172–3

Ebony and Ivory, 33, 72–3, 92

Glory of Life, 99, 102, 144,
176, 215

Henry Hudson, 120, 121; discussed, 118–19

Honey and Gall, 72; quoted, 71

*Hour on Christianity, An. See
The Pathetic Fallacy*, below

Impassioned Clay, 32, 46, 102,
170, 215; discussed and
quoted, 142–4

Letters of Llewelyn Powys, 91,
201; discussed and quoted,
216–19

*Life and Times of Anthony à
Wood*, 119–20, 170

Love and Death, 4, 5, 11, 32,

33, 87, 102, 169, 176; discussed, 207–9

Now That the Gods are Dead,
102, 144, 170, 215

Pagan's Pilgrimage, A, 117,
139

Pathetic Fallacy, The, 139,
148, 170; discussed and
quoted, 141–2

Rats in the Sacristy, 169, 170

Selections from the Writings (ed.
Hopkins), 206

Skin for Skin, 11, 32, 91, 105,
121; discussed and quoted,
102–4

Somerset Essays, 121, 170; discussed and quoted, 173–5

Swiss Essays, 121, 172, 175 n.,
215, 216

Thirteen Worthies, 72; discussed and quoted, 74–5

Twelve Months, The, 99, 170,
175, 176

Verdict of Bridlegoose, The,
67, 72, 102, 118, 121; discussed, 104–5

OTHER WRITINGS

'Butterfly Secret, A' (*Earth
Memories*), quoted, 173

'Cardinal Newman' (*Damnable
Opinions*), quoted, 170–1

'A Grave in Dorset' (*Earth
Memories*), 91, 120, 148

'Morality' (*Damnable Opinions*), 171

'Of Egoism' (*Earth Memories*),
11

'On the Other Side of the
Quantocks' (*Earth Memor-
ies*), 120

'Open Spaces in New York'
(*Honey and Gall*), quoted, 71

'Out of the Past' (*Earth
Memories*), 89, 172

'An Owl and a Swallow'
(*Earth Memories*), 172

'The Oxford Group' (*Dam-
nable Opinions*), 172

OTHER WRITINGS—*continued*
'The Partridge' (*Earth Memories*), 172
'The Poetic Faith' (*Damnable Opinions*), 171
'Stalbridge Rectory' (*Dorset Essays*), 89
'Voyage to the West Indies, A' (*The Pleasure Ground*), 145; quoted, 146
'The White Horse' (*Somerset Essays*), quoted, 173–4
'William Barnes' (*Thirteen Worthies*), quoted, 74–5

Powys, Lucy (Mrs Hounsell Penny), 2, 90, 91

Powys, Margaret Alice (Mrs J. C. Powys), 33

Powys, Marian (Mrs Peter Grey), 2, 20, 68, 89; J. C. P. and Ll. P. with, in New York, 67, 72

Powys, Mary Cowper (Mrs C. F. Powys), 1, 3, 9, 14, 29, 30, 178, 201; character sketch of, by Littleton Powys, 7–8; death of, 33, 34

Powys, (Catherine) Philippa, 2, 22, 52, 67, 195, 254; *The Blackthorn Winter*, 6, 90, discussed and quoted, 147–9; *Driftwood*, 148

Powys, Susan, 131

Powys, Theodore Francis, 3, 4, 5, 12, 18, 26, 29, 33, 38, 40, 51, 52, 54, 55, 63, 66, 71, 89, 95, 96, 103, 104, 105, 147, 148, 152–3, 156, 169, 170, 179, 180, 195, 199–200, 207, 218, 224, 240, 256; ancestry, 1–2; birth, 2; schooling, 9–11; farming, early friendships and writings, 19–24; character sketch when young, quoted from *Swan's Milk*, 20–1; at Studland, 22; marries, 22; settles at East Chaldon, 22; *An Interpretation of Genesis*, 23–4; encounters a Corporal, 35; circumstances of publishing *The Soliloquy*, 43–4; *The Soliloquy of a Hermit*, 45–7;

writing of *Mr. Tasker's Gods*, 53; *The Left Leg*, 77, 78–82; *Black Bryony*, 82–3; J. C. P. on his style, 87–8; first short stories published, 98–100; his writing methods contrasted with J. C. P.'s, 106–8; *Mark Only*, *Mr. Tasker*, *Mockery Gap*, *Innocent Birds*, 109–16; *Mr. Weston's Good Wine*, 124–8; character sketch by Sylvia Townsend Warner, 129–31; *Kindness in a Corner*, 153–5; *Fables*, 162–8; *Unclay*, 166–8; removes to Mappowder, 210; last writings, 211–15; last years and death, 254–5

WORKS
Amos Lear (unpublished), 53
Black Bryony, 77, 87, 106; discussed, 82–3
Captain Patch, 213, 214
Fables (*No Painted Plumage*), 214; discussed and quoted, 162–6
Georgina, a Lady (unpublished), 63
Goat Green ('The Better Gift'), 152, 213
God's Eyes a-Twinkle, 162
House with the Echo, The, 162; discussed, 98–9
Innocent Birds, 106, 110; discussed, 114–16
Interpretation of Genesis, An, 23, 53, 109; discussed and quoted, 23–4
Kindness in a Corner, 109, 166; discussed, 153–5
Left Leg, The, 96, 211, 213; published, 77; discussed, 78–83
Mark Only, 87, 106, 113; discussed and quoted, 110–12
Mr. Tasker's Gods, 43, 53, 77, 82, 109, 110, 111, 124; discussed, 112–13
Mr. Weston's Good Wine, 79, 80, 99, 109, 110, 113, 115,

WORKS—*continued*
   162, 165, 167; discussed and quoted, 124–8
   Mockery Gap, 110, 115; discussed, 113–14
   Soliloquy of a Hermit, The (Soliloquies of a Hermit), 21, 23, 43, 44, 47, 52, 77; discussed, 45–6
   Two Thieves, The, discussed, 212–13
   Unclay, 79, 106, 113, 210; discussed, 166–8
   White Paternoster, The, 153, 162

STORIES
   'Abraham Men' (*The Left Leg*), 77, 79, 213; discussed, 80–2
   'Archdeacon Truggin' (*The White Paternoster*), 110, 128
   'The Bride' (*The White Paternoster*), 109
   'The Better Gift' (*Goat Green:* collected in *Bottle's Path*), 213
   'The Cat and the Rooks' (*Captain Patch*), 214
   'Christ in the Cupboard' (*The White Paternoster*), 152
   'Circe Truggin' (*Bottle's Path*), 214
   'The Clout and the Pan' (*Fables*), 164
   'The Corpse and the Flea' (*Fables*), 165
   'Darkness and Nathaniel' (*Fables*), 110, 166
   'The Dove and The Eagle' (*Bottle's Path*), 214
   'Feed My Swine' (*The White Paternoster*), 109
   'God' (*The Two Thieves*), 212–13
   'The Hassock and The Psalter' (*Fables*), 165
   'Hester Dominy' (*The Left Leg*), 77, 78, 79, 80, 87, 213

'The Hill and The Book' (*Captain Patch*), 214
'The Hunted Beast' (*The White Paternoster*), 153
'In Good Earth' (*The Two Thieves*), 212–13
'John Pardy and The Waves' (*Fables*), 166
'The Key of the Field' (*Bottle's Path*), 152
'The Left Leg' (*The Left Leg*), 77, 87, 213; discussed, 78–80
'The Lonely Lady' (*The House with The Echo*), 98
'The Lost Proofs' (*The House with The Echo*), 110
'Make Thyself Many' (*Make Thyself Many*), 214
'Mr. Pim and the Holy Crumb' (*Fables*), discussed, 163–5
'Nor Iron Bars' (*The House with The Echo*), 98
'Squire Duffy' (*The House with The Echo*), 110
'A Strong Girl' (*A Strong Girl*), 109
'A Stubborn Tree' (*A Stubborn Tree*), 109, 152
'Tadnol', 77
'The Two Thieves' (*The Two Thieves*), 212, 213
'Uncle Dottery' (*Uncle Dottery*), 99, 152, 153
'Uriah on the Hill' (*Uriah on the Hill*), 152, 153
'What Lack I Yet?' (*The White Paternoster*), 153
Powys, Theodore (son of T. F. P.), 129
Powys, Violet Rosalie, (Mrs T. F. Powys), 22–3, 129–31, 218
Powys, William, of Ludlow, 1
Powys, William Ernest, 2, 12, 29, 30, 33, 35, 41, 54, 62, 147, 195, 218
Poxwell (Dorset), 111
Prentice, Charles, 77 n., 162

Principles of Art Education (Münsterberg), 36
Prior, Matthew, 151
Proust, Marcel, 181, 228
Psychology and Industrial Efficiency (Münsterberg), 36
Psychology and Life (Münsterberg), 36
Putney, 15

Rabelais, François, 18, 38, 74, 96, 120, 181, 228, 229–32, 237, 247
Radley School, 18
Raleigh, Sir Walter, 10
Ramsgate (Kent), 25
Random House (publishers), 75
Rationalist Annual, The, Ll. P. writes for, 169
Redwood-Anderson, John, 221
Reid, Ann (second Mrs Louis Wilkinson), 121, 147, 148, 172
Rembrandt, 121
Rennie, John, 85
Review of English Literature, A, 161
Reynolds, Stephen, 147
Richards, Grant (publisher), 73, 74
Richardson, Dorothy M., 180; J. C. P.'s monograph on, 156–7
Rider, William & Sons (publishers), 14, 23
Rochester (New York), 46
Rolland, Romain, 180
Romeo and Juliet (Shakespeare), 28
Rowland, John, 206, 217, 219
Royal Society of Literature refuses to honour John Cowper Powys, 255
Rubens, Peter-Paul, 121
Ruskin, John, 176
Russell, Bertrand, 3rd Earl Russell, 72, 156; debates with J. C. P., 66

Sacramento (California), 134
St John's College (Cambridge), L. U. W. at, 18
Saint Louis (Missouri), 97, 134
St Peter's Court, Broadstairs, Ll. P. teaches at, 25

Saltus, Edgar, 27
San Francisco, 94, 176, 181; J. C. P. and Ll. P. at, 68–9
Santa Barbara (California), 68
Saturday Review, reviews J. C. P.'s *Poems*, 17
Sausalito (California), 68
Scarlet Pimpernel, The (Orczy), 27
Scott, Sir Walter, 80, 237
Sentimental Journey, A (Sterne), J. C. P.'s preface for, 238
Shakespeare, William, 28, 38, 56, 80, 107, 110, 113, 180, 181, 210, 228, 237
Shanks, Edward, writes preface for *Ebony and Ivory*, 73
Shaw, G. Arnold, 21, 35, 37; publishes early Powys books, 43–6; and *Mr. Tasker's Gods*, 75, 185
Shaw, George Bernard, 192, 223
Shelley, Percy Bysshe, 56, 174
Sherborne (Dorset), 9, 30, 31, 32, 40, 63, 85, 101, 136, 191; Ll. P. teaches at, 29
Sherborne School, Powys brothers attend, 9–11
Sherratt & Hughes (publishers), 16
Shirley (Derbyshire), 1–4, 5, 30, 51; J. C. P. and T. F. P. born at, 2
Shirley, Ralph, 14, 17, 29–30
Shoel, Thomas, 6; Ll. P. writes on, 174
Siberell, Lloyd Emerson, writes preface for *A Baker's Dozen*, 215
Sidmouth (Devon), 30, 147
Silverado Squatters, The (Stevenson) 117
Sinclair, May, 156
Sketches by Boz (Dickens), 78
Smart, Christopher, 240
Society for the Protection of Ancient Buildings, The, A. R. Powys secretary of, 84
Southampton (Hampshire), 63, 149
Southey, Robert, 84, 251
Southwick (Sussex), J. C. P. at, 13
Spenser, Edmund, 125, 176

Squire, J. C., 33, 90
Stalbridge (Dorset), 1, 172
Staples & Staples (publishers), 229
Steeple Ashton (Wiltshire), 129
Stein, Gertrude, 180
Sterling, George, 68
Sterne, Laurence, 238
Stevenson, Robert Louis, 31, 67, 117
Strachey, Lytton, 87, 119
Strauss, Ralph, 196
Strong, L. A. G., 28, 177
Studland (Dorset), T. F. P. at, 22
Sutton Poyntz (Dorset), 174
Sweffling (Suffolk), T. F. P. farms
    at, 9
Swift, Jonathan, 102, 251
Swinburne, Algernon Charles, 13,
    15, 56
Syracuse (New York), 134

Taliessin, 222, 223, 228
Task, The (Cowper), 163
Templecombe (Somerset), 89
Tennyson, Alfred, Lord, 56, 246
Tess of the D'Urbervilles (Hardy), 15
Thorne, Guy, 27
Tintinhull (Somerset), 5
Tocqueville, Alexis Comte de, 181
Tolstoy, Leo, 229
Tomlin, Steven, 22, 77
Tomlinson, H. M., 22, 206
Torquemada, 223
'Tortoise and the Hare, The'
    (Aesop), 162-3
T. P.'s Weekly, 26
Treasure Island (Stevenson), 172
Trevelyan, G. M., 238
Trevelyan, R. C., 22, 253
Trollope, Anthony, 112
Trovillion Private Press, 215
Truth, L. U. W. defended in, 18
Turner, Reginald, 27
Twain, Mark, 98,

Ultima Verba (de Kantzow), 16
University Lecturers Association of
    New York, 35

University of Wales honours J. C. P.,
    255
Untermeyer, Louis, 10
Unwin, T. Fisher (publisher), 16
Urquhart, Sir Thomas, 230, 231
Utica (New York), 134

Venice, 34
Viking Press, 77
Virgil, 181
Visiak, E. H., 247

Wake, William, 56
Wallis, John, 206
Walpole, Horace, 253
Walpole, Sir Hugh, 26, 100
Walton, Izaak, 119
War and America, The (Münster-
    berg), provokes The War and
    Culture (J. C. P.), 36
Ward, Artemus, 98
Ward, Mrs Humphry, 22
Ward, Lynd, 144, 215
Ward, Richard Heron, 196, 201, 206,
    233
Wareham (Dorset), 95
Warmwell (Dorset), 101, 102
Warner, Sylvia Townsend, 22, 205,
    211; assists T. F. P. with pub-
    lishers, 77-8; quoted on T. F. P.,
    128-31
'Wasteland, The' (Eliot), 157
Watson, Dr James S., with Ll. P.
    in Rocky Mountains, 90
Waverley Novels, 10
Weld family, of Lulworth, 52
Wellington, Duke of, 101
West Indies, Ll. P. visits, 117
Western Morning News, 17
Weymouth (Dorset), 2, 51, 62, 88,
    95, 101, 102, 105, 129, 136, 186,
    189, 192, 204; setting for Wey-
    mouth Sands, 184-5
White Nose (Dorset), 22, 120, 132;
    Ll. P. living at, 101-2; the
    headland, 142
Whitman, Walt, 57, 181, 228

Wilde, Oscar, 196
Wilkinson, Louis Umfreville ('Louis Marlow'), 3, 6, 9, 11, 12, 15, 17, 19, 35, 63, 77, 95, 112, 117, 121, 124, 132, 147, 180, 204, 210, 216, 223, 238, 252; early years, and first meeting with Powys brothers, 18; character sketch of T. F. P. quoted, 20-1; helps to finance T. F. P.'s first publication, 21; first trip to United States, 27-8; on Ll. P.'s lecturing, 29; with J. C. P. and Ll. P. in Italy, 34; *Blasphemy and Religion*, 43-5; *The Buffoon*, 47-9; editorial work on *Mr. Tasker*, 53; middle years, 196; Ll. P. on *Swan's Milk*, 197; *Swan's Milk*, 196-201; *Welsh Ambassadors*, 201-3

WORKS
    Blasphemy and Religion, 53, 197; discussed and quoted, 43-5
    Buffoon, The, 43, 55, 197, 199; discussed, 47-9
    Forth, Beast!, 197
    Lion Took Fright, The, 147
    Love by Accident, 27
    Mr. Amberthwaite, 27
    Puppets' Dallying, The, 27, 47, 49
    Swan's Milk, 6, 11, 47; quoted on T. F. P., 20-1; discussed, 196-201; quoted on J. C. P., 198-9; quoted on Ll. P., 200-1
    Two Made Their Bed, 196
    Welsh Ambassadors, 6, 17, 117, 147, 196; discussed, 201-3; Littleton Powys objects to, 201-2
Wilkinson, Rev. W. G., 9
William Barnes of Dorset (Dugdale), 4
Williams, John William, 'The Catholic', 19, 38, 48
Williamson, Henry, 157
Wilson, Edmund, 72
Winfrith Newburgh (Dorset), 51
Winterborne Came (Dorset), 4, 5
Wood, Anthony à, 66, 74, 119
Wood, Charles Erskine Scott, 68
Woolsey, Gamel, 206
Worcester (Worcs.), 235
Wordsworth, Andrew, 206
Wordsworth, William, 56, 57, 99, 181, 211, 256
Wuthering Heights (Brontë), 198
Wyatt, Sir Thomas, 10
Wyoming, Ll. P. in, 90

Yeats, William Butler, 15
Yeovil (Somerset), 2, 5, 134, 136, 191